WAY TO GO

Two of the World's Great Motorcycle Journeys

GEOFF HILL

THE
BLACKSTAFF
PRESS

BELFAST

First published in April 2005 by
Blackstaff Press
4c Heron Wharf, Sydenham Business Park
Belfast, BT3 9LE
with the assistance of
The Arts Council of Northern Ireland

ARTS
COUNCIL
of Northern Ireland

Reprinted 2005, 2006, 2007

Typeset by CJWT solutions, Newton-le-Willows, Merseyside

Printed in England by Cromwell Press

A CIP catalogue record for this book is available from the
British Library

ISBN 978-0-85640-765-9

www.blackstaffpress.com

GEOFF HILL is the features and travel editor of the *News Letter* in Belfast, one of the world's oldest newspapers. He has either won or been shortlisted for a UK Travel Writer of the Year award eight times. He is also a former Irish Travel Writer of the Year and a former Mexican Government European Travel Writer of the Year, although he's still trying to work out exactly what that means. He writes about travel regularly for the *Daily Telegraph* and the *Independent on Sunday*. He writes for the motoring section of the *Irish Times* and is an editor for *Fodor's*, the American guidebook series. He has also won one UK and three Northern Ireland Feature Writer of the Year awards, and two UK newspaper design awards.

He lives in Belfast with his wife Cate, a cat called Kitten, a hammock and the ghost of a flatulent Great Dane. His hobbies are volleyball, flying, motorbikes, skiing, and thinking too much.

Geoff's dad, Bob, on a hand-change 1929 Rudge 500
before the 1950 Cookstown 100

Contents

Preface

In *Zen and the Art of Motorcycle Maintenance* Robert Pirsig divides people into classicists and romantics. When a classicist looks at a motorcycle, he sees a collection of nuts and bolts. But I'm a romantic. When I look at one, I think of oil and leather, the bright tinkle of a spanner on concrete in my dad's old garage, the open road, the wind in my hair, the smell of daisy meadows and my mother's perfume when she was young.

To me, it seemed the most natural thing in the world, when I saw a Royal Enfield outside a pub in Belfast and found out they were still being made in India, to imagine riding one back from Delhi; and when I thought of a Harley, to wonder what it would be like to head off down Route 66, all the way from Chicago to LA.

You see, in my dreams, I am still a boy on a bike. Because when I was a boy, every day was an adventure and a new beginning. Because when we are children, we are reborn every morning, but when we grow older, a little of us dies every night: killed by what ifs and if onlys, by mortgages and bills, dry rot and rising damp. When we travel, though, we are children again. And when we travel by motorcycle, we have nothing to think of when we wake but checking out of a motel, throwing a few belongings into our panniers and riding off down the road, unencumbered by regrets and concerns. On a motorcycle, every day is an adventure and a new beginning.

On a motorcycle, I am still a boy on a bike.

GEOFF HILL
FEBRUARY 2005

Acknowledgements

My thanks to the following:

The Nambarrie Run
Delhi to Belfast on an Enfield

Patrick Minne, without whom I would be still be in Delhi trying to work out how to adjust the clutch. Joris Minne for naively asking Nambarrie to give us money to ride two motorbikes back from India. Rosena McKeown and Brian Davis at Nambarrie for even more naively saying yes. Ian Mackinnon, our man in Delhi, for organising everything at that end, in a country where organisation is banned by law. Nanna for preparing the Enfields so beautifully. Steve Pang at Psion for providing a Series 5 palmtop. Luise Smith and Jackie Stephenson, the world's finest copytakers, whose voices were the sound of home for me every evening across the long miles. Geoff Saltmarsh at Saltmarsh PR for persuading KLM to fly us from Belfast to Delhi. Raj Desai at Jet Airways for getting us from Delhi to Calcutta and back. Brian McKibbin for cajoling SeaCat into providing the transport across the wet bits. Philip Rees at Visa Express in London for solving several impossible visa problems.

Miller Miles
Route 66 on a Harley

Rosemary Hamilton at Future Image, Brian Houston at Bass and Mike Hennick at Miller for giving me even more money, not to mention the leather jacket. David James and the guys at

Harley-Davidson for lending me a Road King for a month. Jayne Innis at Cellet Travel Services for organising accommodation and tours at several stops.

My thanks also to Geoff Martin, my editor during both trips, for not noticing that I was gone from the office for months at a time. Gavin Livingstone, the artist who created the brilliant Nambarrie Run and Miller Miles logos. Hilary Bell, my editor at Blackstaff, for getting me to stick to the point occasionally. My current editor, Austin Hunter, for rather foolishly agreeing to give me three months out of the office for my next adventure, Chile to Alaska by motorbike on the Pan-American Highway in spring 2006.

And, most of all, to Cate, for her love and support and for understanding that sanity is not the most important thing in a husband.

Geoff and Patrick Minne with Nanna,
Delhi's finest motorcycle dealer, and their brand-new Enfields
at the start of the Nambarrie Run from Delhi to Belfast

Part I

The Nambarrie Run
Delhi to Belfast on an Enfield

Kitting Out

It all began on Christmas Day 1997. I was happily proceeding in my ancient Porsche 924 around a roundabout in a clockwise fashion on my way to dinner with friends, and the next minute not proceeding at all. So if anyone ever tells you that Porsches don't break down, you can tell them different.

Now, I know that some purists say that a 924 was developed jointly with Audi and isn't a proper Porsche. But stuff them, I say. It's got the badge on the front, and that's all that matters, even if it does make me worry sometimes that, deep down, I'm a really shallow person. I know, too, that Porsche drivers are supposed to have huge egos and tiny dongles, but I can assure you that I don't. In fact, I'm very proud of having no ego at all. As for my dongles, they are a matter which I am not prepared to discuss in this book, since you may well be reading it before the nine o'clock watershed.

Anyway, there I was getting late for dinner, so I made my way to a nearby call box, phoned the man from the AA, and after a while he appeared in his van and took a close look at me.

'Yes, you've definitely been drinking too much,' he said. 'All the signs are there – red nose, bags under the eyes, unsteady hand ...'

'Hang on a second,' I said. 'You're from the wrong AA. It was the Automobile Association I wanted.'

'Fair enough,' he said in an equable manner. 'But remember – a drink isn't just for Christmas, it's for life.'

After a while, the correct chap appeared in a yellow van with flashing bits, and told me that the fuel pump had ceased to pump fuel and was unlikely to do so ever again, but that he was happy to give me a tow back to Belfast.

That evening, halfway through a bottle of wine, which is when I get some of my best ideas, I suddenly thought that rather than buy a new fuel pump, there was a more sensible solution. I would buy a motorbike, which would be cheaper to run, and much more fun than a car. There was only one problem. I was broke, as usual. Still, I was never one to let reality get in the way, and on Boxing Day, a solution presented itself serendipitously to me.

I was on my way to get the morning papers when I found a man called Brian Parke getting off a gleaming Royal Enfield outside the pub across the road.

'That's a lovely bike,' I said. 'How old is it?'

'Only a year, funny enough,' he answered, taking off his helmet and goggles. 'Royal Enfield had a factory in Madras from 1949 to 1955, making Bullet 500s for the Indian Army. When they shut up shop, the Indians bought the factory and the licence, and they've been making them ever since. The only difference is the electrics are twelve-volt instead of six, and they've got indicators.' He gave the bike a friendly pat. 'I bought this one brand new for 65,000 rupees when I was out there last year, rode it around India all summer and planned to sell it before I left, but then I couldn't bear to part with it, so I had it shipped home instead.'

'It's gorgeous,' I said, giving the bike a friendly pat myself. 'How much is 65,000 rupees?'

'Oh, about 865 quid.'

'Good heavens.'

I wandered on to the paper shop, all sorts of strange ideas bouncing around the inside of my head.

Then, on New Year's Eve, serendipity took another turn, as

serendipity will: my old mate Ian Mackinnon paid me a visit.

He used to play volleyball with me on the Northern Ireland Commonwealth team back in 1981, when we were Masters of the Universe, and was now living in Delhi with his German girlfriend.

'Here,' I said, as I opened a bottle of disturbingly expensive wine, 'do you know much about those Royal Enfields they're still making in Madras?'

'Know anything about them?' said Ian, draining his wine glass in a disturbingly expensive way. 'I should say so. I've got one myself and they're wonderful. If you're interested, I know Nanna pretty well. He's the dealer in Delhi and he'd send you one for 800-odd pounds, plus whatever the shipping costs are.'

I drained my glass and thought what a very good idea that was. However, by the time we had finished the whole bottle, and another one, I came up with a much simpler idea.

'It would make much more sense to fly out there, buy one and ride back,' I said to a slightly blurred Ian.

'But you don't know a single thing about motorbikes,' said Ian, who has suffered from common sense for as long as I've known him.

'That's not true. I did my test three years ago. I know they've got two wheels, and go until they stop. Besides, my dad used to race them, so it must be in my genes.'

'And how many miles have you done on a bike?'

'Well, let's see. I've been to Lisburn and back for the test – about thirty, I suppose.'

The thing is, he was right. It was a mad idea.

That evening, in a fit of late twentieth-century post-modern, post-prandial, pre-adventure angst, or possible sobriety, I phoned Carine Minne, a friend in London of the finest Franco-Belgian stock. Carine is a psychiatrist who spends her days helping people solve their problems, although, to be honest, I've always felt that psychiatrists are so expensive that they cause more problems than they solve, since you spend most of the session lying on the couch worrying about how you're going to pay the bill. It's not for nothing, after all, that the traditional psychiatrist's greeting is: 'Good morning, Mr Jones, five pounds. Sit down ten pounds. What can I do for you fifteen pounds?'

Thankfully, since Carine's a friend, she gives me advice for free, so I told her about the Enfield idea and the slight problem that I wouldn't know a tappet if one walked up and introduced itself.

'What a brilliant idea,' she said. 'Why don't you phone my brother Patrick? He's been obsessed by bikes since he was fourteen, and he does all his own mechanical stuff.'

'Do you think he'd be interested in going?'

'Listen, I'll tell you exactly what he'll say. He'll say: "Give me five minutes to make a month's worth of jam sandwiches." Here, I'll give you his number in Edinburgh.'

I put down the phone and called Patrick immediately. He answered on the third ring.

'Brilliant idea. Can you give me five minutes to make a month's worth of jam sandwiches?' he said.

It's spooky how much psychiatrists know about people, even if he is her brother.

I went out to a New Year's Eve party, got far too drunk, and the following afternoon, when I finally got up, phoned Exodus, a London company that specialises in overland trips to the Himalayas.

Camilla, the delightful young woman who answered the phone, said the expedition shouldn't be a problem as long as I stayed out of Afghanistan, where I was likely to be kidnapped and murdered by hill bandits. She suggested I contact the Royal Geographical Society and ask for their Expedition Advisory Centre, where I imagined a chap in a battered tweed jacket sat beside a bakelite telephone smoking a pipe, with a well-thumbed atlas on his knee. And she recommended the Royal Automobile Club for advice on *carnets de passage*, the passports for bikes that would permit transit through countries en route.

Tragically, even on the first day of planning this great adventure, I ran into a tangle of red tape created by the sort of people who have nothing better to do, and whose idea of adventure is wearing coloured socks on their day off and parking their jeeps on the pavement.

According to the RAC, for example, to transport a motorcycle worth £1,000 through Iran, you had to leave a bond of £4,000 at the border, in the optimistic hope of getting it back at the other end. If you hadn't quite got that much on you, the RAC would insure you for that amount, for a sum of £650, £450 of which you would get back if you made it safely through the country. All this for the privilege of riding your own motorcycle through a country where you would be likely to be roasted by day and frozen by night.

Pakistan promised to be even worse. Pakistan customs officials, I was told, would demand such a mound of paperwork that the simplest method of getting a vehicle through the country seemed to be to take it to pieces and post each bit separately to the first post office across the border.

But then, if God had meant life to be simple, he would never have invented the hydraulic suspension system on Citroën cars. And besides, everyone I mentioned it to thought the trip was a wonderful idea and said they'd do it themselves if only they'd been younger/older/mad.

Well, apart from my mother, who said, 'Do be careful of those bandits, dear.' Mind you, my mother says that even when I nip down to the shops.

Now all I had to was persuade Geoff Martin, the editor of the *News Letter*, the Belfast newspaper I worked for, to give me the time off for the trip.

'Mmm. How long do you think all this will take?' he said when I asked him the next day.

At least five weeks, I thought.

'Oh, four weeks at the very most,' I said airily. 'And you'll get a really good column from the road every day. And no newspaper in the UK has ever done something like this before.

And if I get some sort of financial backing, it won't cost you anything.'

This last bit seemed to interest him the most, even though I hadn't a clue what I was talking about, or who on earth I was going to get financial backing from.

'All right, then,' he said, surprising both of us.

It was February before I finally sat down and started organising the trip – and almost at once ran into the sort of apparently insoluble bureaucratic problems that were to crop up every single day for the next four months.

Patrick, now fondly known as Monsieur Minne, the world-famous Franco-Belgian motorcycle mechanic, a title befitting such a grand adventure, discovered that we needed to order the bikes from Nanna immediately, because before we could get the *carnets de passage*, we needed to get the logbooks with the bikes' registration and frame numbers on them. But Nanna would not release the logbooks until he had a letter from the British High Commission in Delhi authorising us to remove the motorcycles from India. Unfortunately, the British High Commission in Delhi insisted that we couldn't get the letter without the logbooks. Furthermore, to get the letter we would have to call in with our passports in person, which was a bit tricky, since I was in Belfast and Monsieur Minne was in Edinburgh.

However, in a stroke of genius, I delegated the matter to Patrick.

By the end of the month we had decided, by a democratic vote of two to nil, to set off in May, and I had been to the doctor to be immunised against malaria, rabies, hepatitis A-Z, meningitis, polio, cholera, anthrax, dysentery, dengue fever, bad taste and writer's block.

Amazingly, everything started to proceed according to plan. We ordered the motorbikes from Nanna, along with a frighteningly comprehensive list of spares, which Patrick dreamed up: namely, light bulbs, brake, clutch and accelerator cables, fuses, HT leads, chains, gaskets, pistons, piston rings and inner-tyre tubes. I never knew there were so many bits on a motorcycle, never mind spares for it. In fact, I felt sure that there were so many bits on Patrick's list that when we got back, we would be able to build another motorcycle out of them and sell it. As for what they all do, heaven only knows. I knew that the piston was the big bit in the middle of the engine that went up and down, and apparently, since the Enfield Bullet is a four-stroke single, whatever that means, the piston is the size of a dustbin and only goes up and down once every 500 miles or so, which means that on the ride back from Delhi the engine would actually only fire, if that's what engines do, about ten times, thus reducing the chances of it breaking down and leaving us in a phone box in the middle of the sands of Arabia trying to get through to AA Relay.

To reduce the chances of breakdown even further, we took on board the advice of Ian in Delhi, that since Indian motorcycle builders are to quality control what German businessmen are to stand-up comedy, most of the things that go wrong with Enfields do so in the first 1,000 miles. We had, as a result, come to an agreement with Nanna that he would get his staff to run in the bikes for us, then put back all the bits that fell off. The danger of this was that if Nanna employed the sort of indolent youths employed by garages all over the world, we would arrive to find that all that was left of our brand new motorcycles was a couple of dented mudguards and a wing nut. Whatever a wing nut is. So, when we heard in mid-March that our Enfields had arrived at Nanna's from the factory in Madras, we wondered fretfully if they were being run in with loving gentleness by his finest mechanics or knackered by the youths he employed at three rupees a week.

In fairness, this tendency of employing indolent youths is not confined solely to Indian motorcycle shops, but extends even to the most luxurious establishments in the West.

Since the offices of the *News Letter* are smack bang in the middle of a slick post-modern industrial estate, where every car dealer in Northern Ireland seems to have made their home,

I was quite used to the sight of large BMWs scorching past at 487 m.p.h., with the only sign of life inside the top of two crewcut heads belonging to the matching pair of garage apprentices on their way around to the local greasy spoon caff for a brace of bacon and egg sodas with extra ketchup for themselves and their mates. But then, if we were all the same, life would be a dull old thing altogether. I just hoped I wouldn't get back safely from the 7,000 miles from Delhi only to be mown down by a 7-Series travelling at just below the speed of sound, leaving me a crumpled heap of tattered leather and bruised ambition on the road, with the faintest aroma of bacon, eggs, ketchup and cheap hair gel hanging in the late afternoon breeze.

In any case, I had more important things to worry about, like the fact that I had no motorcycling gear whatsoever, having borrowed all I needed to do the test from the bike school I'd learnt at. And so, one Friday afternoon at the end of March, when any sensible person was packing up their desk and heading home for the weekend, I found myself standing in the doorway of Silverman's of east London, who are, according to their own publicity, suppliers of expedition kit to the professionals. I wasn't quite sure whether I was going to find inside earnest chaps in pith helmets and tweeds, preparing for a trip up the backwaters of the Amazon, or sad gits who liked to dress up as soldiers and watch Oliver Stone videos all weekend. However, when I stepped through the hallowed portals, I was the sole customer and had three sales assistants to choose from. There was a man who looked as if he hadn't slept for three weeks, an Indian woman who couldn't have been more than five feet tall, and, yes, an indolent youth. There are always indolent youths in places like this too.

'What can I do for you?' said the man pleasantly.

'I need a pair of boots that are cheap, rugged, lightweight enough for hot climates and suitable for riding a motorcycle back from India in May,' I said.

'Ah, you'll be wanting our Magnum boot in Cordura and

nylon at a very reasonable forty pounds,' he said.

'Those sound manly enough,' I replied. 'Do you have them in size twelve?'

'Naturally,' he said.

I put on the boots he gave me and marched up and down in front of the counter, feeling like a one-man Changing of the Guard.

'How do they look?' I said.

'Perfect,' said the man. 'Will you be wanting anything else for your trip?'

'I'm not sure,' I said, scratching my chin. 'Do you have any mosquito nets?'

'Of course. Single or double?'

'Er, single, I suppose,' I said, since I had no particular intention of snuggling up with Monsieur Minne of an evening, mosquitoes or no mosquitoes.

'Impregnated or plain?'

'What's the difference?'

'Well, if you're a mosquito, plain is like a road block and impregnated is like a bear trap.'

'I'll take the bear trap, then.'

'Good choice. You'd better have some prickly heat powder while you're at it. It's £2.99, special offer. What about water bottles?'

'Water bottles?'

'Absolutely. We do these collapsible 2.5 litre ones, which are dead handy. When they're empty, they take up hardly any space.'

'Unlike my brain, for example?'

'You said it, not me.'

And so it was that five minutes later I emerged from the shop laden with boots, mosquito net, water bottles, six bungee cords for general strapping-things-down-on-back-of-motorcycle purposes, and a container of prickly heat powder, even though I was still a little unclear as to what exactly prickly heat was. I imagined it was something prickly you got when it was hot, and if it only cost £2.99 to get rid of it, it was cheap at the price, if you asked me.

I went back to the friend's flat I was staying in, made some supper, drank several glasses of wine and then, although I should probably be embarrassed to admit it, put my new boots on and marched round the flat, admiring them from different angles. Sometimes, no matter how hard you to try to be grown up, you just end up ten years old again.

It soon became clear that our madcap scheme was going to cost us both several billion pounds, which I was unlikely to recoup from the *News Letter's* annual travel department budget of nought pounds and nought pence precisely, and I realised that I would have to lay aside my normal high standards of editorial integrity and plunge willy-nilly into the world of gross commercialism, particularly since I had promised the editor in a moment of wild generosity that this wouldn't cost the paper a penny. A sponsor, that was the thing, and no better man to discuss the issue with than public relations genius Joris Minne, who is, of course, in case you accuse me of vicarious nepotism, no relation whatsoever to Patrick Minne, or to Carine Minne for that matter, apart from being their older brother.

I made an urgent appointment by telephone, hied myself immediately to the sumptuously spartan home of Minne the slightly elder in the mountains, high above the tedious everyday life of Belfast, found him in his favourite armchair by the fire, and broached the matter without wasting a moment in idle frippery.

He stroked his chin, which had only that morning been carefully shaven by his Turkish barber and lovingly annointed with attar of roses, essence of myrrh and several other precious unguents which I am not at liberty to disclose for the simple reason that being from the country I am unversed in such matters, adjusted his handwoven silk tie, in spite of the fact that it had already been perfectly knotted only half an hour before by his Assyrian valet, and said in his immaculately cultivated Franco-Belgian accent, 'Tea.'

'Tea?' I said, being a simple rural lad unused to the succinctly monosyllabic conversations in which men liked to converse to indicate subtly that while few words might be spoken, an entire universe of thoughts, dreams, hopes, ambitions and deeply felt emotions are whirling around below the surface. And indeed, this was to be the case, for it became clear from Joris Minne's next sentence that, while he had only uttered a single word, a scheme both breathtaking in its simple boldness and infinite in its potential had already been formulated behind his noble brow, which had only the evening before been bathed by his Persian maid in olive oil from the first pressing of the season in Naoussa, the unspoilt village on the balmy shores of the Greek island of Paros.

'Tea,' he said again, removing from his elegantly curved lips a fine 1937 Romeo y Julieta rolled on the dusky thighs of none other than Castro's mother, a redoubtable beauty in her day, and entirely without the voluminous beard sported by her son. 'I feel that in this case the best approach would be to a fine, upstanding company such as Nambarrie, which purveys its tea from none other than the very subcontinent from which you intend to make your departure. I shall make a phone call immediately.' He flicked an iota of dust from the flawlessly cut lapel of his cashmere Gieves, Hawkes, Rembrandt and Dormeuil smoking jacket as he left the room. And indeed, in no time at all, he had returned to tell me that Nambarrie was graciously willing to help with the finances.

And not a moment too soon, for in mid-April I received an e-mail from Patrick saying that Nanna had, rather unreasonably, asked for some money for the Enfields. Patrick had wired him the princely sum of £2517.50, which, he itemised, covered the cost of the long-distance spec for the bikes, larger tanks, better tyres, crash guards and hand-built panniers, all the spare parts we ordered, letters from the British High Commission, banking charges, faxes and exchange rate changes between today and tomorrow. 'Ergo,' the message ended, 'you owe me £1258.75.'

I couldn't help but think, as I wrote out a cheque to him, that this trip was supposed to be saving me money on car repairs.

Thankfully, shortly after, a large cheque arrived from Nambarrie to cover the entire cost of the trip, so I immediately sent half of it to Monsieur Minne, then went shopping for a pair of goggles.

And so the preparations continued apace. All the major problems had been taken care of, like the goggles, and only a few minor details, like the flights to Delhi, remained to be dealt with.

It seemed, you see, that in going to India that summer, myself and Monsieur Minne unwittingly found ourselves heralding the dawn of a new fashion in travel. In short, the world and his grandmother were going to India that summer, whereas the previous year most flights heading in that direction contained only the flight crew, the chief stewardess, and a wrinkled matriarch fleeing the unbearable damp of an English summer. Now, while it was somewhat gratifying to have anticipated a trend so successfully, it meant that every airline marketing supremo I phoned up and asked, 'Here, what about giving us chaps a couple of free seats in return for the plethora of publicity you'll get?' just laughed hysterically, thanked me for cheering them up no end, and put down the phone.

Thankfully, KLM finally came up with tickets from Belfast to Delhi, and Jet Airways agreed to get us from there to Calcutta to pick up the first tea leaves of the season and bring them back to Nambarrie headquarters as a publicity stunt.

In the meantime, tragically, the people at Nambarrie turned down our inspired suggestion that they should provide matching Hell's Angels leather jackets, inscribed on the back with the legend 'Nambarrie's Chosen Few', above a tea bag and crossed spoons. Instead, they wanted us to paint the motorcycles in the company colours of pillar box red and canary yellow, which would be a nice surprise for Nanna in

Delhi, since we had already told him we wanted them in elegant grey, then changed our minds and asked for them in black.

Nambarrie also wanted us to slap a company logo on the petrol tank, in a move which would certainly maintain our sense of corporate identity as we trundled across the Baluchistan desert. Unfortunately, it would also make us much easier to spot by passing Pakistani dacoits, the world's most middle-class bandits who, deeply disillusioned with the government's inability to provide them with a job after university, had taken to the hills for a life of kidnapping passing adventurers in a bid to embarrass the government into at least coming up with a job creation agency.

Still, at least it would make the bikes easier for us to find. We had toyed briefly with the idea of painting them in desert camouflage colours, before realising that we would wake up every morning and spend half the day wandering around in the sand muttering, 'I was sure I parked it here somewhere.' And anyway, it could have been worse. Nambarrie also markets another brand of tea, and if we had been sponsored by it, we would have ended up riding two motorcycles, one red, one yellow, a quarter of the way across the world with 'Pratts' in huge letters on the side.

I rang Nanna to tell him about the change of colour. He seemed to take it well, apart from the screaming, so I put the phone down just as Gavin, the artist in work, arrived with the artwork that would appear above my daily dispatches. Below the heroic legend 'The Nambarrie Run', it showed Monsieur Minne and I hurtling west across a map of the route from Delhi to Belfast, coat-tails flapping in the wind and two tea chests strapped to the back of our red and yellow Enfields.

Splendid, I thought. At least we would look well, which was, after all, the main thing.

Now, here is a handy hint for anyone who wishes to avoid being garrotted, beaten to death with rusty barbed wire or shaved all over with a blunt rock.

Do not mention insurance companies to me. Ever.

You see, in a sane and sensible world insurance companies would be there to provide insurance. But it seems they are there to give you several thousand reasons why they cannot. Let me give you an example. A month before we were due to leave I had mailed the firm that provides insurance for the company I work for, to check that I would be insured for the trip. At first they said no. Then they said yes. Then, when I phoned them with less than a couple of weeks to go, they denied they had ever heard of me.

I put down the phone in disgust and called an international insurance company, and got the numbers for their offices in Dubai, Calcutta and, believe it or not, Ipswich. I called Dubai, left a message and got no reply. I called Calcutta and got a recorded message in Gujarati, Hindi, Urdu, English, and left-handed Swahili, saying that the office had closed for the foreseeable future. I called Ipswich and was told that they would not insure motorcycles in any shape or form.

For the rest of that day, I tried every insurance company in the UK, and they laughed at me. Then I tried what seemed like every one in the world, and they just laughed at me in other languages. I was just about to go home when the phone rang. It was Monsieur Minne.

'Listen. This is a cry for help,' he said. 'I've tried everything to get myself insured for the motorbike. I've rung a million companies. I've rung the Association of British Insurers. I've joined the BMF, the IMF, MFI and MI5. And nothing. I can get personal travel insurance, but it won't cover me for personal liability if I cause an accident.'

'It's funny you should say that,' I said. 'There's only one solution.'

'What?'

'We'd better not have an accident.'

On the way home, I bought a bottle of manzanilla, the delicious Andalucían aperitif that smells exactly like old walnuts, and decided to forget about insurance for the time being.

I picked up the phone the next morning for no other reason than that it was ringing, and found a man with a very expensive voice on the other end.

It turned out to belong to Richard Weller, a TV producer who had heard about the trip from Monsieur Minne, and wanted to approach Channel 4 with a proposal to do a programme about it.

'I'm just looking for a bit of background before I talk to them. Paddy tells me your dad used to race motorbikes?'

'Aye, although he never caught one,' I said. 'He used to own a small country garage specialising in bikes, and he was a very good amateur rider in Northern Ireland until he got engaged and gave up racing because my mum didn't want to be a widow before she got married. They're now divorced, sadly, but the ironic thing was that it was only after he gave up racing that he had a bike accident. When I was eight, he was knocked down at a crossroads by his bank manager.'

'They obviously dealt with overdrafts a little more severely in those days.'

'Quite. Anyway, he was pretty badly injured, and he's never ridden a bike since. For years I was interested in bikes but didn't do anything about it, until I finally did my test three years ago, though I haven't been on a bike since then. I guess this whole thing is a rite of passage for me, when I finally become my father's son. You know, following in his footsteps. Or tyre tracks.'

'And what about Paddy?'

'Well, I'm glad he's coming along,' I said. 'Ever read *Zen and the Art of Motorcycle Maintenance*? The idea that people are divided into romantics and classicists? Well, I'm the romantic, interested in the beauty and romance of the whole thing; and Patrick's the classicist, more interested in taking it apart and seeing how it works, and then keeping it working. Perfect combination. Also, he knows what tappets are.'

'So let me get this straight,' said Richard. 'You did your test three years ago and you haven't been on a bike since, and in a few weeks you're going to be getting on an unreliable, heavy, cantankerous British classic, re-learning to ride through one of the most chaotic cities on earth, and then setting off on a 7,000-mile journey through areas like Baluchistan in the deserts of eastern Pakistan where, according to my *Lonely Planet* guide, the advice is, 'on no account set out on the roads without an armed escort organised by the appropriate tribal chieftan, although you should be safe on the main road to the border if you travel in a convoy'. And you're also going through south-east Turkey, where in the unlikely event of you surviving Pakistan, you stand a good chance of being kidnapped by Kurdish bandits.'

'Er, yes,' I said, making a mental note to read some guidebooks before we set off.

'Fascinating,' said Richard. 'Fascinating. Let me talk to Channel 4 immediately, and I'll get back to you tomorrow.'

But nothing ever came of it. It seems that TV companies need several years' notice to produce terrible television, unlike writers, who can produce terrible stories at the drop of a biro. Still, never mind. I always thought I'd a better face for radio.

I popped down to Omagh that weekend to take my dear old dad for a spin up to the coast and say goodbye before Monsieur Minne and I left for our little jaunt in less than two weeks' time.

I found Dad pottering around the living room until he finally discovered, among the thousands of old envelopes, books, newspapers and carefully written notes reminding him to do things which would never get done, what he had been looking for – volume 4 of *British Motorcycles since 1950* by Steve Wilson, which had a section on the 1956 Royal Enfield, the motorcycle which is virtually identical to the machines on which Patrick and I would be proceeding west from Delhi. The book fell open at a suitably reassuring passage: 'In service the dual brakes were good but not exceptional, a lot of braking energy being absorbed by the two cables and the cables' whiffle-tree or beam compensating mechanism.'

Heavens, I thought, I had better pen a memo immediately to Nanna, asking him to ensure that our cables are utterly free of any whiffle-tree or beam compensating difficulties.

Dad, meanwhile, had temporarily forgotten that we were supposed to be getting ready for a trip to the seaside, and had settled down in his favourite armchair to read a magazine article on the Manx Norton. As he sat in that chair by the fire, looking more and more like Moses, you wouldn't have thought that he was once completely bonkers.

'You know,' he said, 'I remember the first motorbike I ever bought. It was a 1926 BSA, the same year as I was born, and I got it from a farmer for a fiver, for it was lying in a barn covered in chicken shit.'

He had borrowed a trailer, and he and his brother Fred hauled it back to one of the outhouses of the big house at Termon, where my grandfather Edward was the butler. There Dad, a brilliant self-taught mechanic and electrician, stripped it down to the last nut and bolt, enamelled the frame and rebuilt the engine better than new. In those days, he thought nothing of jumping on the bike on a Sunday morning, doing an entire circuit of the province of Ulster and being home in time for tea.

'God help that bike,' he said, 'for the only speed I knew in those days was flat out.'

It seemed strange that this old white-haired man had once so happily embraced the madcap joy of youth. I know that we all grow old and grey and full of sleep. It just seemed unfair that it had happened to my dad.

But then I caught the twinkle in his eyes, and realised that no BSA was quite safe yet.

'Right,' he said, 'shall we go to the seaside, then?'

'Do you want me to drive, Dad?' I said as we walked out to his car, an ancient diesel Vauxhall Belmont which might see fifth gear in a month of Sundays.

Although it was a blazing day, like old dads everywhere, he was wearing a vest, a shirt, a pullover and a jacket. I resisted the temptation to ask him if he wanted to bring an overcoat, just in case.

'Well, let's see how far I get,' he said, lowering himself into the driving seat.

In the end, he made it all the way to the Port, overtaking several tractors as a final flourish before handing me the keys and treating himself to a half pint of cider in the British Legion. It was the furthest he had driven for eight years, and the first time he had seen the sea since 1985.

It was early evening by the time we headed home by the scenic route, and twilight by the time we reached Cookstown, where he and Uncle Fred had fought some ding-dong battles with the other top local riders in the early fifties.

Down the long main street and out into the leafy glades, the shadows lengthened towards dusk as he talked about how in the Cookstown 100 of 1952, Fred had been going like the clappers around this 100-mile race on a Norton that my dad had stripped down and rebuilt to full Manx specification. Until he hit a patch of oil and slid into a hedge, which the local farmer had stripped down and rebuilt to barbed-wire specification. Emerging scratched and bruised, Fred bent the bike back into shape and rode on to ninth place, making him the third top local rider of the year.

Dad, until he got married and gave up racing, was no mean shakes himself: riding an underpowered handchange Rudge, he had finished the same race the year before with a nut missing from the front forks, passing on the final bend a chap who had just returned from a 100 m.p.h. lap at Brooklands.

He remembered it all as I drove him around the course in the Belmont: every bend, every oil leak, every pit stop, every rider he overtook until the attack of the missing nut.

'Shame I didn't have a Manx Norton,' he muttered, scratching his snowy beard. 'They wouldn't have seen my heels for dust. Look, this is the final bend where I passed Geordie Brocken going full tilt, with the forks shaking and rattling all over the shop. When I took the flag and pulled into the pits, one of the other mechanics came over to me and said: "Bob, it took a man with a strong back and a weak mind to ride that bike today".' He laughed, a sound I had not heard for a while.

It was a cold and starry night when I dropped him back at the house, and before I left to drive back to Belfast Dad and I stood on the front step looking up at the moon, as we tend to a lot in our family.

'You know,' he said, 'this reminds of the nights I used to ride the old Norton with the straight-through Burgess silencer home late from work, and John Donaghy, who was our neighbour in those days, would come to his back door when he heard that sound – it was very distinctive, that Burgess silencer – and he would listen to it all the way up the lane from the gatelodge until I turned into the courtyard and switched her off, and then he knew the day was done, and he would go in to bed.'

Now, I wouldn't know a Burgess silencer if one walked up and handed me a calling card, but wrapped up in memory and moonlight and the thought of my dad as a young man before age wore him down, it seemed like the most romantic thing in the world, as I drove back to Belfast with, on the passenger seat beside me, volume 4 of *British Motorcycles since 1950*, with its dire warnings about the mysterious dangers of the whiffle-tree or beam compensating mechanism.

If whiffle-trees and beam compensation were our only problems, however, we would have been truly blessed, for the organisation of this trip over the past months had left me so close to going quite gaga that if I survived it, I promised to give up this travel-writing lark, buy a pipe, a large tin of Old Throgmorton's Ready-Rubbed Tobacco and a pair of carpet slippers, and spend the rest of my life in the armchair by the fire with a good book, preferably one I'd written myself.

Take insurance, for example. Now, I know I said that I wasn't going to bother with it, but after several nightmares in which Patrick lay bleeding to death at the side of the road, with me trudging off to spend the rest of my life alone in an Iranian cell for running down a mullah, I decided to have another go. However, after several million more attempts I utterly failed, partly because the bikes were registered in India and we were in the UK, and partly because the trip was so dangerous that the insurance companies could not stomach the fact that they might actually have to pay out something for all the dosh they get, the two-faced, lily-livered bunch of faceless pen-pushers. Not that I'm bitter or anything.

The only glimmer of hope was a friend of a local Indian restaurant-owner called Mohammed Rayees in Dubai, who chuckled merrily when I asked him about the matter.

'If you get into any bother in Pakistan or India,' he said, 'please call me immediately. I have several friends in Pakistan, and my brother is an MP in India.'

I wasn't sure whether he meant a military policeman or a member of parliament. We might need both, I thought, since another little problem was the fact that India and Pakistan, embroiled in yet another dispute over Kashmir and international sanctions, seemed to be engaged in a nuclear-testing contest, a rather curious affair in which each country was testing larger and larger nuclear bombs in its own territory in a frightening game of one-upmanship, which looked as if it would end with the winner being the country that blew itself up first, presumably with Patrick and I sitting in the middle, like two pieces of burnt toast.

And as if that wasn't enough, my passport had just arrived back from the Iranian embassy in London with my visa stamped 'Period of stay – five days', in spite of the fact that the itinerary I gave them in February had nine clearly defined days on it, all of them called different names like Monday, Tuesday and so on, and also in spite of the fact that the only way to get across the vast expanse of Iran in five days is in a military jet.

However, I cheered myself up by buying possibly the coolest motorcycle jacket in the entire universe as a little birthday present to myself. I won't go on about how cool it is. I will simply say this: it's Italian. And when I looked at it, the thought of whiffle-trees, beam compensating mechanisms, insurance, visas, and dying in a nuclear war somehow went clean out of my head.

Suitably attired, I returned one day to the leafy lanes of Tyrone where I was brought up; to a country garage in the hamlet of Ardstraw, to be specific, very much like the one once owned by my father. The Castrol sign was turning slowly in the summer breeze, the mysterious tools were hung in order on hooks along the wall, the boxes of Champion spark plugs sat on wooden shelves, the smell of fresh rubber from the stack of Dunlop tyres in the corner, the redolent tang of ancient oil, and the sweet jangle of a spanner dropped on concrete.

Above the door, and a clue to why I was there in the first place, hung a poster in which a chap, his Army and Navy Store surplus seaman's wool socks folded carefully over his leather motorcycle boots, was hurtling around a country bend, nothing in front of him but the open road, and nothing behind him but the past and the flapping tail of the red and white polka-dot scarf he borrowed from his girlfriend and never quite got around to returning. And above him as he raced endlessly through the gap between perfect childhood and intangible future, on a very fetching parchment background, were the words 'Enfield Authorised Dealer'. For this little country garage was owned by a man called George Miller, who had had a Royal Enfield when he started to ride motorbikes back at the start of the fifties, and now imported them for no other reason than nostalgia.

Not that George will ever get fat on the one or two Enfields he sells every year – but in a world where companies are run by humourless men in grey suits whose vision extends no further than the bottom line on a balance sheet, George has not forgotten the very important lesson that life should be fun.

Like most motorcyclists of his age, he remembers the Enfield as an unsung hero of the fifties, a fast and reliable machine whose fate was to sit in the shadow of the Nortons, Triumphs and Matchlesses, whose marketing men or racing prowess made them the motorcycles on which young men put down their demob pay as a deposit. And this afternoon that unsung hero, like the tortoise who outran the hares, was sitting in the summer sun outside George Miller's garage, being topped up with oil and petrol by Frank Connolly, a man with a moustache worthy of a Bulgarian wine waiter, who I took to be George's trusty assistant, but who turned out to be a man who was just passing by.

'There you are, she's ready to go. Do you want to start her up?' said Frank.

Absolutely, if I knew how, was the answer.

As I found out, the process of starting an Enfield goes something like this: you switch on the fuel tap, the ignition, the electrics master switch and the choke. Then you hold the decompressor lever in and swing the kick-start pedal a couple of times until the ammeter needle is pointing skywards, which shows – although I hadn't a clue why – that the piston is at the top of its travel. Then you release the decompressor, ease the kick-start down until you feel resistance, and kick hard, at which point one of two things happens.
(a) The pedal will kick back viciously, breaking your ankle,
(b) Nothing.
If it is the former, you then fall over, ring an ambulance and go to hospital. If it is the latter, you sigh and repeat the process.

After several attempts, you push in the choke, try again, and finally breathe a sigh of relief as the engine coughs into hearty life.

And if that seems a bit more complicated than just pressing a button, the sound of an Enfield when it starts is worth it. If you could bottle a sound like that, you'd have a really nice sound in a bottle. Like a hippo farting underwater when it's ticking over, it becomes a throaty roar and then an angry snarl at full throttle.

I climbed aboard, clicked first gear with the lever, which is on the right in the old British tradition, slipped the clutch, and

I was off down the leafy lanes of my childhood, becoming at first my father, then me as a boy, and then, as the sun flickered through the branches of a roadside elm, the man in the poster above the door.

I was in heaven.

That evening, with only a few days to go before the grand adventure, I called Ian in Delhi, only to find out that he wouldn't be there when we arrived because he had to leave urgently for Germany.

'Anyway, it's 46 degrees here, so even the locals are dying like flies,' he said. 'I'll be glad to get out for a while. This heat's impossible even for me, and I've been living here for years.'

Good grief, I thought, as I put the phone down. With heat like that and at least four hours' motorbike riding a day and Delhi belly, I'll come home an inch wide and dark brown, like an unusually long shoelace.

To try to stop myself panicking and calling the whole thing off, I sat down and made a complete list of everything you need to get from Delhi to Belfast on an Enfield. And here it is, just in case you ever feel like trying it.

Transport

One Royal Enfield Bullet 500 motorcycle, supplied and run in by Nanna of Delhi and his indolent youths, upgraded for long-distance travel with panniers, heavy-duty tyres, leg guards and 21-litre tank, and supplied with a complete set of spares, including tyres, tubes, gaskets, tappets, fork seals, cables and pistons.

Clothing

One motorcycle helmet, one pair goggles, one pair tinted lens, clear visor, tinted visor, two pairs sunglasses, one lightweight rainbow-coloured scarf, one lightweight astonishingly beautiful Italian motorcycle jacket, lightweight leather gloves, one back support belt to stop kidneys disintegrating, one pair ex-Dutch paratrooper's trousers from Edinburgh Army and Navy Stores, two sets of underwear, one pair lightweight motorcycle boots,

baseball cap, one short-sleeved T-shirt, one long-sleeved T-shirt
for Muslim countries, one polo shirt and one pair chinos for
formal occasions, one pair chino shorts for swanning about
outside Muslim countries, one pair swimming trunks for diving
into Black Sea on arrival in Turkey, three pairs socks, one pair
canvas shoes.

Accommodation

One tent, one sleeping bag, one stuff sack, one sleeping mat, one
impregnated mosquito net, one International Youth Hostel
Association membership card.

Money

£1,200 in traveller's cheques plus £400 worth of US dollars and
£200 worth of Deutschmarks for baksheesh in the Middle East and
Eastern Europe respectively, plus £10 sterling for Turkish visa at
border. Credit cards, emergency loss phone number. Money belt.

Paperwork

Passport with visas for India, Pakistan, Iran and Romania,
international driving licence, medical emergency card, carnet
documents for bikes, covering letter explaining purpose of trip,
customs export certificate for tea, maps of each country as far as
Turkey, European motoring atlas, AA planned route from Istanbul
to Ostend, spare passport photos, photocopies of all relevant
pages of passport in case of loss, four large and two small
notebooks, four fine black Bic biros.

Books

Rough Guides or Lonely Planet guides to each country en route,
plus *Full Tilt: Dunkirk to Delhi on a Bicycle* by Dervla Murphy,
Culture Shock! Pakistan by Karin Mittman and Zafar Hisan,
Danziger's Travels by Nick Danziger, *The Road to Oxiana* by Robert
Byron, *Dervish: Travels in Modern Turkey* by Tim Kelsey and
Culture Shock! Turkey by Arin Bayraktaroglu.

Technology

Psion Series 5 palmtop computer, modem, mobile phone, charger,
spare batteries for Psion, microcassette recorder, ancient Pentax
MX, 12 rolls film. BT phone card if all else fails.

Medical

Vaccinations against malaria, hepatitis A and B, rabies, meningitis A and C, typhoid, polio and tetanus. Basic first-aid box plus sunscreen, lip salve, foot powder, prickly heat powder, iodine, insect repellent, diarrhoea and food poisoning treatment, laxatives, rehydration tablets, water purification tablets, eyebath, antibiotics, sutures, syringes, haemorrhoid cream (a must after four hours a day on a vintage bike), multivitamins, general toiletries.

Hardware

Swiss Army knife, torch, four 2.5-litre expanding water bottles, U-bolt and chain for bike security, padlocks for luggage, ex-army entrenching tool (for no other reason than that Patrick thought that it looked cool), soft seat bag, tank bag, bungee cords and straps for attaching luggage, cargo net, mess kit, and small cooking stove.

The day before our departure, Monsieur Minne arrived from Edinburgh, left all his stuff in the living room, and went shopping.

I was lying in the hammock in the back yard reading a copy of *Biggles Flies West* when, late in the summer afternoon, the doorbell rang. As I went to answer it I could hear a strange yet familiar sound from outside. And when I opened the door, there was a Royal Enfield ticking over, and Brian Parke, the man who on Boxing Day had put the idea into my head in the first place, was standing beside it with a grin on his face.

'Read your piece in the paper yesterday about the trip,' he said. 'Fancy a spin?'

I made us some coffee and we were sitting on the front step under the maple tree when around the corner, carrying a video camera and a shortwave radio he'd just bought, came Patrick. We had a ride up and down the avenue on the Enfield, then we all sat on the step drinking beer and looking at it. I caught Patrick's eye and knew that we were both thinking the same thing. He raised his bottle, in the dappled light below the tree, and I raised mine.

That evening we spread everything we had planned to take on the living-room floor, pared our bare minimum down to an even barer one, and packed it all away.

'Shame about the entrenching tool,' said Patrick, gazing wistfully at the discarded pile.

Finally, we had another beer and went to bed after setting the alarm for 4.15 a.m. But I was too excited to sleep and spent the night dreaming fitfully that I was in a race with a naked Tara Fitzgerald.

She had almost caught me when the alarm jangled me awake at dawn.

India

Our 6.30 a.m. flight from Belfast to Amsterdam on 31 May peeled itself damply off the runway and into low cloud, and the wet green fields slowly faded to white, like that technique Wim Wenders always used in his old movies. Most of the way we just skimmed the clouds, as if we were in an old fifties Douglas Dakota, and I gazed out of the window dreamily, uncertain whether I was going back to childhood or forward to maturity, until my reverie was interrupted by burning my tongue on breakfast.

'There's nothing worse than scorching your tongue on a hot baked bean first thing in the morning,' I said to the famous Franco-Belgium motorcycle mechanic.

'Except for having your dick nailed to a burning building,' said Monsieur Minne, who could always be relied on to retain a healthy perspective on things.

At Amsterdam, our 747 to Delhi was called Charles A. Lindbergh. Monsieur Minne and I crept on board, settled into our soft seats, and accepted, with a pang of regret, a glass of champagne and a bag of elegant toiletries from the stewardess. After all, it was the last luxury we would see for quite some time.

'This is much nicer than the one I've brought with me,' said Patrick, gazing wistfully into his free bag, as I accidentally sprayed myself in the eye with rose water.

At Delhi airport, we counted our bags, with relief, off the carousel and went to the Punjab Bank 24-hour currency exchange desk, at which sat an eager teenager, wearing a white shirt and a black moustache. On one side of the desk was a pillar of rupees about a foot high, stapled together in bundles, and on the other, a column of forms. He sat in between, like a Samson of finance.

I handed him a traveller's cheque and he set to work furiously disengaging the rupees. When he had unstapled several thousand, he turned his attention to the pile of forms, withdrew one at random and handed it over. The typewriter ribbon had given up the ghost at about the end of the Second World War, and I signed somewhere towards the bottom, roughly where I imagined a signature might be required, added the date as an afterthought, and handed the form back.

Laden with rupees, we emerged into the Delhi night. It was 38 degrees centigrade and a few minutes before midnight. Beside us, a man was languidly whitewashing a pillar, and in front of us stood a handsome Sikh gentleman whose metal name tag identified him as I.R. Dhillon. He wore a spotless khaki uniform complete with epaulettes.

'Ah, Mr Hill and Mr Minne,' he said pleasantly, opening the door of a cream Hindustani Ambassador, the copy of the fifties Morris Oxford that is still being manufactured in the subcontinent.

We stepped inside, and entered India.

Two sleepless hours after we had checked into the luxury Ashok Hotel – it was the most expensive night's sleep I've never had – we were driven to the airport for our flight to Calcutta to collect the tea. As we dozed in the back, I.R. Dhillon waltzed the Ambassador elegantly between huge Tata trucks, psychedelically painted from head to toe, whose drivers, keeping themselves awake on a diet of opium, roar vast distances through the night. On the backs of the trucks were painted various exhortations such as 'Blow Horn' (superfluous advice), 'Keep Your Distance' (useless advice), 'Amazing India' (tautological advice), and 'Ex-Serviceman's Carrier' (intriguing advice).

At the airport we had left only a few hours earlier, we tipped I.R. - we never did find out what his initials stood for – a meagre 100 rupees, or £1.80, which later turned out to be more than the average weekly wage, noted with a measure of terrified concern that even at this hour the airport thermometer read 46 degrees, and strode into the domestic departures terminal to find a scene which if it had been a *Star Trek* episode would have been called 'Planet of the Love Goddesses' .

'Is it just me, Scotty, or is everyone on this planet impossibly beautiful?' I said to Monsieur Minne, as two stewardesses glided past and came to land only yards away in a flurry of cayenne, turquoise and lilac, then an entire family fluttered by in russet, emerald and tangerine. Coming from a land of grey suits and rain, it was like going to sleep as the Birdman of Alcatraz and waking up in an aviary.

'Indeed, I'm having trouble controlling my dilithium crystals, Captain,' said Monsieur Minne, who was reading the horoscope in the *Jet Airways* magazine he'd picked up. 'You're a Gemini, aren't you?' he said. 'It says here that this is a bad time for you to jump into anything new.'

'Now you tell me. What does yours say?'

'I'm an Aquarius. We don't believe in that horoscope crap. Anyway, it says this isn't a good time to start a new venture.'

Halfway through the flight to Calcutta he had recovered sufficiently from this bad news to lean over and mutter, 'If you don't want your breakfast, I'll have it.'

'How long have you had this pathological fear over where your next meal is coming from?' I said.

'Since the last one,' he replied.

I made a mental note to save him an extra tea bag for supper as the plane descended towards Calcutta's Dum-Dum airport, not far from the eponymous factory where the British produced the infamous exploding bullet, which ensured that its victims wouldn't be going home for tea that day or any other.

As we stepped off the plane it soon became obvious that our flawless expedition planning had paid off yet again, for we had arrived on the hottest day of the year. And although Calcutta was a piffling 34 degrees compared to Delhi's 46 degrees, it also had 97 per cent humidity – 97 per cent water and 3 per cent steam, that is. If Delhi was a sauna, this was a Turkish bath, and as we walked through the terminal building to be greeted by Rishi Raaj Deb, the tea company's man in Calcutta, we could already feel mushrooms sprouting between our toes and palm trees growing out of our ears.

'Welcome to Calcutta,' was Rishi's greeting, 'have you heard that thousands of people are dying because of the heat?'

We drove into the city and a scene so fantastic that it is difficult to describe, except as a tapestry of images that flashed by – acres of laundry drying on riverside bushes, people bathing in the muddy water, rickety rickshaws, cows contemplating the endless weaving and honking traffic from their position of spiritual sanctity, shacks, the ubiquitous Ambassador taxis competing for space with 75-year-old trams, markets, a cricket game in Victoria Park watched by two vultures too hot to fly, the man with the most pointless job in the world sitting in a car marked 'Calcutta Traffic Police', company signs promising the earth and everything in it, beauty and poverty cheek by jowl, and through it all the sense of some vast, chaotic, madcap system, which finally, more by luck than logic, gets things done.

We stopped outside an elegantly peeling block in the business quarter, and walked through a ground floor that had been gutted by a fire and which was still smoking here and there. We took an ancient lift to the sixth floor, where we were ushered, steaming gently, just as the lights flickered and went out to signal yet another power cut, into the mahogany and leather office of Vijay K. Awasty, founder, chairman and managing director of Bush Tea, Nambarrie's Calcutta subsidiary.

'Ah, good morning, gentlemen,' said Vijay, rising from behind a desk, on which a miniature set of silver golf clubs took pride of place. 'Would you like a cup of tea?'

Indeed, how could we refuse?

For the next hour he entertained us on subjects as diverse as Tea: 'Tea is food to an Indian. You will quite often see a poor chap have nothing more for lunch than a piece of bread dipped in tea, and be bloody happy with that.'

The Partition of India: 'It was bloody horrible. I was only twelve at the time, growing up in Lahore in what is now Pakistan, and it was announced overnight. We had to just leave everything and take the train east. Of course, many of the trains were stopped and all the occupants slaughtered – by both sides – but we got through. Bloody lucky, really. And there is no individual animosity, even today with all this nuclear testing nonsense. It's just the politicians being bloody fools as usual. Look, I even went back to Lahore recently and found my father's old house, and the family who had been living there all this time said, "We are so glad to meet you. All these years we have been living in this huge house, and wondering who it belonged to." They even took me to their club for lunch, in fact.'

The Game of Golf: 'Some lovely courses in the Rockies. Do you play at all?'

And University: 'Of course, all the boys learned Urdu and Persian, and the girls learned Hindi. But we never bothered to learn to write Urdu, until a week before the final exams the authorities decided there was going to be a written examination. Naturally, there was a bloody riot, and in the end they gave us the questions and we mugged them up and passed.'

And so to the tea-tasting rooms, where twenty-one cupfuls in descending order of merit were waiting, from the first aromatic flush of the finest Darjeeling to what would be the last dusty tea bag left on the shelf. In the corner were two large tea chests, and for a worrying moment we thought Vijay was going to ask us to take those back to Belfast, but in the end we were presented with a discreet silver canister filled with the finest, and first, Darjeeling leaves of the season.

Mission accomplished. Now all we had to do was get it home.

'You do realise we won't be able to keep this Darjeeling,' said Patrick, as we headed for the airport through the rush-hour traffic.

'Why ever not?'

'Because all proper tea is theft,' he said.

I was proud of him. Puns that bad show a rare talent.

As we descended through the roseate dusk on our return flight, the Captain came on the blower.

'Ladies and gentlemen, welcome to Delhi. The temperature is 42 degrees,' he said. Now, that's an oxymoron if ever I heard one.

I.R. Dhillon drove us through the night back to our hotel, and we finally fell into our beds at 1.20 a.m. We had not slept for over forty hours, yet, insanely, Patrick took out his new shortwave radio and started learning how to work it, and I began to write down everything that had happened during the day.

The next morning the front page lead headline of the *Times* of India thundered: 'Petrol Price Raised Sharply', and below it the line, 'Not enough for a kick start'. Thankfully, closer inspection revealed that the latter referred to the economy, not Enfields, so we breakfasted on coffee and omelettes and set off in a rickshaw in the direction of Nanna's motorcycle yard.

Having finally fallen asleep the previous night just before dawn, we had slept so late that it was now noon, and 44 degrees in the shade. Still, at least it was so hot that the mosquitoes were refusing to come out. We ignored the rickshaw driver's fervent attempts to sell us sightseeing and shopping tours, life insurance, and his family, and then ignored his attempts to charge us 10 pounds, handing him instead 100 rupees and finally stepping down at Nanna's in the middle of a slum only 200 yards from the front door of the Delhi Hilton.

It was a typical small garage, down to the girlie calendar on the wall advertising spark plugs, except that since this was India, the girlie wore a full-length sari and an expression of syrupy coyness which suggested that for the appropriate fee she might cover you in warm yoghurt and beat you gently with a poppadom.

A small man with a large smile emerged from the shadows and came towards us wiping his hands on an oily rag.

'You must be Geoff and Patrick. Welcome to Nanna's,' he said, shaking our hands.

'Hello, hello. Are you Nanna?' I said.

'No, he had to go out. He'll be back in a few hours, if you'd like to wait. Can I get you some tea?'

We sat down to wait in the shade of a bo tree, surrounded by Enfields old and new, a 1936 Norton, and a goat of uncertain vintage and a truculent nature. In one sun-dappled corner of the yard sat the two most beautiful motorcycles we had ever seen, one cinnamon red and the other lemon yellow. And the best thing of all was that they were ours.

We sat sipping tea and admiring them until Nanna returned half an hour later.

'Listen, I'm very sorry, but we didn't really get these run in as you requested. It was too bloody hot to go out, you see,' he said.

Oh well, never mind. Neither of us had ever owned a brand-new vehicle before. We kicked them into life, had a couple of practice spins around the block, shook hands with Nanna and set off back to the hotel

I think it was at this moment that, sitting in the saddle of the Enfield looking out into a maelstrom of vehicles, I truly realised simultaneously that I had only ever ridden 30 miles on a motorcycle before, that I was 7,000 miles from home, that I was sitting on the only thing capable of getting me there, and that if I was accused of sanity, not a court in the land would convict me.

One hundred and fifty people die every day on India's roads, and after ten minutes in Delhi traffic I was, frankly, surprised that I wasn't one of them. I could see now why Siddhartha, the founder of Buddhism, recommended the middle way as the proper method of proceeding through life. The middle way is the only way of staying alive on Indian roads. To make matters worse, the engine kept stalling because the clutch refused to disengage, and I just couldn't find neutral on the neutral finder. I stalled at a junction, looked up, and to my utter dismay Monsieur Minne was nowhere in sight. I was lost in a heat wave, without a map, in one of the most chaotic cities in the world, and rush hour was only minutes away.

After several seconds' rational analysis of the situation, I decided that the only option open to me was to panic. So I panicked.

After I had finished panicking, I asked eight people, from the large crowd that had gathered to watch me panic, for directions, and got nine different answers. They weren't being mendacious, of course, just helpful to the point of unhelpfulness.

Finally, given the choice between lying down in the road and crying and coming up with a solution, I had the bright idea of asking a passing taxi driver to lead the way back to the hotel while I followed, and after fifteen minutes I was home, drenched in sweat and poisoned by the taxi's diesel fumes, but alive.

'Ah, there you are,' said Monsieur Minne. 'I was just reading that driving in Delhi traffic is the equivalent of smoking forty a day. Just think of the money I'm going to save.'

I garrotted him playfully for several minutes, and then, after I calmed down, we compared injuries – burnt fingers because the controls were so hot and burnt legs from the engine. But having survived the first day, we made plans to go out and celebrate. Burns night, naturally.

In the meantime, I penned a memo to God. Dear God, why in the name of, well, yourself really, have you organised so much heat for that part of the world when there are other parts crying out for it? When Lapp woodsmen sit shivering in their woolly socks as they wait for the mighty tundra rabbit to appear over the frozen horizon. When Siberian farmers realise that the reason they never made it big in wheat is because the grains they sowed twenty years ago are still lying on the surface of the permafrost with baffled expressions on their tiny frozen faces.

By the will of Allah and the seven sainted Sultanas of Constantinople, I never knew there was that much heat in the world, or I would have started a movement to ban it. I was reminded of the words of the much-travelled English clergyman Sidney Smith: 'Heat, ma'am! It was so dreadful here that I found there was nothing left for it but to take off my flesh and sit in my bones.'

Throughout India, during the previous seven days, 1,359 people had died because of the heat, and here in Delhi, there were riots against power cuts and water shortages as the temperature hit 48 degrees, one degree above the temperature at which aerosol cans start exploding spontaneously.

The next day at noon we climbed aboard our shiny new motorcycles and roared off to Nanna's to pay our last bills, collect our last spares, and say our last farewells.

Nanna was sitting in his yard wearing black lace-up shoes, trousers the colour of hot chocolate before you put the milk in, and, unbelievably in this heat, a vest under his shirt. He was talking to Dilip Surana, a young businessman who organised Enfield tours of the Himalayas. Watching him, with that peculiar expression of benign malevolence that they have, was Nanna's goat, which he had bought for three dollars from a street butcher who was about to slaughter it.

'I was just walking past and this goat head-butted me. I

thought he was asking for assistance, you know,' said Nanna. 'Mind you, he still head-butts me, but in a friendly sort of a way.'

So Nanna not only saves classic motorcycles, but classic goats as well.

As we waited for our bill to be totted up, Nanna showed us photographs of old Enfields he had restored, new Enfields with astonishing paint finishes, and ingenious mechanical adaptations he had dreamed up in the long, hot summers when work was scarce. He had photographs of his customers from all over the world. Most of them had bought their Enfields there while on holiday, then had them shipped home, but one plucky Frenchwoman had spent two months learning to ride on Nanna's own Enfield, then bought one and ridden it back home to Paris. So we weren't quite alone in our lunacy.

Inside the workshop, under a corrugated tin roof, several small boys were sorting nuts and polishing tanks, and in the paint room a chicken was cooking in the wood-fired oven, out of which an Enfield, resprayed British racing green, had just been removed.

'We always have a chicken after baking the paint. Shame to waste the heat,' said Nanna.

Back in the yard under a jungle fruit tree, the goat had reached the end of its tether and been freed by one of the boys. It was now wandering around licking the batteries of old Matchlesses, NSUs, Nortons and BSAs because it liked the taste of the sulphur.

We returned to the hotel to pack, and went to bed early to rise at dawn for the start, at last, of the great adventure. Except that five minutes later the phone rang. It was Dilip, the young man we'd met at Nanna's earlier.

'Hey, Nanna and I are going out for dinner,' he said. 'Want to come?'

Half an hour later he and Nanna pulled up in a large white Nissan and we drove out to a restaurant and disco complex called The Sahara. On the way, Nanna and Dilip talked about motorcycles in a strange mixture of Hindi and English, which sounded like: 'Poppadom spark plugs Peshwari brake pads tikka masala spare tyre.'

We arrived at The Sahara to find from the waiter that it no longer served beer.

'What, the Sahara has gone dry?' said Dilip, who laughed so uncontrollably at his own joke that we thought he was going to burst a vein.

We ate there anyway, then drove ten miles north to the strip of no-man's-land between Delhi and Haryana, where the city's strict alcohol laws do not apply. And there, in a large sandy space off the road, dozens of cars with couples in them sat in front of a vast shed of booze, surmounted by a large flickering sign advertising Seagram's Royal Stag Whisky, and fronted by flamboyant Punch and Judy drapes. It was like being an extra in a Bollywood sequel to *American Graffiti*.

'I think our hopes of leaving at dawn are fading fast,' said Patrick, as Dilip went off to get the first round.

'Why on earth do you want to leave at dawn?' said Nanna, twisting around from the driving seat.

'To miss the heat and the trucks,' said Patrick.

'And because it sounds good,' I said.

'No, no, the truck drivers sleep all night and start at eight,' said Nanna. 'The best time to leave is at 1 a.m.'

I looked at my watch. It was five minutes to midnight.

'Here's the beer,' said Dilip, arriving back with four one-litre bottles of Kingfisher. 'When are you chaps actually leaving?'

'I told them to start at one,' said Nanna.

'No, no,' said Dilip. 'It's far too dangerous to drive at night, because everyone drives with their lights off to save the bulbs. Also, the truck drivers never drive in the heat of the day. Best time to leave is at nine.'

Several hours and beers later, when we finally did crawl into bed, we decided we would just leave when we woke up.

By eight in the morning we had checked the bikes and I was

packing everything on board when the yard man came up.

'Good morning, sir,' he said, saluting smartly.

'Good morning.'

'You are checking out?'

'Yes, in about one hour.'

'Tomorrow?'

'No, today.'

'What time are you checking out?'

'About nine.'

'This evening?'

'No, this morning.'

'Tomorrow?'

'No, today.'

Thankfully, at this stage, Monsieur Minne appeared with eight litres of water.

'Fancy an expedition, old chap?' he said to me.

'Don't mind if I do, actually.'

It was, I must say, one of the most exciting and yet nervous moments of my life kick-starting the Enfield, climbing on and pulling out into the Delhi traffic. My heart felt full to the brim as we wound our way out of the city for the last time and turned north-west along the Grand Trunk Road towards Pakistan.

At times the countryside around us was like France, with poplar trees lining the road all the way to the horizon. The only difference was that, at 46 degrees, it felt as if someone was blowing a hot hair dryer in your face all the way.

Half an hour out of the city I pulled alongside Monsieur Minne and lifted my goggles, blinking in the heat.

'We've just passed a brewery,' I shouted over the roar of the engines.

'Why?' he laughed as we slowed for a row of hay carts pulled by bullocks, at the front of which a camel was being harnessed. 'Here I am, the king of the bleeding desert,' his splendidly haughty face seemed to say, 'looking after this lot. What a load of old bullocks.'

Further on a Tata truck was leaning drunkenly against the ditch, its back axle nowhere in sight. The driver, unperturbed, lay asleep on the front seat, waiting for God or a mechanic to rescue him.

A mile after that, I was riding along minding my own business and thinking how wonderful life was when a Tata, coming the other way, suddenly pulled out and overtook a bus, its driver blithely ignoring the fact that I was occupying the other lane at the time. As he hurtled towards me in a cloud of thundering dust, I swerved off the road into deep gravel, almost went flying headlong and skidded to a halt about a foot from a large tree, my heart racing.

'Bloody hell,' I said to a large heron, who had seen the whole thing from the riverbank alongside. 'That Tata was almost bye-bye.'

He didn't even chuckle. No sense of humour, herons.

I could see now why so many people died on the roads. Not to mention the people dying of the heat. Mind you, with almost 55,000 babies born in the country every day – although not all to the same woman – there was little risk of the country ending up deserted.

At lunch time, after several more near-death experiences, all involving Tatas hurtling towards us on the wrong side of the road, we stopped at a roadside rest house north of Panipat at which only one small boy spoke English.

'What's good?' we asked him, lifting the lids of a row of mysterious pots.

'Cheese tomato masala everything,' he said brightly.

'We'll have that,' we said.

We dined surrounded by flies, since Panipat is allegedly the most fly-infested place in India after a local saint banned them, then returned them a thousandfold when the people complained that he had done too good a job.

'I seem to be getting a springy-spongy sound from the forks when I go over a bump,' I said to Monsieur Minne, keen to expand my mechanical knowledge.

'That'll be the fork springs,' he said, his mouth full of cheese tomato masala everything.

And so our first day passed entirely agreeably, until at nightfall we found ourselves in Chandigarh, designed by Le Corbusier as a model city in the fifties. Unfortunately he had not designed in enough hotels, and we arrived to find every decent one full. We trudged around glumly, being turned away from one after the other, until we finally found the Motel Shiwa, where the morose and unshaven proprietor painstakingly checked us in as we sat under a photograph of his morose and unshaven late father and a cheesy calendar for a forestry company.

Wearily we climbed the stairs to our derelict room, clutching carbon copies of the eight separate forms we had been required to fill in to register – since along with the railways, the great British legacy to India has been a love of paperwork, a tradition maintained so successfully by the smug and bloated Civil Service that it has practically ground the country to a halt.

By the grubby window, I watched as, in the square below, a diligent policeman stopped every scooter with more than four people on it and ticked them off, after which they all apologised profusely, climbed back on the same scooter and rode off again.

Patrick was in the bathroom with a case of the Nambarrie runs, and I was trying to become resigned to the fact that I was probably the only person ever to come to India and get constipation.

I was knackered and covered in dust from head to foot. What I needed, as Carol, my colleague in the office back home was fond of saying, was a good rub down with a wet lettuce.

After the harsh rigours of our first day on the road, the next morning was like an English summer's day, an effect heightened by countryside that looked eerily like Kent. We breakfasted at a roadside diner, where a magnificently hirsute Sikh chef cooked us two perfect omelettes.

As we sat in the dappled shade, an elderly gentleman

crawled slowly by on one of the hand-powered tricycles, below which only pedestrians rank in the hierarchy of Indian roads. Above the tricycles come the bicycles, of which the Hero company alone turns out three million a year. After that are the bullocks, pedal rickshaws, then tractors, mopeds, scooters, auto-rickshaws and Enfields, thus completing the two-wheeled section. Bottom of the four-wheelers are Ambassadors, then normal cars ranked according to the same Murphy's Law system that applies in the UK – that is, the slower ones are always in front of you. Top of the pile are the Tatas, which, as we know, hurtle down the roads day and night, driven by wild-eyed men who overtake on blind corners as a matter of course, forcing everyone and anyone out of their way. Well, everyone except buses, which have precedence over trucks, presumably because they have more voters on board, and India is the world's largest democracy.

Still, at least first sight of an Indian bus solved one mystery I had wondered about for all the years I had worked as a journalist, which is why, every Saturday night, a story would come in from Reuters, headlined: '58 die in Indian bus smash'. Why always fifty-eight? I wondered. Well, now I know. That's exactly the number you can cram onto a bus designed to take half that.

Exempt from this pecking order of the roads are sacred cows and strange people-carriers made from what looked like old Douglas Dakota fuselages powered by lawnmower engines. They were so slow when crossing a junction that any drivers approaching it stopped their vehicles, went to the nearest milk bar and came back in an hour.

By evening we were motoring into Amritsar, near the Pakistan border.

'Welcome to the holy city. Are you insured?' said a huge yellow advertising hoarding.

Indeed it had a point, for Amritsar is not only the centre of the Sikh religion, but a dangerous spot at times. In 1919, almost 2,000 unarmed Indians demonstrating for independence were shot indiscriminately by the British, and in 1984 Sikh extremists occupying the Golden Temple were evicted by the Indian army, with at least 1,000 killed.

That evening, though, reflected perfectly in the water which surrounds it, the eighteenth-century temple was a beautiful and peaceful place.

Almost as beautiful as Mrs Bhandari's guesthouse, where we stayed, which had a garden, a swimming pool and unlimited cold beer. Compared to the previous night, when we had been unwillingly seduced by the lusty attentions of several large bedbugs, we were now, in the holy city of the Sikhs, close to paradise.

Pakistan

'On a normal Friday night,' said Monsieur Minne as we had our breakfast of coffee and eggs under an awning in the garden of Mrs Bhandari's guesthouse, 'I'd get home from work, put on three loads of laundry, fall asleep in front of the TV for half an hour, watch *Friends*, *Have I Got News for You* and *Frasier*, go to the pub with some mates, have several beers, get a curry, take a cab home and go to bed. Last night, I got a rickshaw pedalled by a man called Jo-Jo through the crowded, chaotic streets of Amritsar, saw the Golden Temple at dusk, then had dinner under the stars.'

'Did you notice much difference at all?' I said, helping myself to another slice of mango.

In the garden beside us an elderly Sikh was planting begonias and a young boy was trimming the hedges, while in the kitchen of the rambling mansion, which Mrs Bhandari the elder and her husband had built in the thirties, Mrs Bhandari the younger was organising the servants' rota for the day. Thirties house, fifties bedrooms, timeless hospitality, and we were enjoying our last morning of it, for today we would ride across the border into Pakistan, and, by all accounts, into cowboy country.

'You are now leaving civilisation,' was how Phil, an English engineer, had put it at dinner last night.

How right he was, for as dusty, chaotic and poverty-stricken as India had seemed, Pakistan was to make it look like Switzerland by comparison.

A couple of miles from the border I had my last vision of India: a woman walking by the roadside wearing a kingfisher blue sari and saffron scarf, carrying on her head a large canvas bag overflowing with hay. It was a perfect symbol for the country: burdened by a rocketing population, falling water levels, pollution, poverty, heat, dust and apparent chaos, it still fed its people and produced the most sublime beauty almost by accident.

At the Indian side of the border we were interviewed by a charming and elderly Sikh gentleman immaculately turned out in khaki uniform with matching turban. He was called Mr Singh, as was his young assistant, and indeed most Sikh gentlemen.

'What is your occupation, please?' said Mr Singh the younger.

'I am a writer,' I said, working on the principle that if I said it often enough, it would come true.

'Ah, I too am a writer,' he replied. 'I am writing poems and music, and I am in the band of the Civil Service. If I may send you my poems, may you publish them in UK?'

'Please do.'

'And will you send me copies of your articles on India?'

'Indeed I shall.'

'Thank you very much, you are most kind.'

On the Pakistani side, the customs post was a gloomy barracks block, in the doorway of which stood a young man in a grimy shalwar camise, the long shirt and loose trousers favoured by both sexes.

'Come in,' he said.

We sat on a wooden bench, and our friend put his feet up on a chipped wooden table and came straight to the point.

'How much money do you have?'

We told him.

'Give me 100 Deutschmarks. You will be out of here in half

an hour. For some people it takes three days,' he said.

Patrick dug out a 100 Deutschmark note and handed it over for both of us.

'No, I mean 100 Deutschmarks each.'

He went out with the money, and a large, heavily moustachioed man came in and sat at the table.

'Passport and carnet documents, please.'

He studied them closely.

'What is your opinion of the nuclear testing?' he said.

'I hope the situation will return to normal soon,' I said diplomatically.

'I see. What is your opinion of the sanctions against Pakistan by several foreign powers?'

'There have been none by the UK,' said Patrick.

'Quite. What is your opinion of the Kashmir situation?'

This was a reference to the mainly Muslim state whose Hindu maharajah had opted to stay with India at the time of partition, against the wishes of his people. A ragtag army of Pakistani forces was dispatched to seize it, but, showing an early aptitude for the chaos that has been the national hobby ever since, did so much plundering en route that India got there first, and Kashmir has been an open wound between the two countries ever since.

'We think it should belong to Pakistan,' Patrick and I said simultaneously, as the younger man came back with a wad of Pakistani rupees.

'Here is the money for your Deutschmarks. I have given you good rate. Now we must look in your bags.'

'Of course,' we said, surprised to be getting the money back at all.

We went outside, and the intensity of the heat – it was 46 degrees – must have suddenly struck him.

'Tell me, for you are good man. Have you any alcohol?'

'No.'

'Very well. You may go.'

We rode off down the dusty main road and into Pakistan. At

times we were bumping along what looked and felt like a dried-up river bed, choking on the dust of everything from lumbering bullock carts to gaudily painted vintage Bedford trucks, like tarts on wheels, and constantly at risk from drivers who would see you coming and still pull out, forcing you to slam on the brakes. At least in India everyone, except bus and Tata drivers, pull out in a charming and apologetic sort of way.

Lahore was even worse. Back in Delhi, Nanna had told us: 'Lucky you learnt in Delhi traffic. It's nice and slow compared to Lahore.' As we had stood in his yard looking out at the maelstrom on wheels storming past, we had thought he was joking, but the scene that greeted us in Lahore was one of Wild West anarchy.

We parked the bikes in front of the train station, Patrick went off to phone the wonderfully named Wing Commander Butt, our contact in Lahore, and I was surrounded by about fifty curious onlookers, some more curious than others.

'What is your country of origin, please?' said the one at the front, an elderly man with only two front teeth and a wild look in his eye.

'Ireland.'

'Ah, Holland.'

'No, Ireland.'

'Ah, Iran.'

'No, Ireland.'

'Ah, Holland.'

'Yes, Holland.'

At this stage there was a furious commotion and a young, very earnest man forced his way through the crowd to my side.

'Please do not stay here,' he said. 'It is very dangerous. Here is my card if you need any help.'

'Muhammed Ali Khan, finest quality housery and shoe exporter', it read.

Of course, since I had two motorbikes to carry, no idea where Patrick was and a large crowd in front of me, I wasn't going anywhere.

About five minutes later, Patrick came back.

'The Wing Commander says the only safe place in town is the Ambassador, but it's about 35 pounds each,' he said. 'Nice to see you've made lots of friends.'

We rode to the Ambassador, avoiding death several dozen times over, more by the will of Allah than any judgement on our part, and found that the room was actually 50 pounds each, way beyond our budget. Still, better broke than dead, as my granny was so fond of saying in her later years, and we retired to our over-priced room, watched the Asian indoor windsurfing championships on television and waited for the Wing Commander. He was a friend of Major Mogh-Rees, who was a cousin of Monsieur Minne's brother Joris's friend Miah Khan, a highly respected patriarch of the Pakistani community in Northern Ireland and the owner of an excellent restaurant in north Belfast. I hope that's all clear. If there are any children reading this, Miah Khan is no relation whatsoever to Shere Khan, who is a tiger, which are banned from owning restaurants because they eat the customers.

The Wing Commander eventually knocked on our door. He was without Major Mogh-Rees, which was a pity, for we had been looking forward to meeting him.

'I'm sorry the Major cannot join us. His wife insisted he go to his daughter's birthday party in Islamabad,' said the Wing Commander.

'Yes, what a shame,' said Patrick. 'Are you married, Wing Commander?'

'A bit,' said the Wing Commander, leading us out to a 1963 Ford Cortina. 'My apologies,' he added. 'My personal car has just been sold.'

'Not at all. My parents had a car just like this. It was even the same colour,' I said, climbing in and feeling like I was going for a family picnic, as we set off for a splendid Chinese meal in a flashy Las Vegas-style strip.

'Crikey, what a place,' said Patrick. 'Who owns all of this?'

'The army,' said the Wing Commander, dishing out the

crispy duck, tucking into an extra bowl of won-ton noodle soup with extra chilli sauce, then going on to spend the evening describing in detail what Pakistan (population 117 million) would do to India (population 1.1 billion and rising) if the Indians escalated the nuclear testing crisis. It had been a long time since the chaotic partition of India on religious grounds in 1947, when Muslims fleeing west to the newly created Pakistan were slaughtered in their hundreds of thousands by Hindus and Sikhs, who then suffered the same fate as they fled east to India, but memories, it seemed, were just as long.

'If they declare a jihad, I feel sorry for them,' he said, then insisted on paying for the meal.

Total war, total generosity. Pakistan was going to take a bit of getting used to.

The next morning the Wing Commander's eyes widened in horror and he almost choked on his Sunday breakfast.

'No no, you must not even consider going by road through Pakistan at the moment. It is much too dangerous. People are getting kidnapped every day, and are never seen again,' he said.

And so, later that morning, we found ourselves sitting in the first-class, air-conditioned waiting room for gentlemen at Lahore railway station. With its deep turquoise wainscoting and cream walls, and its oak sideboard, fireplace and oval table, it looked exactly like a Victorian dining room, and it seemed that at any moment a butler would appear bearing tea.

And indeed, an elderly, bespectacled gentleman in a white shalwar camise arrived with a battered tin tray bearing a pot, milk, sugar, and a plate of custard creams.

'Chai, sirs?' he said.

As we munched our biscuits, all around us on low benches were men in various states of repose, while in a corner one knelt towards Mecca, which lay equidistant between platforms four and five. Outside, our motorcycles, emptied of fuel, sat waiting to be laboriously loaded into the luggage car of the 12.45 train for the 27-hour journey to Quetta. No space had been available, but after the appearance of 200 rupees, some had miraculously been found.

At 1.15 the train lumbered in, and a porter swathed in orange robes, with the hawkish nose and fierce expression of a Pathan tribesman from the north, bore our luggage to the carriage. There we found that, due to an over-booking error, our compartment was filled with a family of four from Peshawar, a major from Islamabad, and a very elderly couple from Lahore. But immediately, grandmother was hoisted onto an overhead bunk, grandfather was squeezed into a corner to read the paper, two babies were stacked on their mother's knee, and their father offered us half his family's lunch.

And so, for the rest of the day there was little else to do but indulge in that most Zen-like of activities – sitting in a train watching the world roll slowly by.

Betweentimes we snoozed and discussed cricket with grandfather: 'Well, in my youth I was a five-day man, but today people do not have the time for it.'

Politics with the Major – particularly the argument that has bedevilled relationships between India and Pakistan ever since partition: 'Well, of course, Kashmir is rightly ours, and I will now give you a million reasons why, in alphabetical order' (even though, on the other side of the border, we had heard the same million reasons why it should be Indian).

And life as a one-and-a-half-year-old, with the eldest of the two babies: 'Ooh, ah, goo, crash' (sound of glass falling off window shelf).

At Kot Radha Kishan a small boy with a spanner about three feet long was adjusting the tracks, and at Okara a huge dust storm blew up, enveloping the world in an orange pall. Trees bent like whips, families huddled by the roadside with scarves wrapped around their faces, jaunting cars ground to a halt, and bullocks cowered in massive silence. It was eerily evocative of a nuclear winter, sweeping across the land between two nations which in the past six years had spent 70 billion US dollars on defence and 12 billion on education. Why they spent so much on defence was quite beyond me: no one would invade Pakistan because they couldn't afford the bribes, and no one would invade India because there simply isn't room for anyone else in the country.

But then the rains came, bringing relief from the sullen sky.

The couple and their baby daughters disembarked at Mian Channon, and the rest of us spread out and, not without difficulty, lit the dim reading lights by the window. As we sped west into the gathering dark, with the grandfather praying, his wife dreaming of her university days in Madras, Monsieur Minne wondering out loud why on earth there was a distillery in Quetta, since no one was allowed to drink, and the Major reading an article in the *Reader's Digest* entitled 'Hypnotise Your Way to Success', our carriage was not unlike a small Edwardian sitting room, outside which the sun finally set on a land not much changed since the fourteenth century.

After about an hour grandfather leaned over and confided: 'I used to sing, you know. I sang with that famous American once, but I have forgotten his name,' he said, then burst into a pitch perfect rendition of 'Can you remember her name, Miranda?'

The Major disembarked at Multan after giving us each a mango, leaving the four of us – Patrick, myself, grandfather and grandmother.

We climbed at last into our separate bunks, and just as I was nodding off grandfather tapped me on the elbow. 'I have remembered now. It was Paul Robeson,' he said.

We breakfasted on the Major's mangoes, and throughout the morning grandfather lectured Patrick on God and cricket. Patrick, who believed in neither, was visibly nodding off. Outside, the landscape was flat and arid.

'Did you know that the Baluchi language has over 160 words for date?' I said, trying to rouse him from his languor.

'Really? What are they?' he said, apparently without moving his lips.

To while away the long hours before the train arrived in

Quetta, we played I Spy.

'I spy with my little eye something beginning with S,' I said.

'Sand,' said Monsieur Minne.

That was the end of the game.

All afternoon we climbed into the dry mountains, then just before tea time the train plunged into a short tunnel and emerged into a dramatically different landscape – a fertile valley dotted with nomads' tents and camel trains, orchards and wheat fields. A few miles to the north lay the Afghanistan border.

We disembarked at Quetta, the regional capital of Baluchistan and home of feudal warlords over whom the Pakistani government does not even pretend to have control, making the region the kidnapping centre of the country. North of here they build houses exactly on the border so they can smuggle drugs in the back door and out the front, not wishing to bother the customs officials with tiresome procedures, and in Quetta itself they all live on Sariab Road, from which they emerge from time to time to race through the streets in armed motorcades. It was a one-horse town until they kidnapped the horse.

Unfortunately they also seemed to have kidnapped the train to Mirjave on the Iranian border. According to our guidebooks, one was supposed to leave the following day, but the stationmaster was adamant that the next one was not for five days. Like Shergar and double-breasted jackets, it had vanished as if it never existed. People in Quetta looked baffled when we mentioned it, and small boys ran away screaming; when they were not trying to sell us hashish, that is.

We booked into a hotel quaintly called The New Lourdes. Presumably the bandits had stolen the old one. But worst of all, they had also stolen the satellite TV which the guidebooks promised us was a feature of the hotel, and on which Monsieur Minne was fervently hoping to watch the Scotland v. Brazil World Cup game. For him, this was the greatest tragedy of the trip to date.

We made plans to go to the tourist office in the morning to enquire about the missing train. And a new guidebook. In the meantime, we dined on a surly chicken, and went to bed in our bare ground-floor room, while the Enfields slept outside in the pale moonlight.

After a light breakfast of tea, toast and marmalade, we walked into town to encounter everything from the fourteenth to the twentieth century: merchants selling peaches, grapes, cherries, melons and apples, bookshops with everything from Enid Blyton and Tintin to 227 Ways to Unleash the Sex Goddess in Every Woman. However, since I had read all the Tintin and I had no wish to unleash the sex goddess in Monsieur Minne, I declined to make a purchase. Inside the general stores were interiors recognisable to anyone over the age of forty – mahogany and glass cabinets, and shelves piled high with cardboard boxes containing everything from shoelaces to spark plugs.

From an Afghani merchant in a tiny room lined with carpets we bought two camises. The loose, long-sleeved shirts would ensure we were not stoned to death in Iran for the near-genocidal crime of baring our forearms. The merchant's friend appeared, conjuring mirrored prayer hats, fantastical waistcoats, bejewelled rugs and blocks of hashish out of thin air. Our opinions and our cash were sought over endless bowls of green tea. But our wallets were empty and our bladders were full, and we left with apologies.

On Sariab Road, a steady stream of supplicants wearing the exotic robes of the tribes – the Brahuis, Baluchis, Pashtuns, Meds, Khoras and Makranis – queued at the heavily guarded entrances of the tribal chiefs, seeking safe passage through the hostile desert. But even in our new camises we could not have passed for the most Aryan of Pashtuns, and we found ourselves instead in the office of Mr Miqubal Kasi, the local chief of the Pakistani tourist information tribe, seeking advice on whether to ride to the Iranian border or wait five days for the train.

'Kidnapping?' he scoffed. 'Pah. You have been reading those bloody guidebooks, haven't you?'

We nodded shamefacedly, not wanting to confess to him that we had also been warned off by the Wing Commander.

'Listen, the road to the border is perfectly safe. You can get petrol, you can stay in Dalbandin, you can stay in Mirjave,' he assured us. 'The manager of the tourist motel in Koh-i-Taftan, near the border, is Qayyum Khan. Here, I will write it down. Tell him I sent you.'

We walked back to the hotel, thinking that we would purloin a second opinion from Malcolm Bennett, the British warden of the town, and if he said yes, we would leave at dawn. Allah and Royal Enfield willing, we could be in Iran in two days. But fate was to have other plans for us, for as we let ourselves into our room, the phone was ringing. It was Malcolm, who had heard we were in town, and he had some terse technical advice on the risks of travelling by road to the border.

'We're having an ex-pats party and a few beers tomorrow night,' he said. 'Come to that instead.'

Ten minutes later the phone rang again. It was Nigel Langdon, a 28-year-old irrigation engineer from Sheffield and a friend of Malcolm's.

'Take the train. The road is bad, dull, hot and long. Anyway, I'm riding back to the UK in three weeks on a '57 Triumph Thunderbird. Fancy going out to dinner tonight and comparing notes?' he said.

Mind you, I wasn't sure either was right when they said the train was safer – a bomb had exploded on the Karachi to Peshawar express that morning, killing 26 people and injuring 45. Pakistan's Information Minister, naturally, blamed the Indians.

And the horoscope in the *Khaleej Times* had been even less help on whether to leave now by road or wait for the train. Monsieur Minne's said: 'Play a waiting game. If patient you win, otherwise you invite loss.' Mine claimed: 'Funding available, so full steam ahead.'

Suddenly there was the sound of a large diesel engine outside the door, and we stepped out to find that Nigel had arrived in a Toyota pick-up truck and a cloud of dust. If we had expected a safari suit, pith helmet and carefully clipped moustache, we were in for a shock – he was wearing combat trousers, a black vest and a ponytail.

'Welcome to Pakistan, officially the second most corrupt country in the world after Nigeria,' he said, as he slotted into the cassette player what I believed from Monsieur Minne was known as a mix of intelligent house and ambient techno, and we drove off in search of a pizza parlour on Jinnah Street. 'The Pakistanis were really pissed off at that one. They reckon if they weren't so good at hiding the corruption, they'd have been first,' Nigel added. 'Damn, what's happened to the pizza place?'

'Closed,' said an elderly Pashtun sitting on the pavement.

'Damn. That was the only good one in town. The Baluchis never did cotton on to the concept of pizza. Wait, I know a good Chinese.'

We crunched into second gear and raced across a roundabout, forcing a motorised rickshaw to stand on what passed for its brakes. Nigel used the traditional Pakistani driving technique of full speed ahead and no mercy, but since he slowed down slightly for junctions, it was really Pakistani Lite.

'By the way,' he said, 'if you guys are looking for anything cheap, everything that's stolen in Europe ends up in Afghanistan, then here. Olympus cameras, Sony TVs, brand-new motorbikes – you name it.'

Chinese takeaway safely on board, we raced to his house in a nearby compound.

'Mixers. Bloody hell, we need mixers. I've got gin, whiskey and Cossack vodka from the local distillery. All highly illegal, of course,' he said. 'Foreigners get a booze allowance here, you see. The Germans get the most, then the UN, then aid workers, then elderly diplomats, who donate what they can't drink to the communal bar, and if all else fails, we drink the local stuff.'

On his front porch, as we opened the gates and drove into the courtyard, sat Nigel's driver Aslam. Aslam, who had a magnificent white beard which made him look like a photographic negative of Abraham Lincoln, was cradling his two baby daughters, Asha and Aksa, and Aslam's friend Abdul was reading back issues of *Classic British Bike* magazine.

'How do you do?' said Aslam. 'You're the chaps with the Enfields, I hear. I have a '61 Bonneville myself.'

'Asalaam aleikum,' said Abdul, who, it transpired, was restoring the 1952 ex-army Triumph Speed Twin we had noticed sitting outside a garage in town earlier that day.

In the courtyard sat Nigel's own immaculate Triumph, the plaything of a tribal chief who had grown too old for it, and as slim and lethal as a shark.

Since Nigel was paid at the local rate, it had taken him a year to save the 800 pounds for it, unlike the Germans, who have bought up virtually all the classic British bikes and spares in Pakistan and driven prices so high that even the simplest parts cost Abdul and Aslam two months' wages. We may have won the war, but we've lost the Nortons.

We ate on the porch and talked of old motorcycles, as Aslam's daughters fell asleep to the whisper of the pines, the light of the full moon and the distant crackle of Kalashnikovs from over on Sariab Road to announce the start of an Afghani wedding ceremony, which apparently lasts longer than most British marriages.

We drove home at two in the morning. On Jinnah Street, an old man with a flute played the tremulous refrain from an old Baluchi song, which ends: 'Our drink is from the flowing springs, our bed the thorny bush, the ground we make our pillow.'

We went to bed with no intention whatsoever of rising at dawn. This adventuring lark was all right, but a beer and the Scotland v. Brazil World Cup match was a whole different kettle of ball games altogether.

We spent the next evening before the match learning the arcane intricacies of a 1957 Triumph Thunderbird wiring system from Nigel, and then retired to the Quetta ex-pats bar night, a weekly movable feast of illicit distilling pleasures. It was like a cocktail party in Kent, upon which God had visited the curse of Babel.

There was a bunch of twenty-something Italians from Fiat, building a power station, which, by all accounts, will turn out to be as reliable as their cars, or as Nigel put it tartly: 'I wouldn't be surprised if the bloody thing blows up the moment they switch it on.' There was also a beautiful Italian woman with a hypnotic navel, but sadly she was with her beautiful Italian husband.

There was a handful of very drunk French thirty-somethings, whose white Toyota Land Cruisers with UN number plates were parked in a neat row outside. 'Oui Oui, we are all from the Antarctic. We are all penguins there,' said François, the tallest, with a Freddie Mercury haircut and a dangerous look about him. For a penguin, that is.

And then there was Edgar, who was wearing a suspiciously striped polo shirt and had just spent three weeks' leave decorating his flat in Hamburg. 'Ja, in Africa I vas a bush pilot. Quite often I vud look out of ze window and zee the clouds gazzering, and by ze time I got up, zere vere zunderstorms tventy zousand veet high. So I vud fly down ze river to ze zee, zen hop along ze vaves, like zis. Vun day I take up a nurse and she pissed her pants, ha ha ha. No, really.'

I must have nodded off at zis point, for the next thing I knew it was the following morning and I was faced with the most difficult problem of the trip so far – rousing Monsieur Minne from his deep gloom over Scotland's 2-1 defeat at the hands of Brazil the previous night. Having lived in Edinburgh for the past thirteen years, he had become a fervent Scotland supporter by a process of cultural osmosis, to the extent that his first words on waking were: 'Soooo unlucky. If only Tommy

Boyd hadn't been there. If only the ball hadn't bounced off him.' He was inconsolable, and to make matters worse, he had lost his shirt in a wildly impetuous bet with Mr Kasi of the tourist office and split the brand-new pair of trousers he'd bought in a Quetta bazaar from stem to stern while rising to adjust the TV volume control in a bid to silence the jubilant clamour of the Brazilian fans.

What to do? We could go on a jaunt to the old British hill station of Zirat, but that was three hours away, over roads that had last seen tarmac around the time of partition.

We could go to the movies, but all the Delite Cinema had to offer was that old Pashto favourite *Da Karni Karkha*, and according to Nigel all Pashto films consisted of three minutes of extreme violence, followed by three minutes of a winsome brunette singing in the rain, and so on, ad nauseam. Or we could round up a few Baluchi twenty-somethings for a big night out, but apparently a big Baluchi night out consisted of going to a bar, ordering Pepsis all round, giggling at the girls/boys (delete where appropriate), cruising around town (allow five minutes), more Pepsis all round, firing your Kalashnikov in the air if you have one, and going to bed.

No, a picnic was the answer, at scenic Lake Hanna in the mountains east of the city, which, according to the guidebook, promised stunning views, a playground and a little café. And indeed, it was a rip-roaring success. The hotel failed to produce a picnic lunch, and we failed to find the road to the lake. Still, a soldier manning a checkpoint took pity on us and gave us an apricot each.

In the end, we went out for a mango milkshake at Flora's with Nigel, Aslam, and Aslam's nephew Usman, who was limping after being accidentally shot, not once, but twice at an over-exuberant wedding celebration. It was the best mango milkshake I had ever had, and not just because it was the first, if you know what I mean.

Afterwards we stopped by a little Afghani restaurant for some *korai*, a hill tribe speciality, which involves beating lamb bone with a lump hammer until it shatters. All around the dimly lit room men sprawled on carpets beside low tables, industriously removing splinters of bone from their gums, while in the corner, a huge Sony TV screen announced: 'Please wait – satellite dish is turning', eventually coming to rest on *The Magnificent Ambersons* with Orson Welles.

Then back at the hotel we took green tea and water melon on the lawn, by the light of a full moon.

Before we went to bed, a long talk with the hotel receptionist finally sorted out the mystery of the Tuesday train from Quetta to the Iranian border. The Tuesday train leaves on a Friday, except when Wednesday falls on a Thursday, so we would be leaving in a couple of days, on Saturday.

Having got to the bottom of it all, I slept peacefully, woke early the next morning and walked over to the hotel campsite to say goodbye to Andrew and Rupert, two motorcyclists we had met who were heading in the opposite direction to us, aiming to be in New Zealand in six months. Keen and fearless, they were of the sort of young Englishmen who would have been Spitfire pilots in the forties. But they had already gone, leaving a rectangle of pale yellow where their tent had been.

It was time we were away as well, for we had been delayed too long in Quetta, no matter how good the mango milkshakes were, and ahead of us stretched the grim prospect of crossing the vast deserts of Persia at 40 m.p.h., since the bikes would not be run in until Tabriz. At that rate we wouldn't be home until Christmas, I thought, and I didn't mean this year.

As I made my way back to the hotel a storm blew up out of nowhere and shrouded me in sepia dust, so that when I looked in the mirror back in the room, I had become the image of the old photograph of my grandfather that Dad kept on the sideboard at home. I felt, for half a second, a bit too old for this adventuring lark. But only for half a second.

To lift my mood, I got out a rag and bucket and washed the bikes, proving yet again that I fell into Pirsig's definition of the romantic, fascinated by the surface beauty of things. Then, as a flamboyant gesture towards pragmatism, I repacked the panniers so that the load was equally balanced on both sides and directly over the back axle, to improve the handling.

As I finished, Patrick woke inside. 'What's the forecast?' he shouted out through the open door.

'Hot and sunny. Get up for breakfast, you lazy bollocks,' I shouted back.

At two, we walked over to the town's archaeological museum, which contained a small but poignant section on Colonel Sir Robert Sandeman, the indefatigable Scots Presbyterian who brought order to the region, won the respect of the tribal chiefs, saw his wife and two young daughters die of diphtheria, retired to Ireland and became an expert on the problems of the country's fishing industry. Then, persuaded to return to settle yet another tribal dispute, he stayed for ten years, established revenue, irrigation, medical and communication schemes and died there in 1892. Since the guidebook had assured us the museum would be open it was, naturally, closed, but a spell of spirited ringing on the doorbell eventually produced a languid Pashtun.

'Are you open?' we shouted through the letterbox.

'No.'

'When are you open?'

'No.'

'Are you open tomorrow?'

'No.'

'Ever?'

'No.'

Allah was speaking to us, and he was saying it was time to leave Quetta.

To celebrate our imminent departure, we rode five miles out of town and spent the rest of the afternoon watching Gulab try to kill himself.

Gulab was a local legend. At first it was just him and his mates, practising their motocross skills by riding stolen Japanese trial bikes up the side of a nearby mountain. Then word got around, and a few people started coming out to watch them, and that afternoon there were hundreds applauding every leap, wheelie, madcap dash up the mountain and even madder-cap dash down. At one stage a spectator, inspired beyond logic, tried it in a Suzuki jeep, got stuck and slid all the way down backwards, emerging with a dusty grin to an appreciative tsunami of applause.

At dusk, having been invited over to Nigel's for a farewell dinner, we arrived to find his living room the scene of a horrific crime. Someone had killed a goat, sliced up the pieces and covered the body with thinly sliced roti bread, in a bid to hide the evidence.

'Come on in, we're having *sajji*,' said Nigel, appearing suddenly from the kitchen with a token bowl of salad as a ludicrously ineffectual counterpoint to this most primeval and delicious of meals.

We ate with our bare hands, folding chunks of goat into parcels of roti, posting them first-class into our mouths and washing the lot down with slugs of the highly illegal Cossack vodka, which by law must be exported to non-Muslim countries.

We went to bed with our bellies as tight as drums, and woke to our last morning in Quetta. And we were sorry to leave – it was a Wild West town for sure, but the people had been monumentally generous, making it like Dodge City run by the Rotary Club.

It was an impression confirmed by the noon train to the Iranian border, which, of course, left at two, with the Enfields tied down in a freight carriage at the back. Nigel had come to see us off, with Aslam and Asha and Aksa – his little mouses, as he called his daughters when he thought no one was listening.

The train looked as if even Butch Cassidy and the Sundance Kid would have refused to rob it, and our compartment, the best to be had, looked as if it had been raked with Kalashnikovs, then finished off by a mad axeman. The windows were unglazed, and the toilet was so rusted through that sitting on it would have required a leap of faith worthy of Kierkegaard, the Danish philosopher who spent long hours sitting on the hanging toilets of Copenhagen while he dreamt up his gloomy theories on religion in revenge for the sorry state of his love life after splitting up with his fiancée.

And yet amidst all this poverty, the first act of Ali Hamza, the elderly gentleman we sat down opposite, was to leap up, race out to the stall on the platform and buy Pepsis for us all.

The stationmaster's whistle blew, and our farewell party got off. As the train lurched and began to move forward, they walked outside our window all the way to the end of the platform, waving all the while. We waved back until at last Nigel, Aslam and the little mouses were lost to sight, then set our faces, if not yet our hearts, to a new land.

At four, the chai wallah brought around tea on the ubiquitous battered tin tray, and a battle royal ensued as we attempted to pay. Eventually our new-found companion, Ali, who looked like Charles Bronson and spoke fluent English, Baluchi, Pashto, Urdu and Farsi, won by dint of insisting the loudest.

'Chūb kārı nakon,' (you put me to shame with your generosity) said Patrick, who had been learning Persian on the sly.

We drank our tea during one of the interminable halts, while dust devils danced in the distance, and beside a nomadic sheep herder's tent a camel regarded us with exactly the expression Margaret Thatcher always reserved for journalists. Camels are particularly Tory beasts anyway, I've always thought: the looks of Leon Brittan, the personality of Cecil Parkinson, the belly of the pre-diet Nigel Lawson, and the charm of the Great Satan herself.

Beside the track for a deal of the journey lay the infamous Quetta to Koh-i-Taftan road, which we had discussed for so long, and which all the guidebooks had said not to travel on except as part of an armed convoy. But it seemed innocuous enough, with a teenager cycling whimsically along it, looking as if being kidnapped by bandits was the last thing on his mind.

In fact, the greater dangers lay inside our compartment. As darkness fell, Patrick, after successfully hot-wiring the ceiling fan into life using the two live flexes dangling from the wall, took to the flimsy bunk above, leaving me worrying out loud that he would crash down on me during the night and I would end the trip, not kidnapped by bandits, but crushed to death by a falling Franco-Belgian motorcycle mechanic.

'And bloody good electrician,' he muttered from above.

However, hubris is a terrible thing, and five minutes later the lights went out and the fan ground to a halt, leaving us in darkness with only the desert moon to guide the train through the night. Oh, and the railway tracks, of course.

We fell to silence, and as I lay propped up on my elbow in the moonlight, gazing out of the window at the vast desert of Baluchistan, with its mud houses and nomadic tents, and wondering at the logistics involved in moving armies, from Alexander the Great's to the British, across it, a strange series of questions and answers came to me out of nowhere.

What would you do if you were out here instead of in there?

I would return home.

What if you could not?

I would stay here and find a wife.

What if you could not?

I would turn to the spiritual rather than the physical life.

How would you do that?

The spiritual life is not a question of doing, but of being.

Thankfully, just as I was about to self-destruct in an implosion of introspective existentialism, Monsieur Minne's voice broke the silence.

'Here, what are we having for dinner?'

'Beef Wellington, gratin dauphinois and petits-pois, washed down with a bottle of Gevrey-Chambertin, the wine of which Victor Hugo said, "I cannot remember the town, and the name of the girl escapes me, but the wine was Chambertin."'

When dinner did come it was, naturally, goat and roti.

'Another glass of the Chambertin?' said Patrick, passing down a bottle of tepid water. 'It's the '74; I think you'll like it.'

'A splendid choice,' I said, as the train lurched suddenly to a halt in the middle of nowhere.

Rousing himself, Patrick went off with Ali to buy two melons for dessert from the trackside traders, who, during the rest of the night, would materialise from the desert every time the train stopped in the middle of nowhere, then vanish again.

'Fags out there are only 18 pence a packet,' he said when they returned five minutes later, laden with fruit. 'More Chambertin?'

'No, I think I'll move on to the Chateau d'Yquem with pudding,' I said, opening another bottle of tepid water and dumping an iodine tablet in it.

In darkness we fell through the dunes to the desert town of Nushki, like Antoine de Saint-Exupéry descending from the stars which filled the desert sky, perfect and true, and the entire length of the Milky Way was visible, draped like a blanket across the sleeping body of the night.

And soon we had joined it, rocked to sleep by the tickety-tack of the track.

We arrived at Koh-i-Taftan at 5 p.m. the next day, despite the fact we had been variously told by station staff, conductors, chai wallahs, melon sellers, and people who were just passing by, that the train would arrive at 9 a.m., 11 a.m., 2 p.m., 3 p.m. and 4 p.m. And since the luggage car had stopped short of what passed for a platform, the Enfields had to be physically lifted down through the open door of the freight carriage by an instant gang of willing helpers. Apart from them, however, Koh-i-Taftan proved to be a den of pocket Hitlers.

The stationmaster insisted we go to the customs office, even though we told him we were not crossing the border from Pakistan to Iran until the morning. Then the customs official, a man with a face like a sponge that had soaked up all the sadness in his life and none of the joy, told us to go back to the station, where the stationmaster insisted again that we go back to the customs post, where the customs official met us with irate gloom, stamped our documents and told us we had to leave Pakistan immediately.

We told him that since it was seven on a Sunday night, since the border closed in an hour, since we were tired, hot, dirty, thirsty, hungry, and low on fuel, we had no intention of going anywhere. A heated argument ensued, which we ended more in hope than expectation by simply walking out and riding off into the desert, thinking that if we waited until after dark before returning, he would have given up and gone home.

Unfortunately, after about five miles, we discovered just how low we were on fuel by conking out simultaneously.

'Well,' I said, as Patrick pushed his Enfield alongside, 'it's almost dark, we're in the middle of the desert, we've been thrown out of the country and we've run out of fuel.'

'At least things can't get any worse,' he replied, as from the nearest dune came two swarthy Pashtuns armed to the teeth and with bandoliers crossed over their not insubstantial chests.

I turned to Patrick, but he was as speechless as I was. This was the end: murdered by bandits, as all the guidebooks had warned us.

The taller of the two stopped in front of us.

'Sorry to bother you, chaps,' he said, in an accent that owed more to Balliol than Baluchistan, 'but do you need petrol?'

'Yes, we do, actually,' I stammered, as he and his compatriot pushed the Enfields around the dune to reveal a Mad Max encampment of mud huts surrounded on three sides by stacked barrels of smuggled Iranian fuel. One was dragged over, a hosepipe and a muslin filter fitted, and both our tanks were filled for the princely sum of fifty pence.

We shook hands with the entire village and rode off into the desert. I began to breathe again, and Patrick started to laugh and did not stop until we arrived outside Koh-i-Taftan's only motel just as darkness fell. There, the proprietor, Abdul

Qayyum Khan, anointed us with such hospitality that, fed, watered, showered and human again, we practically fell at his feet in supplication.

'Please, please,' he said, 'I see myself as a missionary for travellers. For me, helping others is a form of prayer.'

If so, he is the holiest man in Taftan. He had even planted two little trees on either side of the front door to brighten the place up, and every morning, when he and his staff waken from their beds on the porch, they sweep the dusty sand all the way to the front gate.

Before we went to bed we had asked him if the bikes were safe, and in the morning we found that two of his staff had slept beside them to make sure they were.

And so, after breakfast of eggs, bread and honey, to Persia – fabled land of Xerxes, Tamburlaine, Alexander the Great and Persepolis, not to mention rugs. However, if Alexander and his mates had had to go through Iranian customs, they would have given up and gone home.

After having our passports checked, we passed a long wall bearing the graffito: 'All we want is the establishment of Islamic laws and rules everywhere in the world.' Fair enough. But the Iranians should bear in mind that if that happens, the entire population of the planet will be stuck at customs posts for eternity.

After what seemed like several days of being sent from one office to another in the two-storey customs building, we found ourselves on the front doorstep again in the baking heat, looking at the unremittingly flat desert stretching all the way to the horizon.

'If they ever need to build an airport here, they won't have much bother deciding where to put it,' I said.

'Or a Dutch theme park,' said Patrick. 'Bloody hell, it's hot.'

Eventually I was called back in to an office in which, behind a desk, sat a man with a moustache that had obviously taken a lifetime of careful cultivation. Unfortunately, it had also used up so much of his energy that it had left him incapable of movement, for after another ten minutes he was still sitting motionless in front of our carnet documents, which only needed two stamps and signature for us to be gone and never darken his door again.

Then I spotted a strangely familiar object under the desk.

'Is that a volleyball?' I said.

He looked up and raised an eyebrow, and in a gesture as surprising as if he had torn open his shirt to reveal a basque and launched into a rendition of 'I'm just a sweet transvestite from trans-sexual Transylvania', he picked up the ball and volleyed it to me.

It wasn't a bad volley, either, although his elbows were a bit far apart. But just at that moment, he could have had three left hands and still been on my team, and thirty seconds later, all our documents stamped and signed, we were on our way across the border, passing a large thermometer that informed us that it was 51 degrees in the shade.

If there had been any, that is.

Iran

The long road north from the Pakistan-Iran border was the sort of journey that would have been very dull in a car: 300 miles of desert and mountains with Mantovani on the stereo and whoever was in the passenger seat saying: 'Heavens, Cyril, isn't nature exquisitely brutal!' But on a motorcycle, you're right there in the middle of it: the sun flayed us, fierce sandstorms poured salt on the wounds, desert rains cooled us, and the hot wind blew us dry. And through it all, the Enfields plugged away, God bless their little tappets.

When we weren't being toasted, sandpapered, soaked and baked, there was little to do but appreciate what a Zen-like activity riding long distances on a motorcycle is, since, alone with your thoughts, there is plenty of time to contemplate the stillness at the centre of your being, which, as we all know in traditional Buddhist thinking, is one inch above your navel at a point called the *hara*. Which is, funny enough, about the only part of you that remains still on a motorcycle like the Enfield, with its series of rhythms all designed to reduce your bones to marrow and your internal organs to jelly.

You see, whereas German bikes are built on the theory that, like the Third Reich, they will last a thousand years, old British bikes are constructed on the Zen principle that everything changes. At rest on an Enfield there is the slow heartbeat of that huge piston lolloping up and down; at cruising speed, a deep purr, like a lion after a particularly satisfying wildebeest, which slowly unscrews all the large nuts and bolts on the bike; and at high speed, there is a finer, more subtle threnody, like the wind in telegraph wires, which loosens all the small ones. Patrick would probably know a technical term for them all, but to me they sounded like the music of the stars.

Talking of which, after finally arriving in the ancient walled town of Bam, which is famous for its dates, we spent what remained of the evening discovering the amazing variety of solids that nine hours on a motorcycle in the desert leaves up your nose. If some of mine had been asteroids heading for earth, they would have destroyed a city the size of Boston. Patrick, meanwhile, with commendable environmental foresight, was planning to take his home and use them as the basis for a rock garden.

After dealing with our noses, we dealt with our stomachs, eating dinner below one of the portraits of Ayatollah Khomeini that still hang everywhere in Iran, nine years after his death. To me he looked like Sean Connery, and I expected at any moment a voice to appear out of thin air, saying: 'On shecond thoughts, better make that a double milkshake on the rocksh, Mish Mullahpenny.'

How strange today was, I thought. I had expected it to be a monumental ordeal, but in fact it was one of the happiest days imaginable. Even the bad bits were good. The Buddha obviously knew what he was talking about when he said that if you expect nothing, everything is a gift.

It seemed remarkably unfair, however, in a country with no booze, to wake up the next morning with all the symptoms of a hangover. Still, it served me right for not drinking enough water the day before in the desert, so I downed a couple of litres over breakfast in Bam, while Patrick went off hunting for postcards to send to all his friends in Edinburgh, since 'bam' apparently means something unmentionable in Scottish.

On the early morning road north to Kerman, I thought again of what it is that makes motorcycles so romantic. Perhaps it is because, if you think of old cowboy movies, the people inside the stagecoach or the train were always the passive victims of circumstance, whereas the lone figure on the horse was always the rescuer who did the good and necessary thing, then rode off into the sunset, a symbol of freedom and the nomadic spirit which the writer Bruce Chatwin thought was in us all, wanting to break away from the tithes of settlement. Free of all that, the only relationship that lone figure has is with himself, whatever he happens to be sitting on and wherever he chooses to lay his head that night.

Think of all the solitary romantic figures that spring to mind – Jesus, Hamlet, Lawrence of Arabia, Dr Zhivago, Charlie Brown. Indeed, sitting dusty, unshaven and saddle-sore at a rest stop in the desert with the snow-covered mountains in the distance, it was difficult not to feel like Clint Eastwood, the archetypal high plains drifter. I wondered what he would have made of Iran, considering that both he and that other icon of late twentieth-century man, Father Jack, share the view that fine wine and fine women are probably the two most important things in life.

Here, the Iranians have banned one and wrapped the other up comprehensively in chadors, the all-enveloping black garment with, at times, only a narrow rectangle left for the eyes. Even in practical terms, it seems incomprehensible to wrap everyone up from head to foot in such a hot country. If you are going to have a Muslim nation, why not make it somewhere like Iceland? And I'm sure it saves Iranian women a lot of time deciding what to wear every morning, but it's very disconcerting being surrounded by women cruising silently through the streets like Stealth pillar boxes with slots through which you feel you should post notes saying: 'Is there anyone in there? Are you as hot as I am? Fancy going down the pub tonight?' But there's no point. The nearest pub is in Turkey.

Just before dusk in the old bazaar of Kerman, above our heads, swallows swooped in the endless blue of summer. And from all around, beneath the vaulted brickwork arches, drifted the aroma of a thousand spices and the ring of the metalworkers as they hammered out everything from exquisite jewellery with Koranic inscriptions so tiny they were almost invisible, to copper tubs you could bathe the family in.

We were looking for a famous restaurant which had been recommended to us, but when we got there it was closed. Naturally. Outside the bazaar we found a man pushing an ancient Hillman Hunter, which were produced here under licence in the Shah's days.

'You want taxi?' he said.

'Not if we have to push it,' said Patrick.

'No, no, not at all,' he said, jumping in and starting the engine, leaving it a mystery why he had been pushing it in the first place.

Back at the hotel the television had been tuned to the Scotland v. Norway match in honour of Monsieur Minne living in Edinburgh. We gathered around to watch with the entire staff of the hotel; the chef was so engrossed that there was no possibility of dinner until after the final whistle.

We were joined by an American, who announced that his name was Trigger. Short for Happy, presumably. He had just come from Turkmenistan, where he had spent three days on the tenth floor of a hotel with no electricity or water, so waiting until the end of a football match for dinner was little hardship to him.

The Iranian TV coverage of the match, meanwhile, showed endless replays rather than crowd shots, in case the watching male populace would be whipped into a frenzy by the sight of an uncovered female elbow.

I'm afraid I have little time for societies which live in such fear of the naked human body, like Iran, Pakistan and Ballymena.

The desert night was cold, and we slept wrapped in many blankets, then left early for police headquarters to have our visas extended. We still hadn't worked out why the Iranian embassy in London had asked us for a nine-day itinerary then given us a five-day visa. It seems that this nonsensical behaviour is standard practice. The strange thing is that the Iranian people themselves are invariably as helpful, friendly and happy-go-lucky as your average Dubliner. I mean from the north side of Dublin, of course. It is only when the veil of bureaucracy falls across their eyes that they become unseeing, unmoving and unhelpful.

At the emigration office, the woman in charge – the first we had seen in any official position in Iran – told us we would need one photograph, a photocopy of the relevant passport pages and 10,000 rials (about £1.20). Could we get the photocopy and pay the money there and then? Of course not: that would have been too simple. We had to go to a photocopy shop around the corner, then lodge the money in a bank and get a receipt.

We did all this, and returned at nine.

'Thank you,' she said. 'Now come back at eleven.'

Still, all this is nothing new. As Robert Byron said in *The Road to Oxiana*, published in 1937:

> The Persians have a talent for cutting off their nose to spite their face. They stopped the Junkers air service because it exhibited foreign superiority. They make roads, but their customs duties prohibit the importation of motors. They want a tourist traffic, but forbid photographs because someone once published a picture of an Iranian beggar, while conformity with their police regulations is a profession in itself.

Early the next morning, I visited the temple of Ateshkade in Yazd and found a fire of apricot wood burning in the centre of the room. Nothing remarkable about that, you may say, except that it has been burning since AD 450 as a symbol of purity and hope, kept alight by the Zoroastrians as they were bullied from pillar to post by all the bigger religions. It's hard to see why, since the basis of the religion is a relatively harmless belief that life is a constant struggle between good and evil, making it one of the easier faiths to follow, with only two rules – do good and for God's sake don't let the fire go out. On the wall near the fire hung a portrait of Zoroaster (also known as Zarathustra), who founded the religion six thousand years ago. He looked uncannily like Gene Wilder.

Apart from the temple, Yazd was made almost entirely of mud. Even the fourteenth-century mosque looked from a distance as if it was made out of mud, although closer inspection revealed it to be fine sandstone, while its tall, elegant minarets were veiled in a tracery of cobalt tiles as if they were attempting communion with the sky.

The taxi driver and I crept in as quietly as mice, while above our heads a colony of swallows flitted and darted below the vaulted dome. The driver spoke no English and I spoke no Farsi. We got on splendidly. At the mausoleum of Sayyed Ja'far, one of the line of holy men descended directly from Mohammed, the entire interior had been decorated in modern mirror tiles, and hundreds of women in black chadors were at their morning prayer.

I tiptoed out, returned to the hotel to find Monsieur Minne yawning and scratching himself, and we took the road north to Esfahan.

For the first two hours on a motorcycle in the morning, all the stiffness, aches and pains and rattles in your body from the day before vibrate slowly all the way down and fall out through the soles of your boots, where they are collected later by the Iranian road service. The second two hours are for cruising aimlessly along, with Patrick either half a mile ahead or half a mile behind, depending on whether he was languishing in the joys of Franco-Belgian mechanics or cursing the vagaries of Anglo-Indian motorcycle engineering. And the final two hours are for thinking about how sore your bum is, sitting on one buttock then the other to relieve the pain and trying not to admit to yourself how much you're looking forward to finding a little hotel with a warm shower, a hot dinner and a soft bed.

We arrived in Esfahan at dusk, and I fell in love with it

immediately. If it was a woman, you would want to marry her. Well, unless you were a woman, in which case you would wish it was a man. Er, unless you were bisexual, in which case you wouldn't mind, or a priest, in which case you shouldn't care. As Robert Byron said, unlike the Taj Mahal or the Alhambra, the beauty of Islamic architecture lies in form rather than decoration, and there is no finer expression of that truth than Esfahan. 'Before you know how, Esfahan has become indelible, has insinuated its image into that gallery of places which everyone privately treasures,' was how he put it.

Arriving at a hotel recommended by the guidebook, we met someone coming out of the front door muttering that it had the biggest cockroaches he had ever seen. Turning on our heels, we found another place around the corner, where the following morning, we were presented with a breakfast of egg and tomato puree masquerading as an omelette. Mind you, it was that kind of place: the room minibar was full of tinned peaches and the restaurant was only distinguished by a fine water list.

On our way to the Meldun-e-Imam, the seventeenth-century square, second in size only to Tiananmen and surrounded by some of the most beautiful buildings in the world, we were stopped by a small, dapper man called Iraj in an olive suit and black faux-crocodile loafers.

'Where are you from? Ireland? I have friends in Ireland,' he said excitedly, producing a postcard of Dublin and then leading us down an alley into a subterranean teashop.

The walls were lined with carpets and swords and the vaulted ceiling was covered, above a dangling plethora of lamps, bells and a First World War German Pickelhaube, with sepia photographs of Iranian soccer heroes and wrestling champions with magnificent moustachioes. In the centre was a photograph of Khomeini, looking suitably disapproving.

Beneath this vista of faded virility and quaint Edwardian charm, men sat all around at low tables drinking tea and smoking hookahs, both of which were duly brought and placed at our table, while Iraj produced photographs of travellers he had befriended on their way through Esfahan. Uncannily, we had met two of them, Marcus and Sonya, at the India-Pakistan border. He had also met Rupert and Andrew, the two Englishmen we had met in Quetta who were on their way to New Zealand. Iraj was obviously a full-time befriender.

We drank the pale, slightly acerbic tea and smoked the wild sweet tobacco, while from all around came the soothing hubble-bubble of the tall glass and walnut hookahs. It was very pleasant, and soon I began to feel so light-headed and mellow that the only way not to fall asleep would have been to leap up and challenge one of the regulars to a hearty wrestling match.

Fortunately, at that stage we left and arrived at last in the square, where the Shahs once played polo and where the mosque of the Imam and the smaller mosque of Sheikh Lotfollah sit in contrapuntal harmony. They were, naturally, closed – in this case for Friday morning prayers – so we went to sit by the pool in the peaceful, exquisite gardens of the Temple of the Forty Columns, where Persian noblemen once welcomed foreign courtiers and then engaged them in languid orgies.

We stood for a long time outside the city's art museum, a building which is stunning in its simplicity, and returned to the mosques in the afternoon. Both astonish the European: Robert Byron remarked that he had no idea that abstract pattern was capable of so profound a splendour. The sense, both in the larger, more fabulous mosque and the smaller, simpler one, was one of immeasurably deep peace and contentment. Until the cantankerous caretaker threw us out, that is. Otherwise we could have sat there all day, watching the tiles change colour in the sunlight and moonlight. It was as if all the spiritual beauty in the world had been distilled into one drop, and its name was Esfahan.

We left, late in the day, for Qom, holy city of the mullahs. However, it seemed that the Nambarrie Run had been sabotaged by the Tetley Liberation Front, because 100 yards down the road from our hotel, Patrick's bike spluttered and stopped.

As he got out the toolbox, we were surrounded within the space of a minute by every child in Esfahan, two village idiots who quickly became engaged in a punch-up, presumably over who was more idiotic, a schoolboy eager to practise his English, and a man claiming to be a mechanic. Fortunately, he actually was, and soon the problem was diagnosed as a dead battery, its terminals clogged up by sandstorms.

'Although I think you have some other electrical problem there,' he said. 'You should get it looked at.'

We jump-started the Enfield, then around the corner saw a vision walking down the street: a young woman wearing a white wrap and orange trousers with blue polka dots. Heavens, the next thing would be a couple of mullahs calling around to see if we wanted to nip down to the Old Shah and Peasant for a few jars of best Tehran mild and a singsong. Even better, behind her we found a little hostel with a courtyard, a fountain, and four people sitting at a table playing multilingual poker. Dave and Jane were biking from England to Sydney to start a new life, and two Dutch girls, Martje and Jolanda, were making a documentary on the build-up to the Iran-USA World Cup game.

That evening, the holy night of Friday, all of us went for a walk down by the river, past picnicking families and the four beautiful bridges of Esfahan, until under the arches of the last we found a tearoom as festive and atmospheric as the inside of a Christmas tree, and sat on carpets in one of the arched windows with the river rushing by below.

Inside, the women were unspeakably daring. Some of them had flung their chadors back wantonly to reveal an earlobe, and one dazzling beauty wearing a white silk wrap flung decadently over her chador was flaunting both shamelessly.

Even more remarkable, the women here spoke to us.

'Do you not find this delicious?' said one sultry temptress, eyeing us coyly around the corner of a hanging carpet.

I wasn't sure if she meant the tea, the hookah, the almond biscuit I was foolishly holding halfway to my mouth, or herself, so I nodded anyway.

'Kheili khúb (very good),' I said, since I'd been practising my Persian.

'Well done,' she smiled sweetly.

I was in love, and not for the first time that day. Eventually we were getting on so well that the proprietor came over and told us to keep the noise down. I had just become Iran's first hookah hooligan.

Tragically, she left with her mother, but after a few minutes, Sultry Temptress II approached in a particularly fetching chador.

'Please take this seat,' I said.

'Thank you, that's very kind. Do you like Esfahan?'

'Yes, you must be very proud of it.'

'Why no, I'm from Atlanta, Georgia,' she said, popping her bubble gum.

We took a taxi home, six of us and the driver in a Hillman Hunter, and at the hostel we ate apricots in the courtyard, while exotic people came and went silently on the surrounding balconies, like a production of *Othello* directed by Marcel Marceau. We fell asleep at two, the fountain tinkling outside the French windows of our little room.

If Monsieur Minne's motorcycle had not broken down, we would have met none of these people. Esfahan had blessed us twice, at first by welcoming us, then by refusing to let us leave.

The next morning, Patrick spent half an hour cleaning his battery, kicked the Enfield into life, and declared himself satisfied. With a sweet sadness in our hearts, we climbed into the saddles and set off on the road for Qazvin: a road which we quickly discovered was not for the faint-hearted.

Iranian truck drivers, you see, see themselves as latter-day equivalents of German fighter pilots. Their enemy is anything coming in the opposite direction, and their favourite technique is lurking behind a slower truck then leaping out playfully as you approach, flashing their lights to indicate helpfully that your only alternative to death is to swerve into the quicksand that the Iranian road service habitually uses for verges.

'I'm fed up with this,' announced Monsieur Minne at one water stop, after he had been forced off the road for the third time that morning. 'I'm going to take them on at a game of chicken and see how brave they really are.'

He lost one-nil, swerving aside at the last minute as the truck clipped the Enfield's wing mirror, then vanished in a cloud of dust.

We gave them the benefit of the doubt for the rest of the day, and just observed from a safe distance how, like fighter aces, they stencil their kills just below the cockpit, and decorate their vehicles gaily in the colours of their choice, with rakish symbols taken from a deck of cards, and religious slogans such as 'Ya Allah' (Hurrah for God) or 'Allah u Akbar' (God's a jolly good fellow), or romantic ones such as 'Anjel' (sic) and 'My Heart' beneath portraits of two unlikely *belle époque* virgins. One which almost killed me that afternoon, I could not help but notice as I skidded into the quicksand and began to sink, bore the legend 'Only You', beneath a painting of an Iranian siren who looked as if she was about to perform the Dance of the Seven Chadors, although you got the feeling that no matter how many she removed, there would always be one more, so that you would eventually die of frustration or boredom.

In fact, in spite of the vision in polka dots and the earlobes incident, I had become increasingly convinced that, like nuns, Iranian women had no bodies, and that their heads simply floated along five and a half feet above the ground like hovercrafts, supported on an invisible cushion of spiritual wellbeing.

We could have done with a similar transport system ourselves, for the 300 miles north on the long road to Qazvin was a ride dogged by fiddly, irritating problems, with tiny bolts consigning themselves, willy-nilly, to the wayside, and cables setting themselves free with gay abandon. Then at last there was one blessing: late in the afternoon, I finally passed the mystical 3000 km barrier on the odometer, which meant the bike was finally run in, and I could take the stabilisers off the back wheel and reach the giddy heights of 50 m.p.h., a speed I had previously thought certain to cause blackouts due to lack of oxygen and the G-forces involved.

By early evening we had been eleven hours on the road and for the last two, as we raced north with the setting sun throwing a shawl of shadow over our shoulders, all I could think of was how sore my bum was and how much I was looking forward to a shower, dinner and bed. But then the storm clouds that had been gathering over the lilac mountains disintegrated into lightning and re-formed into a rainbow, and the last rays of the sun lit the scene with a chiaroscuro Caravaggio would have given both arms to paint. As it were.

By dark, finally, we came to Qazvin, a pleasant, tree-lined town, which Byron said was noted for homosexuality and stupidity, although not necessarily at the same time. At our hotel, a vast building containing only us and the proprietor, the foyer was marble and the room glum. It would have been better the other way around.

Robert Byron had a better arrival in the town: 'Stopping at Qazvin on the way back, I discovered the local white wine and bought the whole stock of the hotel. How comfortable that hotel seems now!'

I know what he meant. I slept fitfully on a reluctant mattress and dreamt of Tara Fitzgerald again. This time we were playing nude Twister, so you can imagine my disappointment when I woke up to find only Monsieur Minne, waking and scratching his hairy bits. Which are most of them, now that I think of it.

The people in Azerbayzan, as we crept ever closer to Turkey, were noticeably more European in their looks and manner. Mind you, they still had that quaintly charming and lethal Iranian habit of pulling up beside you on a moped or leaning out of a car window and engaging you in lengthy conversations just as you are arriving in a strange town and are in the middle of the life or death struggle to negotiate yet another anarchic roundabout. They usually cover topics such as where you are from, where you are going, what your name is, whether you are married, the state of your health and your considered opinion on Iran in general and their city in particular. 'Hello, how are you?' is their universal greeting.

The landscape changes in northern Iran. All around us were fields of wheat and a colour that had been lost to our vocabulary – green. A rich, sap-filled green, alien to the parched south. And in the middle of this sea of fertility rises a sight as dramatic as Mont-Saint-Michel or the cathedral of Chartres – the gigantic, turquoise dome of Soltaniye, proof that the Mongol hordes of Genghis Khan were as nifty with a builder's trowel as they were with the sword. Built in 1313 by the Mongol Prince Oljeitu, it is, as Robert Byron said, the prototype of the Taj Mahal and a hundred other shrines, with the difference that it breathes power and contentment, while its offspring achieve only scenic refinement. Beside it is the dusty village of the same name, which in the fourteenth century was the greatest Mongol city of all.

I left Monsieur Minne snoozing by the bikes, and was shown around the shrine by a tiny woman in a chador, beneath the hem of which peeped a pair of exquisite Italian court shoes. In Esfahan we had seen entire wings of bazaars given over to shoes, about the only chance an Iranian woman has to express her individuality.

I returned to find Patrick in a state of scenic refinement himself, having his teeth inspected by the local dentist with an audience of every man and child in the village. On the dentist's desk tea was brewing on a spirit stove, while behind a shower curtain with an aquatic theme lurked a foot-powered drill and a rack of medieval instruments. Fortunately, they were not needed, and the only payment for the inspection was half an hour's amusement with the aid of useful expressions from the phrase book, like *saghf tark khōrd* (the ceiling has cracked) and *Jāsūs nīstam, zartoshti hastam* (I'm not a spy, I'm a Zoroastrian).

In the evening we descended through fields of lavender to the village of Miyane, found a little guesthouse, and sat down in the lobby that night with the entire male population to watch Iran play the USA in the World Cup. Iran won 2-1, the hotel proprietor celebrated grandiosely by buying everyone tea and biscuits, and for the rest of the night, cars drove up and down the street outside honking their horns. In Tehran, we were to hear later, young men and women danced and clapped illegally in the streets, in scenes unprecedented in a country that has been governed since 1979 by men who never smile.

The next morning, the proprietor woke us at six and insisted on giving me an ad hoc tour of the hotel, including a rather impressive collection of Swedish toothbrushes he had for sale. He then asked for payment of the bill. When I pointed out that we had paid it the previous night, he apologised profusely, demanded a tip, then woke us again at seven to ask when we were leaving.

To make matters worse, I had caught a cold. The temperature had dropped below 30 degrees and I wasn't a bit used to it.

The next day, in Miyane, I visited the family home of a young Iranian woman I had become friendly with in Belfast, and with whom I had stayed in touch when she later moved to England. I spent that afternoon with her father, talking and eating apricots, which we picked from the tree beside the swimming pool. Beneath my slippered feet was an antique carpet worth much more than money.

It was a large and beautiful house, filled with sunlight and the memories of laughter. But they were only memories, because this was a family, like so many others in Iran, which had been split asunder by the revolution of the mullahs. I cannot even give the name of this charming and civilised man, and much as he would have liked to, he could not invite us to stay in his home for fear of repercussions, months of questioning, or even jail. He was careful throughout our conversation not to discuss politics. But then he hardly needed to – virtually everyone else I had met in Iran was bitterly critical of the current regime and longed for the return of a liberal government.

Even when Ayatollah Khomeini returned to Iran in 1979, many of the Iranian middle classes had their doubts. There was a general feeling that the Shah had been foolishly persuaded by US arms merchants to squander the country's vast oil wealth on an enormous arsenal of weapons that would never be used. Many hoped that with the return of Khomeini, the country's wealth would stay in Iran for the good of the people. But it soon became clear that life under the mullahs was exactly like life in Northern Ireland would be under the Free Presbyterians – an endless wet Sunday in Portadown.

The Iranians must have known what they were letting themselves in for when Khomeini returned from exile in Paris to be met by scenes of hysterical adulation.

'What do you feel?' a reporter asked him when he stepped off the plane.

'Nothing,' was the unsmiling response.

Of course, the present regime will come to an end, as all extreme societies do, whether decadent or puritanical. But in the meantime, all the people of Iran can do is count the long wasted years. In this particular family, the three teenage sons went to the United States, missing almost certain death or injury as conscripts in the vicious Iran–Iraq war of 1980–88, which saw poison gas and wholesale slaughter in trenches for the first time since the First World War. Their mother followed to look after them, and then their sister went too, unwilling to don the chador and with it a life of insufferable boredom without concerts, books, television, parties, dancing or clapping.

Her father alone remained in that lovely house. There was no one to pick the apricots, laughter was only a memory, and the swimming pool was as empty as an ayatollah's heart.

Turkey

The road curved north to the Turkish border, with hot red hills to the right, deep green meadows before us, and, for a time, the river winding alongside the railway track to our left. Sadly, for part of the way I was seeing it through a glass darkly, for I was stuck behind a tar lorry, which covered me in a delicate tracery of black lines, so that I looked like an Iranian road map. And since I was more accurate than the one we had, which often depicted dirt tracks as superhighways and vice versa, I just threw it away and followed myself to the border, where we had our last Zam Zam – the local equivalent of Pepsi – in the last bar in Iran, beneath the inevitable picture of Ayatollah Khomeini. We gave him a cheery wave as we left, as it was the last time we would see him, but he was as unsmiling as ever.

The Iranian customs were a little more relaxed on the way out than they had been on the way in, either because we were leaving the country or because a little *laissez-faire* had seeped across the border by osmosis. On the Turkish side, they really did it in style – the customs officer stamped our carnet documents while talking to his girlfriend on the phone.

'Be careful on the road,' he said, as he handed our papers back to us. 'The PKK kidnapped a German biker two weeks ago.'

'Remind me who the PKK are again,' said Patrick as we

walked back to the two street urchins we had paid a few coins to mind the bikes.

'The Kurdish Workers' Party. They've been kidnapping tourists in this part of Turkey in a bid to get the government to give them a land they can call their own. Personally, I hope they get it.'

'Why, because you agree with their cause?'

'No, so I can write a headline in the paper back home saying, "Kurds get their way".'

We changed the last of our rials on the black market and crawled west beneath the vast and snowbound splendour of Mount Ararat, where the remains of Noah's Ark allegedly rest, looking down upon a landscape reduced to its most fundamental elements – the dark mountains beyond, the green meadows below and the silver road winding in between.

Mind you, I use the term 'road' loosely. The series of potholes joined by threads of tarmac was so bad that most drivers gave up and drove along the hard shoulder, which was in better condition. But the good news was that the kidnapping of the German biker meant that the Turkish army was out in force, and every few miles we passed a heavily armed unit in the back of a truck, idly examining their machine guns or their fingernails.

In the fields, women and children were making hay and bringing in the cows and the rather doleful-looking Anatolian sheep. The women had their heads covered, as in Iran, but with the sort of headscarves that my mother would have worn in the fifties.

On the road, fat artisans on bicycles wobbled west, with cigarettes clamped between their teeth. It was delightfully homely and reassuring, particularly because we all had one thing in common – we were heading home for a beer after riding through a country whose leaders took the same view of booze as the Reverend Ian Paisley – that it was the devil's buttermilk. There had been times in the southern deserts of Iran, you see, when I had turned into the man in every beer advertisement ever made. If someone had walked up to me then with a can of beer so cold that it had those little sexy goosebumps of moisture all over it, I would probably have sold them the motorbike, my soul, Patrick's soul as a two-for-one special offer, the house and the car.

We arrived at last, shaken half to death by the potholes, in the unsung town of Agri, and after some searching found its only hotel, a grey building that resembled a Siberian mental asylum. Our room was a grey cell containing two beds with rusted springs and infested mattresses. The shower down the hall was a pipe in the wall, from which a stream of icy water poured onto the concrete floor, one 40-watt bulb lit the entire building and gibbering idiots paced the corridors, mostly Patrick and myself.

Still, at least it was cheap. And that evening I saw four things I had not seen for quite some time. A driver using his indicators. A man wearing a tie. A woman's hair, as beautiful as a waterfall of jet. And the can of beer I had long been dreaming of. Since this part of Turkey is strongly Islamic, we had bribed a fourteen-year-old boy to smuggle four cans of Heineken in, and we drank them in our gloomy room, then went to watch the Scotland v. Morocco match on television. But all the Russian refugees in the asylum's moth-eaten TV lounge turned out to be watching a Turkish soap opera, which consisted entirely of a buxom teenager running from room to room in a suburban bungalow, then flinging herself pneumatically on her bed in tears. We could see the attraction, but it was not what we were after.

Eventually we tracked down a café owner, who, in return for us buying every pastry in the joint, let us tune his television to the soccer channel – only to find Brazil v. Norway, and of Scotland not a sign. Patrick sat watching the match, munching his pile of pastries despondently. After a day in the hot sun wearing his motorcycle goggles, he looked like the saddest panda in Belfast Zoo.

When we returned to the asylum, from the window in our

room we could just see the snowy peak of Ararat piercing clouds, through which, in the moonlight, it did not take much of a leap of faith to imagine God poking his head and muttering, 'I was sure I left that boat around here somewhere.'

The next morning, we checked out of the hotel and breakfasted at the little café next door, on tea and baclava. Not the headwear favoured by Turkish bank robbers, but the sinfully sweet pastry the Turks share with the Greeks, and which shows that they have more in common than a disagreement over who owns Cyprus.

And so to Erzerum. But not before the shoeshine boys of Agri had descended on us like a plague and left us sparkling but penniless.

'No, no!' we shouted as they chased us around the bikes with brushes and cloths.

'Yes, yes, yes,' they chorused.

We gave in, eventually. After all, there were more of them, and we are by nature democrats.

My heart lifted as we rode west from Agri along relatively pothole-free roads, through a scene for all the world like a Technicolor version of the Tyrone of my childhood – since I am so old that I grew up in black and white – with the Anatolian mountains standing in for the Sperrins and the white minarets of the mosques rising up from the green meadows as innocently as village steeples. Indeed, much of this trip was a return to the life of a boy, especially in Iran – a spin out on your bicycle in the summer hols, then home for tea and a glass of lemonade.

We rose through glades of lavender, poppy and buttercup into the mountains, which divided graciously at a river gorge to let us through, and an hour later we had reached the snow line and had to stop and put on everything we possessed to stop from freezing to death. There had been several times in the burning deserts of Baluchistan and Iran that we had discussed leaving behind our Nambarrie fleeces to save space and weight, but as I zipped mine up now, then put my jacket on with icy fingers, I thanked the Lord that we had not.

In Kurdish villages, tiny children ran out to greet us, geese scattered and women waved from the kitchens of white cottages. At Erzerum, high in the mountains, we found a splendid inn, and went out looking for insurance. So far we had proceeded safely only by the will of Allah, and we both thought that since Turkey was on the edge of Europe, we might have some luck in finding a company to insure our bikes.

'Ah yes,' said the hotel receptionist. 'There is an insurance office only nearby. Go to the corner down there, turn left, and it is straight in front of you. You cannot miss it.'

We strode down to the corner, turned left and walked into the first large building we came to. Behind a number of desks, an equal number of men were bent studiously over files and papers. We walked up to the first.

'Good afternoon,' said Monsieur Minne. 'We are riding back from India on two motorcycles, and we were wondering if you could possibly organise insurance for them.'

The man looked up and took off his tortoiseshell spectacles. 'Why, no, I'm afraid that would be quite impossible,' he said.

'Oh? And why is that?' said Monsieur Minne, summoning up as much Franco-Belgian imperiousness as he could muster.

'Because this is the office of Turkish Airlines,' said the man, with an air of regret.

In the building next door, which was the one we should have been in, we proceeded through several smoky rooms until we found a man sitting behind a desk. On the walls were photographs of ancient Land Rovers and a Raleigh bicycle. This looked more hopeful.

'Can we insure motorcycles here?' I said.

'Certainly,' said the man, pulling from a drawer a calculator wrapped in cling film and tapping at the keys. 'That will be 4 pounds.'

'Does that cover us for all of Europe?' said Monsieur Minne.

'Ah, all of Europe,' said the man, tapping some more. 'That will be 6 pounds.'

Fifteen minutes later we emerged, somewhat surprised, with two pieces of paper which assured us that both ourselves and the motorcycles were insured all the way to the leafy boulevards of south Belfast, and for a full year beyond. Not only that, but the staff then took us back to the hotel. Now why can't all insurance companies be like that?

To celebrate we went to the local Turkish baths, at which we were lightly boiled, all our skin was carefully sandpapered off and we were lovingly torn limb from limb, then wrapped in swaddling clothes like the baby Jesus and his big brother. After which we went out for a slap-up meal and a bottle of wine. The road from salvation to sin, you see, is always shorter than the other way round.

But how we longed for the purity of Islam when we woke the next morning dry of mouth and dull of head from the previous night's bacchanalian carousing. Still, nothing like a run in the mountains to clear the cobwebs, and as we climbed the high passes with the morning sun warm on our faces I could see for the first time what my father meant when he said once that the sound of a Norton cresting a rise was like a song. At 7,000 feet, however, the carburettors began to struggle for air, and we stopped to rest, eating plums on a grassy verge, with the valley spread below our feet.

Many Turkish soldiers had died defending these passes against the Allies in the bitter winter of 1916, and today a simple monument and a Turkish flag pay mute testament to that long, almost forgotten struggle, which those who fought it hoped would be the war to end all wars.

We climbed higher still, plunging into long tunnels as cold as black water, then swooped to the valley floor, pausing briefly while the authorities rebuilt the road after an avalanche, then continuing past tiny communities clinging to the mountainside, like children to their mother's skirts.

By evening time we had arrived at last in Sumela, veiled in mist and memory. This thirteenth-century Byzantine monastery, whose name means 'virgin of the black rock', was founded by the Athenian monk Barnabas, who turned up with an icon he claimed had been painted by St Luke. Evacuated in 1923, it was gutted by fire six years later. Then, in 1931, one of the monks returned secretly and exhumed the buried icon, which was taken back to Athens, thus undoing all Barnabas' hard work bringing it there in the first place, not to mention climbing 1,000 feet up the mountain to found the monastery.

I followed in his footsteps, only to find when I got to the top that there was a car park 220 yards away. The climb was worth it, nevertheless, even though many of the exquisite frescos had been scrawled over by vandals, including Antonio Hudson, USAF, 1965. Shame on you Antonio, wherever you are. He wasn't the only one, however. In 1983 art thieves were caught prising out whole slabs of the frescos.

Down below, the souvenir shop was doing an intriguing line in pink plastic winkle-pickers. As worn by Barnabas, presumably.

We found an inn for the night, which was, for all the world, like an Alpine chalet. We unloaded our baggage, discovered that most of the nuts had fallen off the bikes during the day, except for the two sitting on top, and approached the proprietor about the matter of dinner.

'Trout fish,' he said.

'Is it fresh?'

He disappeared and reappeared half a minute later with a family of trout fish flapping in a bucket.

We ate two each with a bottle of red as bitter as a widow's curse, while the proprietor's budgerigar perched on Patrick's head.

And so to bed. We had chosen the garret, which had headroom of about five feet, so that by the time I finally climbed beneath the covers I had banged my head seventeen times. Lucky there's nothing in it.

Over breakfast on the terrace, Patrick was strangely listless.

'Look, we're just about halfway home,' I said, trying to perk him up and spreading the world map over the bread and olives.

'But if we were coming the other way, we'd still be in Newfoundland,' he said. 'I wonder if we can catch the ferry from Trabzon to Istanbul, and save ourselves a few days.'

I went off, phoned the tourist office in Trabzon, and returned.

'Do you want the bad news or the good news first?'

'The bad news.'

'The bad news is the ferry left two days ago,' I said.

'What's the good news?'

'The good news is it arrives in Istanbul about an hour from now, so the passengers are waking up to a lovely view of the Bosporus. Also, I've booked us into the Hotel Antique in Istanbul several days hence, since the city's going to be bunged at this time of year.'

Patrick dropped his head on his forearms with a sigh.

There was only one thing for it – we would go to the seaside. That would shake us out of our torpor.

But first, the small matter of our missing nuts.

We had replacements for them all, except one on my motorcycle that held together something called the frame, which is apparently quite important. The nuts on an Enfield are a quaint mixture of imperial and metric measures, and this particular one was imperial, which was where the problem lay. Fortunately, the local garage turned up a mechanic with a lifelong hobby of collecting imperial nuts and he donated one from his collection, then refused payment, like everyone else on the trip who had done us a favour. Well, except maybe the Iranian Revolutionary Guard, who had stolen my torch at a checkpoint while his colleagues were demanding dollars from Monsieur Minne.

We headed for the sea at Trabzon, which was last interesting between the thirteenth and fifteenth centuries when it was part of the Silk Route and a town of legendary beauty. Today, however, the only legendary beauties are the Russian prostitutes who haunt the hotel foyers, and the town's main point of interest is the monastery of Aya Sofya, which contains some of the finest Byzantine frescos in the world. Unlike the vandalised ones at Sumela, these had been beautifully restored between 1957 and 1964. But since our visit fell on a Friday, and us being still on the final fringes of the Islamic world, I was unable to find out exactly how beautifully, because it was closed.

From the mosque, as we left the town limits, the muezzin was calling the faithful.

'Come to prayer. Allah is great,' he was saying.

But a minute later we were passed by a purple, California-look Beetle cabriolet.

'Come to the beach. The babes are great. And surf's up,' it was saying.

Just at that moment I looked to the right and caught our first sight on the journey so far of the sea. And how our hearts lifted to see the fresh salt smack of it glittering in the sun, and to understand fully, after the long days in the deserts of Iran, why the old Persian word for water is the same as the word for blue, the colour of so many of their tiles and an expression of an almost tangible longing for what we now saw before us.

We parked the Enfields, tore off as many of our clothes as was reasonably possible, and plunged into its cold and welcoming heart.

Still dripping, we arrived some time later in the remarkably unremarkable town of Sinop. Its most famous son was Diogenes the Cynic, who lived in a barrel for most of his life, which just goes to show what cynicism does for you.

When Alexander the Great visited the Black Sea town in the third century BC, he asked Diogenes if there was anything he could do for him.

'Yes,' said the grumpy philosopher. 'Stand aside, you're blocking my light.'

The town itself takes its name from Sinope, an Amazonian queen and daughter of a minor river god, who attracted the attention of Zeus. He offered her anything she wished if she would sleep with him. She asked for eternal virginity, and Zeus had no option but to keep his promise. Honestly, some women are never satisfied.

Anyway, since there seemed little point in visiting a town filled with cynics and eternal virgins, we turned inland, heading west across the wooded hills of north-eastern Anatolia. And within half an hour I knew we had made the right decision when a woman blew a kiss at me from a passing bus – proof that at last we had begun to descend from the cold crags of Islam to the lush slopes of western decadence.

It had taken its time, for even along the coast towards western Turkey women had still been sitting glumly on beaches in headscarves while their husbands and sons played in the surf. It was hardly surprising that in a recent newspaper poll on wife-beating, 45 per cent of Turkish men supported it, half claimed intellectual superiority over their wives and two-thirds saw women as subject to their whim. Ataturk, the founder of the modern secular Turkish state who introduced suffrage for women in 1934, would have been appalled after his efforts to drag the nation into the West to see it turning its face once again towards the East.

I was lagging behind Monsieur Minne, who had taken to speeding ahead so that he could stop for a cigarette, when a sudden downpour coincided exactly with my realisation that I had somehow neglected to buy a pair of waterproof trousers as part of my preparation for the trip. Soaked to the dongles, I pulled into a service station, and the staff fed me yoghurt and peanuts until a patch of blue sky appeared in the far distance.

I leaped aboard and raced towards it like Dorothy down the Yellow Brick Road, reaching the unprecedented speed of 75 m.p.h., until I was in sunlight again and could proceed along at a more leisurely pace, steaming gently past a stream of farmers, who were riding ancient Russian motorcycles with red sidecars piled high with hay and their wives sitting on top as ballast.

After a while I passed Gordion, where Midas had turned

everything to gold and Alexander cut the knot. But of Monsieur Minne there was no sign, and at nightfall, by which time I had ridden 400 weary miles, there was still no sign. I checked into a gloomy railway hotel, in which all that was to be had for supper, according to the chef slumped over a table in the dining room, was beer and raki. I had one of each, left the entire staff of two watching *The Road to Bali*, and went to bed, my belly empty and my head full of wonderment as to what had become of Patrick.

The next morning, in sunlight and in shadow. I rode alone across the Bosporus, and entered Europe.

Coming into Istanbul brought with it an almost palpable sense of excitement. There it sat astride two continents and seven hills, the mirror image of Rome, which the Emperor Constantine built in the third century BC as the new capital of the Roman Empire. My heart quickened, and even the motorcycle seemed to feel it, gaily casting off nuts, bolts and finally the horn as we clattered through the streets in search of the Hotel Antique.

And there, sitting in front of its faded pink façade, was the familiar yellow Enfield of Monsieur Minne, which, it transpired, had come to rest with a rattle of loose tappets 200 miles east of the city. While he had retired to the bushes to powder his nose, I had roared past unseeing in the pouring rain to spend the rest of the day peering in front of me for someone who wasn't there.

Patrick, meanwhile, had tightened his tappets temporarily and limped to the nearest mechanic, who proceeded to snap the pushrod in half. Whatever a pushrod is. By this stage it was 10 p.m., and his only alternative to spending the night in a ditch was to hire a truck for 250 US dollars to drive him and the bike through the night to the hotel in Istanbul – honestly, he'll stop at nothing to stay ahead of me – which was where I found him sitting on the hotel steps looking surprisingly happy.

'I'm happy because about two minutes after we set off, the driver pulled the truck into a darkened lane and I thought I was going to be raped. But he was only collecting his mate to share the driving. Not to mention sharing the three mammoth dinners we had en route. We only got here at five this morning,' he said, burping gently.

'At least you've eaten,' I said gloomily, 'Food has not passed my lips since breakfast yesterday morning, apart from a mouthful of yoghurt and a handful of peanuts.'

'Well, the good news is we've gained two days by getting to Istanbul today,' he said. 'The bad news is we've lost it again until I get Nanna to send me a pushrod from Delhi.'

We took some coffee up to the hotel's roof terrace and sat looking over the Bosporus to Asia, home of Enfield pushrods.

'Let's us have a day off then. We deserve it,' I said.

The fabulous Topkapi Palace and the Mosque of Süleyman the Magnificent could wait until tomorrow, and the only item on the agenda this afternoon was aimless wandering through the streets and past the Hippodrome, being approached from time to time by amiable youths whose friendly enquiries as to our wellbeing invariably led to the subject of their brother's little carpet shop, which was just around the corner, only five minutes away, cheapest prices in town, free shipping, etc., etc.

We returned to the hotel and had a beer on the terrace while solving the *Independent* crossword, listening to John Lee Hooker and the singsong voices of the two French girls from the room next door to us, as the sun sank slowly over the Bosporus in a scene that had not changed in five centuries. Apart from the satellite dishes, cars, skyscrapers and container ships, of course.

Just at that moment, however, the peaceful scene was interrupted by the ear-shattering, taped wail of the muezzin from the mosque calling the faithful to the fourth of the five prayers of the day.

'You'd think everyone would know the bloody prayer times by now,' I muttered darkly, realising that at four in the morning we would be woken by more of the same wailing from the mosque.

'Why don't we sneak in tonight and replace the tape with "Rock the Casbah" by The Clash?' said Patrick.

I had to remind him that visiting hours in Turkish prisons are 29 February, from nine to five past.

Over breakfast of bread and honey on the terrace the next morning, Patrick looked up from the fax he was composing to Nanna in Delhi requesting the urgent delivery of a new pushrod.

'I was just checking this morning. According to our original schedule, we're in Belfast by now,' he said.

'I don't think I'll go home after all,' I said, trying in vain to stop honey running all over my trousers. 'I think we should go out to dinner tonight, where I will fall in love with an extravagantly beautiful Turkish girl, get married, have children with blond hair and olive skin, live in a house in the forest and swim naked in a deserted lake every evening,' I said.

'Can I have your bike, then?'

'No, we'll need it for pottering about on until the children come along.'

In the meantime, we were stuck here until the pushrod arrived, but there are worse places to be stuck for a couple of days than Istanbul. Besides, every day was another story and the chance to think how much I loved travelling, and writing about it. For no matter how content you are as an adult, travel makes you remember what it is to be a child again, experiencing everything for the first time. Like being in love, it makes the ordinary seem special, like even the bread, honey and coffee I was having for breakfast.

We walked to Topkapi Palace, the symbolic, commercial and political centre of the Ottoman Empire for four centuries. To get an idea of the scale of this place, bear in mind that the staff numbered 4,000 – there were 1,500 in the kitchens alone. The queue for the harem was surprisingly long, considering it was no longer operational, and many people had given up and were trying to content themselves in the room next door by admiring the footprints of Mohammed (he was about a 12 EEE, since you ask) and samples of his hair, his beard, the dust from his hands. If we'd looked carefully enough, his first toenail clippings were probably in a sideboard somewhere.

Elsewhere, the whole impression was of fabulous, sumptuous extravagance, from the gilded suits of armour to an exquisitely worked silver model of an entire palace and grounds, complete with tiny birds and crabs; from solid gold candlesticks 5 feet high and the 86-carat Spoonmaker's Diamond to the wickedly curved Topkapi dagger itself, hero of a thousand Peter Ustinov Saturday matinée re-runs. Layer upon layer of it, representing the layers of power and intrigue in the palace hierarchy, from the lowest deaf mute to the Chief Black Eunuch; from the janissaries to the Halberdiers of the Long Tresses; through the whispering corridors of the harem to the most favoured concubine, and finally to the princes kept by the reigning Sultan in the suite of rooms above the harem known as The Cage until they were ready to accede to the throne, by which time they had been driven insane by years of gilded debauchery. Like Osman II, who practised archery on his own pages, or Ibrahim the Mad, who in a fit of sexual jealousy drowned his 280 concubines in the Bosporus. Only two survived: his favourite, Seker Para, whom he spared; and another, who escaped from the sack in which she had been bound, swam to a passing French ship and retired to a life of fascinating dinner party conversations in Paris – 'So tell me, *ma chère*, what did you do before you moved here?'

It was all too much. Just as all the spiritual beauty of the world had been distilled into Esfahan, it seemed as if all the sybaritic excess of the world had hauled its vast bulk out of the Bosporus and collapsed here with a groan onto a golden throne. I escaped to the cool, white spaces of the kitchens, like a sorbet after too rich a feast.

That evening we met a man called Miron Sulo outside a backpackers' café, watching a World Cup game on a TV, which was sitting on a table so wonky, you feared that every time the players ran to one side of the screen, the whole lot would come crashing down. Miron's father was half-German and half-Italian, and his mother, half-Finnish and half-Estonian, was born in a Siberian gulag. He should have been deeply confused, but in fact he seemed the most contented person on earth. For the past two years he had been travelling around the world working as a jobbing carpenter and meeting his Danish girlfriend whenever he could, and he had no intention of stopping.

Behind us sat a vast black Dodge limousine, one of the fleet imported from the USA as part of the Marshall Plan after the war, and now used as communal taxis. Sadly, the Turkish government was phasing them out after deciding that they were environmentally unfriendly, although it was hard to see how, since they were so long they didn't actually need to go anywhere: passengers just got in the back, walked to the front, and they were at their destination.

Even more tragically, though, the fact that Miron's grandparents came from four well-known drinking nations meant that he drank four times as much as normal, and after keeping up out of politeness, I woke the next morning with a head in which an entire company of whirling dervishes was practising with hobnail boots on. As a result, it was all I could do to stagger to the nearby Museum of Islamic Art, housed in the Ottoman Palace, built in 1524 for the grand vizier Ibrahim Pasha.

Ibrahim controlled the affairs of war and state for thirteen years, but got too big for his boots and was strangled in Topkapi Palace, probably on the orders of Süleyman the Magnificent's jealous and scheming wife Roxelana. She also persuaded Süleyman to murder his son, Mustafa, leaving the throne free for her own offspring, the magnificently ineffectual Selim the Sot, whose death after falling downstairs in a drunken fit began the long decline of the Ottoman Empire.

Inside the museum were as many Persian carpets as you are ever likely to want to see, instructions on how to build your own yurt and a breathtaking temporary collection of Japanese pottery, which, like everything in Japan, was very simple in an extremely complex sort of way.

In the museum bookshop I was leafing through a ground-breaking study of Turkish earthquakes from 1500 to 1799 when one of the strangest creatures I have ever seen walked in. A man in his early fifties, he was dressed entirely in white – patent leather shoes, lace socks held up by suspenders, plus fours and shirt, topped off with a floppy bush hat. He looked like a gay Crocodile Dundee advertising soap powder.

I'd obviously been out in the sun too long, and there was no better place to get out of it than in the Kapali Carsi, the world's largest covered bazaar, with four thousand shops to spend all your money, five banks to get more and a mosque to pray for forgiveness. I went in planning to buy a T-shirt, but it was like that old problem of going into Sainsbury's looking for a loaf: there's so much choice you spend an hour trying to decide, then go home and order pizza instead. In the end, I looked at several thousand T-shirts in the market, but bought nothing.

In the evening the swallows soared between the eight minarets of the Blue Mosque, whose golden tips were glowing as I lay on the bed looking at the world map. 'Look, we've come the same distance across Turkey as it is from Istanbul to Austria, then from Austria to home, so we're only two Turkeys from Northern Ireland,' I said.

'Speak for yourself,' said Patrick.

We walked out into the cooling streets and ate on a rooftop terrace by candlelight, while on the grassy spaces of the Hippodrome a huge crowd sat drinking tea and watching the World Cup on a giant screen. At the table next to us, a couple touched their glasses and uttered that most beautiful of Turkish toasts: 'Cam cam'a degil can can'a' (Not glass to glass, but soul to soul).

When the pushrod had still not arrived by the following morning, we bought a paper, which contained the happy news that the kidnapped German biker had been released unharmed, and went for a walk along the old sea walls, built in

439, and the crumbling façade of the great palace of the Byzantine emperors. One of the Crusaders who sacked the city in 1204 described it like this:

> Within the palace there were fully 500 halls all connected with one another and all made with golden mosaic. And in it were fully 30 chapels, great and small, and there was one of them that was called the Holy Chapel, which was so rich and noble that there was not a hinge or a band nor any other small part that was not all of silver, and there was no column that was not of jasper or porphyry or some other precious stone.

But by 1261 it was virtually destroyed, saddening Mehmet the Conqueror so much that the only words he could find were those of the Persian poet Saadi: 'The spider holds the curtain in the Palace of the Caesars. The owl hoots its night call in the towers of Athrasiab.'

In the afternoon I took a boat to the islands, home of Princess Zoë in 1012, Leon Trotsky in the 1930s, and all Istanbul's stray dogs in 1911, when they were shipped out and left to starve, a decision which hopefully returned to haunt the councillor responsible when he died and arrived at the pearly gates to find St Peter was, in fact, a St Bernard.

Today, there is peace in this place, in the peeling façades of the neoclassical wooden villas built by Greek and Armenian bankers at the turn of the century, with their gardens of mimosa, magnolia and jasmine. And in the simple white home of the novelist Sait Faik, a sort of dissolute Turkish version of Mark Twain, who died of cirrhosis of the liver in 1954.

I took one of his stories to the forest above the village, with four peaches and a bottle of water. It was about a thief who fell from a tree, and as he lay dying, the silk handkerchief he had stolen blossomed suddenly from his opening hand.

I fell asleep there reading it, in the shade of a pine tree, and woke to find that as the day died too, the softest of rains had brought blossoming from the forest the scents of myrtle, lilac and wild rose.

Foolishly, I then caught the ferry back to the wrong shore of the Bosporus, so that I had to pay a taxi driver 9 quid to take me from Asia to Europe.

That night we solved the problems of Turkey. As we were returning from the quaintly named Vitamin Restaurant, a carpet seller called Ali dragged us into his shop for apple tea and a ninety-minute monologue on government corruption, Islamic fundamentalism, the Kurdish question, police brutality, feminism and the Turkish male, the solution to Cyprus, the importance of free enterprise and the mysterious unavailability of fresh peas in Ankara, during which he did not noticeably pause for breath.

So there's the answer to Turkey's political difficulties: Ali for PM, and let the politicians take over his shop and see how they fare selling carpets. Although, not too well is probably the answer – a fine Turkish carpet has 196,000 knots per square metre, and Istanbul has about the same number of carpet shops per square mile. How they all stay in business remains a mystery.

Meanwhile, the pushrod had still not arrived. Patrick appeared at the receptionist's desk so regularly that he had earned the permanent nickname: 'Packet? No packet.' So all we could do was kick our heels in the listless heat and wait.

Confined to the hotel by feet that had become blistered on the bottom and sunburnt on the top, I reread *Full Tilt*, *Zen and the Art of Motorcycle Maintenance* and *The Road to Oxiana* from cover to cover, not to mention every guidebook from here to Calais and back again. And betweentimes, I looked out at the Bosporus and hummed old tunes that it was too hot to finish, and which the chambermaid happily continued for me, whistling as she went from room to room below, dusting and folding.

And between those times, we made the acquaintance of tourists like Natasha, over 6 feet tall and as black as four in the morning, and her boyfriend Richard, who was so nervous that anyone sitting near him developed a twitch out of empathy.

They were stuck here too, waiting for money to be wired from London to replace a wallet they left behind in an Istanbul taxi.

And so, like languid sultans in a gilded cage, we returned always to the roof terrace of the Hotel Antique, to drink beer and watch football, and to concoct from Patrick's new Turkish phrase book fantastic excuses for not buying carpets, from 'I am allergic to knots' to 'I am going to die in five minutes from a mysterious illness, so there seems little point'.

However, I had my doubts about the efficacy of that phrase book, for while attempting to explain on the phone to a local mechanic that his pushrod was broken, Patrick managed only to say that he had diarrhoea, then apparently suggested to the mechanic that he carry out an act which, with the best will in the world, was not physically possible.

That evening a great storm blew up as we sat under a café awning. Thunder rattled the rooftops, lightning brought a branch crashing down 30 yards from us, and the wind sent menu boards flying and entire Japanese families bowling down the hill, with muffled squeaks of unaccustomed scrutability, into the Bosporus. And then the rain came, washing languid frogs from drains and dispossessing spiders of their ancestral gutters.

After it was over, the streets were carpeted with maple leaves, like the aftermath of a Canadian liberation. As waiters swept up the debris and Patrick went off to buy a flute, I ordered another bottle of wine and settled down with Eric van Zant, an economics journalist from Toronto, to write a best-selling novel which would combine romantic lyricism with a sound awareness of financial structures.

Tragically, when I looked at it the next morning, all it said was: 'It was a dark and stormy night in old Istanbul. In a corner of the Café Gramofon, Murphy sipped a Guinness, reflecting bitterly on the events that had led to the disastrous fall of the Austrian schilling and left him a single man for the first time in twenty years.' It obviously needed some work, and in the meantime the storm had returned, rendering impossible a plan Patrick and I had formulated for me to leave for Bulgaria, Romania and Hungary and for him and the Enfield to follow on by freight train when the pushrod arrived. The rain battered the shutters and disgruntled the hotel owner's budgerigars. By lunch time it had lifted a little, but not enough for me to go on to Bulgaria alone, so we ditched the idea and took a boat up the Bosporus instead.

This was where, in the fifteenth century, the Ottomans built their fortresses and then, after they had stormed Constantinople, their delicately filigreed wooden mansions on the shore. The houses loomed out of the mist, then vanished once more, as if we had dreamed them new and then old again. Today, some of them are collapsing so daintily that they look as if they have become part of the forest behind, while others have been restored by Istanbul's *nouveau riche*, who park their beautiful yachts in the boathouses and their beautiful wives on the balconies.

At the ferry's last port of call, we disembarked and found our way to a restaurant, where we were each served with a tuna the size of a whale. Fish, I thought as I chewed stolidly, is the television of its day, in that it ruins the art of good conversation. Furthermore, you spend the entire meal concentrating on not swallowing a fatal bone, and then find at the end of it all that you have expended more calories than you have consumed.

We returned to the shore to wait for the last ferry home, and just as it arrived the sun came out at last, turning the three chandeliers in the white waiting room from gilt to solid gold.

And when we returned to the city, the entire hotel staff were standing on the steps.

'Packet, packet!' they shouted, holding aloft the key that would free us at last from the gilded cage of Istanbul.

It felt strange at first to be back on the motorcycle again, as if it were a separate object, but then after an hour or so I began to feel once more as if we had become one elemental entity, in the way the Aztecs, who had no domestic animals, thought when they first saw the mounted conquistadors of Hernán Cortés in 1519, that man and horse were one beast. Or maybe I had just become living proof of Flann O'Brien's theory in *The Third Policeman* that if you rode a bike too much, your molecules mingled with its molecules, so that you became half-man, half-bicycle and could not walk into a room and stop without leaning against a sideboard to avoid falling over.

Whatever it was, I remembered what it was to ride a motorcycle. I remembered, too, all the riding positions: lean back, and you were an American motorcycle cop; lean forward, a Second World War dispatch rider; lean forward more, on your way to victory in the 1957 Manx TT.

We stopped for fuel and I saw the first Bounty bar of the trip, and bought it from a shop assistant who ran it through a bar-code scanner. Europe was getting ever nearer to us.

The storms of the past few days had left as suddenly as they came, and we rode west under a cloudless sky between verges of foxglove and fields of sunflowers. The sun sank before us, the full moon rose behind, and a scattering of crows rose over a lake, as in the lilac dark we saw at last the minarets of the Selimiye Camii of Mimar Sinan.

Built in 1569, when Sinan was eighty, it was the finest achievement of the finest architect of the Ottoman Empire. But until we saw inside it, we were left to muse over the tragic circumstances which had seen us arrive in Edirne just too late to see the annual Turkish wrestling championships, in which thousands of hefty chaps arrive in the town, strip down to a pair of leather Y-fronts, cover themselves in olive oil and have a manly tussle. Not that we were planning to enter, you understand, since all I had with me was a bottle of Johnson's Baby Moisturiser, which I believe was banned at the 1994 convention of the Turkish Wrestling Federation.

Still, never mind. The next morning, we took comfort in a wander around the great mosque, its interior vaster than that of Aya Sofya in Istanbul and its minarets the second tallest in the world after those of Mecca. Beneath the celestial dome, covered in calligraphy proclaiming the glory of Allah, a small marble drinking fountain tinkled, symbolising life, and ancient patriarchs padded to and fro, almost translucent in the sunlight streaming through the windows.

Bulgaria, Romania and Hungary

At the Turkish–Bulgarian border we were met by a customs official with eyebrows like privet hedges. If they had been fences in the Grand National, Red Rum would justifiably have refused them. Above his upper lip, meanwhile, was a moustache of a shape and density that would not have looked out of place on the head of a fully grown water buffalo.

We were definitely in Bulgaria, where the cultivation of facial hair is a national pastime. And, it seems, motorcycle maintenance. In contrast to the Turkish mechanic who had fixed Patrick's pushrod for good by snapping it in half, the Bulgarian garage owner we asked to check my noisy front wheel bearings was a genius. Within five minutes, he had stripped down the entire wheel, declared the noise to be a wonky speedometer unit, re-greased the bearings anyway, given us a new spare oil can to replace the leaking one, which had left a trail of fossil fuel all the way from Delhi, checked our tyre pressures and reluctantly accepted the equivalent of 90 pence by way of payment.

Bearings, speedometers, oil and air safely in place, we hummed west across the Plain of Thrace, the fertile downs that had attracted conquerors from Philip of Macedon to the Romans. Bulgarian legend has it that God had already divided the world among different peoples when a delegation of Bulgars pointed out that he had forgotten them. Feeling guilty, he gave them this piece of paradise instead.

Indeed, the scene all around was unashamedly jolly, with roadside merchants selling fruit and vegetables and simple farmers leading simple donkeys to simple homes. Even more idyllically, it was a scorching day, as I soon found out when I realised that, in the middle of worrying about the bearings, I had neglected to put on any sun cream and had become frizzled to a frazzle. However, at this stage my attention was distracted from the sunburn by riding into a bee which was reversing at 60 m.p.h. with no lights on, leaving its sting in my neck. And then, as I was attempting to dislodge it, we rode into a fierce storm, in which we were pelted with hailstones while fork lightning crashed down all around us.

If we had had any sense, we would have been frightened, but it was, in fact, hugely exhilarating. And as a man from Fermanagh once said to me, it doesn't matter how cold and wet you are, as long as you're warm and dry. So that was how we arrived in Plovdiv: sunburnt, soaked, frozen and stung by reversing bees.

Sofia, the capital of Bulgaria, is full of buildings in the socialist massive style, all unsmiling façades and brute force, while Plovdiv is winding streets and elegant charm. In architectural terms, Sofia is a rape, Plovdiv a seduction. Nowhere is this more evident than in the grand houses of the nineteenth-century merchants which line the cobbled, hilly streets of the old town. Since taxes were based on ground area, these were built in an upside-down sort of way: the ground floor is the size of a telephone box, and they expand upwards by means of timber-framed oriels until the top floor is the size of Topkapi Palace, although decorated in such a quaint and homely manner that you feel you have accidentally stumbled into the home of the Bulgarian grandmother you never had.

We found a hotel, checked in, and I changed a 20 pound note into a wad of leva that would have choked a donkey. Then Patrick and I made a lovely discovery. The remarkable thing about Plovdiv was that every single woman in it was breathtakingly beautiful. And I don't just mean the single women. The married ones as well.

The ancient Thracians practised polygamy, allowed young women unlimited sexual freedom before marriage, tattooed both sexes, and smoked hemp. And that evening, I am proud to say, Patrick and I continued this tradition of giddy excess, starting with dinner in the hotel restaurant. The appetisers included brains in butter, grilled goose hearts and breaded gizzards, and the special was calf tripe, tongue, brains and mushrooms, which were presumably added to make the menu more attractive to vegetarians. We asked for the best wine of the house and the waiter brought us a bottle of Sainsbury's Merlot Reserve. The West was growing ever closer still.

Afterwards we retired with several of the staff to the hotel's Hawaiian cocktail bar in the garden for a night of wild carousing, although I am sorry to say that the tradition of unlimited sexual freedom for young women seemed to have gone the way of all flesh, since they went home with their boyfriends at two in the morning, leaving me alone with Monsieur Minne, whose sexual charms are, thankfully, lost on me, although if I was a woman I would probably find him good-looking in a handsome sort of way.

As we rode west toward Sofia the next morning, the rain cleared and we stopped for lunch at a little village, where the only restaurant had a sign outside advertising 'soyps, viands, grog and bulion'. Inside had a wonderfully dated feel about it, with everyone wearing fifties tweed jackets and coats. Since I had been born in the fifties, the whole atmosphere created for me the strange feeling of being simultaneously a child and an adult. Getting back on the Enfield, full to the brim with soyps, viands, grog and bulion, I felt that if I crept up to the window and looked in, I might see my parents at one of the rough wooden tables, dandling on their knees a little me with the same look of baffled optimism I still have today. I almost tapped the window and gave a wave and a thumbs-up to my tiny, imagined self.

We rode on, across dun plains that were once the market gardens of the Balkans, the colour washed out of them now by the long, hard winter of communism and the painful thaw into capitalism. Strange things happen in this derelict world. A dim light comes on in an apparently abandoned building, or you are looking at the rusting skeleton of a bus when it coughs into life and trundles across the plain towards you. After a while, you begin to long for the colours that years of poverty have drained from Eastern Europe – lilac, butterscotch, orange, indigo or terracotta. But then the sun came out, and in a roadside puddle rainbow were all the colours I would ever need.

At Sofia we stopped to tighten some nuts, then turned north for the Romanian border, climbing the twisting road into the mountains, then falling again to the plains, through villages whose entire populations seemed to have turned out to sell buttermilk by the wayside. In a forest, we stopped at a level crossing as a train pulled in at a tiny station, letting off a dark-haired woman in her twenties. There was no one to meet her.

It was evening, and shepherds everywhere were bringing in their sheep. As we rounded a corner, the belated stragglers of a flock dashed across the road. Patrick braked sharply, but he was already too late.

On an Enfield, the drum brakes are so bad that had he wanted to stop in time, he should have started braking three days earlier, at about lunch time. Enfields actually come supplied with a braking diary for just this purpose, so that you can languidly fill a pipe of Old Throgmorton's Ready-Rubbed, take a fountain pen from the pocket of an ancient tweed jacket, and make entries like: 'Wednesday, began braking. Saturday, hit sheep.'

And so it proved. There was a sickening thud, the last sheep went sprawling into the ditch and Patrick and the motorcycle went sliding down the road on their side.

I cut the engine and raced over as he got groggily to his feet.

'I'm all right, I'm all right,' he said.

The same could not be said for the sheep, which was so badly hurt that the shepherd slit its throat, and looked a sorry man as he did so.

As for the motorcycle, Patrick took one look at its twisted forks and muttered grimly: 'Well, that's the end of this adventure.'

However, the tank of the Enfield bears the legend in gold: 'Made like a gun'. We had laughed at it often enough, for Indian economics meant that the solid construction of the original British Enfield had evolved into parts apparently made from old cutlery and tinfoil. But it was time to take it all back, for Patrick climbed on his twisted motorcycle, started the engine and found that, in spite of front forks which looked like bananas, it was rideable after a fashion.

He paid the shepherd 50 US dollars for his dead sheep, as a result of which he probably started up a McDonald's franchise and is now the richest man in northern Bulgaria, and we limped into Vidin on the Romanian border, where the town drunk insisted on getting on the back of Patrick's bike, grabbing him by a badly twisted shoulder and directing us to a hotel.

Inside, a visiting party of Romanian dignitaries had used up all the hot water and were attempting to do the same with the wine, while a bar pianist played them 'Strangers on the Shore'.

We checked in, retired to our room, designed several decades ago by two blind men who had obviously not been on speaking terms, and fell asleep. In the car park below sat Patrick's wounded Enfield, and beyond that the Danube glinting in the moonlight, with Romania on the far shore. Only tomorrow would tell if we would reach it and continue.

In the morning I woke to the whisper of trees outside the window, and Patrick went in search of a mechanic while I walked through the park past statues of various socialist heroes who had had their noses chopped off by the disgruntled mob. And came at last to the fortress of Baba Vida, whose beetling brows have glowered down at the Danube since the thirteenth century.

In spite of the open-air theatre in the grounds, it is a strangely unsettling place, for in the late eighteenth century it was the home of the despotic warlord Osman Pazvantoglu, whose favourite hobby was inventing new tortures. Peering into the windowless dungeon, it is impossible to imagine what screams have soaked into the walls.

There was little else to see in Vidin. In 1941, Lovett Edwards had described it as 'one of those marvellous cities of eastern fairytale ... with spires and cupolas and minarets piled one upon another in a fantastic medley of creeds, ages and styles'. But since then the Soviets had moved in, tearing down the fairytales and replacing them with architectural bad jokes in which the punch line was always the same.

I returned to the hotel to find three American cyclists who had just come from a Serbian village, where they had been taken in by a local man and his family. At first all was well, but as the night wore on, their host became increasingly drunk, and when they went to bed one of them woke to find a gun at his head. He grabbed the man's arm, three shots rang out, and the Americans jumped through the open window and fled into the forest, where they were rescued the following morning by the police.

So maybe we weren't so badly off after all, I thought, as Patrick came limping down the street, looking very weary after a night in which he had hardly slept because of the pain of his bruises.

'The local mechanic's trying to straighten the forks with a huge vice. I can't bear to look,' he said.

An hour later he limped off again, and half an hour later, limped back again.

'Now he's sawing one of them in half. I can't bear to look even more,' he groaned, slumping into a chair and burying his head in his hands.

But he returned to the garage after a while, and then I heard, to my intense relief, the familiar cushioned thump of an Enfield engine coming down the road.

'The good news is that mechanic's a bloody genius,' said Patrick as he got painfully off the bike. 'The bad news is he charged me 18 quid. Fancy a beer?'

We left Vidin the next morning. The sky was overcast and we were both feeling a little glum, as if it were the end of the summer holidays.

'What time is the ferry?' we asked the Bulgarian customs official on the banks of the Danube.

'There is no time. Whenever there is people, there is ferry,' he said.

We crossed the grey Danube and rode off the ferry through a pool of disinfectant, presumably formulated to rid us of any Bulgarian traits, like a fondness for pickled cucumber. And after riding around Calafat several times, being directed to every point of the compass by the impish ragamuffins of the town, we finally found the road north to Timişoara.

Like Bulgaria, Romania is so pastoral it is almost medieval, but many of the villages were so threadbare that it looked as if the last time anyone had cared about them was a long, long time ago, before Nicolae Ceauşescu tore the heart of out this spirited, anarchic nation. Here and there were the crumbling remains of the monstrous tower blocks he had built as part of the lunatic village systemisation programme, in which the farmers were moved into apartments as part of the country's entirely inappropriate drive towards mass industrialisation. What the farmers were supposed to do with their animals or how they were supposed to earn their living was anyone's guess.

But then, that was only one of Ceauşescu's mad schemes, like levelling the most beautiful part of Bucharest to build the grotesque People's Palace and forcing the country's women to have more and more children, who then ended up in orphanages because their parents couldn't afford to feed them. How such an idiot got himself in charge of a country was beyond me, and probably most Romanians. At least in a democracy we get to choose our own idiots.

My musings on contemporary politics were suddenly interrupted by a monumental downpour. It soaked us both so completely that to distract myself from my sorry state for the next half-hour I found myself making up the lyrics to a new Bob Dylan song, sung more or less to the tune of 'Shelter from the Storm'.

> It was a quarter after seven
> On an evening in July.
> We were heading for Timişoara
> And we didn't even know why.
> Maybe it was something to do
> With that revolution they once had.
> But that was many years ago
> Before it all turned bad.
>
> It all turned bad
> It all turned bad,
> Like every revolution,
> Started happy, ended sad.
>
> Tomorrow we ride to Hungary
> Another day, a different town.
> Once I got engaged there
> Now I wish she'd turned me down.
> It all turned bad,
> It all turned bad,
> Like every love affair,
> Started happy, ended sad.

Fortunately for the future of contemporary music and Bob's career, we arrived in the village of Lugoj, a gothic setting befitting the birthplace of Bela Ferenc Blasko, who adopted the Hungarian name of the village, Lugos, and as Bela Lugosi became Hollywood's archetypal Transylvanian count. It would have been a nice touch if a lightning flash had revealed the castle where we were to spend the night, but instead the sun came out and we rode along, steaming pleasantly, towards Timişoara.

After a day spent tasting at every turn the bitter fruits of Ceauşescu's reign, it was appropriate that by nightfall we had arrived in the city that sowed the seeds of his downfall.

Naturally, the hotel in Timişoara we had chosen from the guidebook was full, but as the manager was turning us away, a Romanian wedding party spilled out and insisted that we get our photographs taken with the happy couple. Then he insisted that we stay in the bridal suite.

'But what about the bride and groom?' we protested, imagining a scene in which we would have to hide in the bathroom while the happy couple consummated their marriage, or, even worse, a scene in which the groom drunkenly staggered into the room late at night and mistook one of us for his new bride, and … well, you can imagine the rest.

'Don't worry, don't worry, there are two bridal suites,' said the groom's mother.

So Monsieur Minne and I were firmly installed in the bridal suite, although we couldn't decide who was going to wear the dress.

We had dinner and later, while Patrick went to bed to sleep off the last of his Bulgarian sheep bruises, I went walking through the beautifully tangled baroque streets and squares, coming at two in the morning to the Romanian Orthodox cathedral, where many of the protesters were shot in 1989, including thirty-eight children, as they tried to stop the eviction and exile of the dissident priest Lászlo Tökes.

In the moonlight, a simple plaque said: 'A la mémoire des enfants roumains morts pour la liberté'. I shivered, and went home to my bed.

The last time I had been in Romania was only days after the revolution, reporting on the cataclysmic events of a country struggling to get to its feet after years on its knees. At

Heathrow on the outward journey my luggage vanished, and for days in temperatures around minus 10 degrees centigrade I wandered about in the clothes I stood up in, writing and filing day and night. By the end of the fourth night, I had only slept for seven hours since I arrived, but I spent it walking around Bucharest in the icy darkness writing in a notebook with a ballpoint pen that kept freezing solid.

I had brought with me this time around a copy of what I wrote that night, and I read it now in bed by the light of the moon, looking out of the window at the squares and streets of the town where the revolution had begun. This is what it said.

Bucharest, 1 a.m., Wednesday 17 January 1990: In the darkness, at minus 10 degrees centigrade, I am standing at the beginning of the Boulevard of the Victory of Socialism, where once the peasants brought their food in open wagons down through the winding streets of the old city to sell in the market. Half a mile away, through the mist of ice crystals which hangs in the air, is what looks like a hill dotted with buildings, each lit from top to bottom.

I begin to walk, slipping on the ice and snow, beneath the ornate wrought-iron street lamps and between the rows of deserted apartments built for privileged members of the Communist Party. Beneath my feet, the ice is 6 inches thick.

When I am halfway there, the shape at the far end of the boulevard emerges from the frozen night, its edges solidifying into the astonishing truth. It is not a hill. It is the ultimate folly of Nicolae Ceauşescu, the 2,700-room palace he built to house the government and his family, and what I had thought were individual buildings are in fact the windows. It is impossible to believe the size of the place, even when I walk across the frozen plain at the end of the boulevard and stand before it. It fills the sky, blocking out the stars.

One of the two teenage soldiers who stand guarding it comes to the gate and looks at me.

'Englezeste?' he says.

'Da.'

He looks over his shoulder and taps a gloved finger against his temple in the universal sign of madness. 'Fortress Ceauşescu,' he says, and pulls an imaginary trigger.

1.30 a.m., near Palace Square: The wind moans through the blackened windows of the University Library, headquarters of the Securitate, Ceauşescu's secret police. There were manuscripts here dating back to the fifteenth century. They were all destroyed. There were no copies. The Corinthian columns lean drunkenly against each other, and through the broken glass of the ornate front door, in the dim light of a single bulb, a great dark stain seeps across the mosaic floor. The 40-watt bulb and the bloodstain. Rather than the monumental folly at the end of the boulevard, these are Nicolae's legacy to his people.

2 a.m: In front of the balcony where Ceauşescu came out on 22 December to condemn the uprising in Timişoara to the crowds in Republic Square, and where the entire nation watched him on TV as his face distorted with shock after the people in the square began to boo him. From the roof above, he and Elena fled a day later by helicopter.

The shrine below the balcony, a great wall of fir branches, has been hung with wreaths, white garlands and little baskets of early snowdrops. On it is draped the Romanian flag, the red, yellow and blue tricolour, with the dead heart of the Soviet symbol torn from its centre. The eternal flame that burns on the ground in front, fired by cheap paraffin and twigs and flanked by the thin yellow candles that flicker everywhere in the city where people died, is guarded day and night.

Tonight, Sgt Dorin Taraboanta of the Transport Corps is the keeper of the flame. He is nineteen years old. 'Make love don't war,' he says. On his face is the happily nervous smile of a man who has just been handed his first child. It is an expression everywhere in Romania these days, that fearful glee.

2.30 a.m: In the centre of Romania Square, there is a raised circular garden containing only a Christmas tree, which will stay up until the end of January. Taped to the garden wall, among the wreaths and flowers and poems to the dead from sisters and friends, and a little cardboard Santa Claus, are photographs of what really happened to the protesters of Timişoara. There is a picture of a man in a mass grave, holding up the body of a newborn baby. A bearded man, his face frozen in disbelief as he tries to hold his intestines in. A pregnant woman, her torso sliced from neck to groin.

In front of the photographs stands one of the old stooped women in shawls who pickaxe and shovel the streets clear of ice during the day. She has just lit one of the yellow candles below the photographs, and now she is standing before them. I do not even think she knows I am there. In the darkness, in the candlelight, there are tears on her cheeks, clouding slowly as they freeze.

3 a.m: Below the great chandeliers in the foyer of the Hotel Bucaresti, two soldiers stand on the marble. They cannot be much more than seventeen. In Transylvania the day before, Cristina Demetrescu, an English teacher, had said to me: 'This has been the children's revolution. They freed our country while we were still in our pyjamas.' And now the children who freed their country are guarding it, guarding the little flames all over the city until the dawn comes, in an hour or two.

I fell asleep, and at some time in the night, in the free city of Timişoara, the piece of paper slipped to the floor and lay there in the moonlight.

And so, another day, another border. How tiny the countries of Europe are, like pocket handkerchiefs compared with the vast carpets of Asia. But the border was closed, and an utterly humourless customs official told us that this road was for trucks only, sending us on a one-hour detour in needle-sharp rain. His pettiness was balanced by a motorcyclist from Budapest who stopped and made sure we found the right road, and we finally found ourselves at a border post that accepted vehicles with less than eighteen wheels. I withdrew my sopping passport from a top pocket and handed it to an official, noting as I did so that my signature and several visas had become so smudged with rain they were almost unreadable.

Hungary, which even under communism had always described itself as the happiest barracks in the block, was much more prosperous than Romania: the houses were freshly painted and the cars were new and foreign compared to the ubiquitous Dacias and Trabants across the border. You know you have been in Eastern Europe too long when a passing Volkswagen seems impossibly exotic.

At Kecskemet, a lovely town of neo-romantic houses with gay wooden flourishes on every eave, we found a beautiful little hotel with hot showers, feather beds, a charming receptionist who spoke perfect English, good food, cold beer and the World Cup Final on television. Bliss, utter bliss. The poet Endre Ady described Hungary as a 'river ferry, continually travelling between East and West, with always the sensation of not going anywhere but of being on the way back from the other bank'. On this night, we were firmly set for the western shore.

I fell asleep peaceful and happy, but woke in the middle of the night, and lay awake for several minutes trying to work out what it was that had wakened me. Then it came to me. Something I had been trying to forget, but which still crept up on me sometimes in the hollow of the night.

I dressed and walked out into the starlight, then stopped in a square in front of a wooden church. Sixty miles to the north of here, I had arrived in Budapest on the morning of Valentine's Day two years before with my girlfriend. We had left Belfast at dawn, but it was London before she knew where we were going.

'What a lovely surprise,' she said, disappearing and coming back ten minutes later with a beautiful little pair of heart-shaped cufflinks she had bought for me.

As we landed at Budapest airport it was snowing, and the arrivals lounge was thick with the aroma of cheap cigarettes and damp wool as women wearing tweed jackets and rubber boots rolled in from the frozen plains of Pest and embraced lugubrious men wearing splendid moustaches and superannuated greatcoats.

We took a bus into the white city, snow flurrying around us and the sun a distant amber in a mother-of-pearl sky. I had taken a grand suite at the Gellert, the wonderful art nouveau hotel built between 1912 and 1918 on the site of an old Turkish bath house.

The place to stay in Eastern Europe between the wars, the Gellert was slowly being renovated, so that it was impossible to know which decade we were in as we wandered around on faded carpets, swam in the ancient spa baths in the basement or tried to find Radio Moscow on the old steam wireless in our bedroom, a walnut affair the size of a sideboard still tuned to the ghostly crackling of stations long dead.

That night I took her out to dinner at Gundel. Founded in 1910 by the legendary Karoly Gundel, this was the restaurant where the wealthy of Europe came to dine in the heady twenties, and it is still thought to be the best in Middle Europe. The dining room was hung with paintings by nineteenth-century masters, the tables were laid with Zsolnay porcelain and sterling silver, and the service was of an older, more gentlemanly age.

We had goose liver with Bugac and walnut brioche, trout from Szilvasvarad, consommé of pheasant with miniature ravioli, hot Csongrad Purse filled with paprika chicken, grilled Cemenc venison garnished with pear poached in Merlot, pine-ripened sheep's cheese from Zala and chestnut pudding, each course served with a perfect Tokaji or Merlot recommended by the sommelier.

It had been the most expensive and the most splendid meal of my life, and not just because of the food, because somewhere between the trout and the venison, as the snow fell outside the window and the string quartet played Lara's theme from Dr Zhivago, my girlfriend became my fiancée. And as midnight drew near, we took a taxi back through the blizzard to our suite at the Gellert and opened a bottle of vintage Bollinger, which I just happened to have brought with me.

We found ancient, crackling waltzes on the Lvov channel on the radio and drank champagne on the balcony, with the snow and the music swirling around and the ice cracking as it shifted on the Danube below.

And then we realised how sleepy we were, and went to bed. That morning I had woken up with my girlfriend, and that night I fell asleep with the woman who was to be my wife. It had been the perfect end to a perfect evening, at the end of a perfect day.

Except that we never did get married. We had separated a year later almost to the day, and she had gone away to live in another country, and I still had not quite worked out why.

I now looked up at the white walls of the church before me, the sort of little church you would get married in. And then I realised that I was crying, for the first time in a long time.

Austria, Germany and the Home Straight

We set out in sunlight for Vienna, meeting on the way a ponytailed truck driver from East Anglia, delivering mechanical diggers to Bucharest.

'Call me Hippy, everyone else does,' he said, rolling up his sleeves to reveal forearms covered in tattoos extolling the virtues of every old British motorcycle ever made, before going on to treat us to a one-hour treatise on the drawbacks of the Enfield – which we already knew – the architectural highlights of Eastern Europe, some of which we knew, and minutely detailed directions to every cheap inn and truckers' café between Budapest and Calais, which we now knew whether we wanted to or not.

This all took so long that our chances of reaching Vienna were fading with the daylight, so we found ourselves instead in the serendipitous choice of Gyor, a medieval town. We stayed in a restored eighteenth-century Carmelite priory. Mind you, it was 40 pounds a night, so it's no wonder all the monks left. It overlooked a choice of three rivers and eight streets, down which the entire population of the town was promenading in the evening sun between beautifully preserved ochre mansions in the Hungarian nationalist revival style, which is a sort of baroque minimalism, if such a thing is possible.

After tiring of marvelling at how women could wear such tiny dresses and not get arrested, we took a seat at the Mozart Café, a sort of shrine to the greater glory of the coffee bean. I had a Cappuccino Neujahr, which was described as 'hot black coffee poured over sweet frothy milk, made crazy with chocolate and orange syrup, and sprinkled with a pinch of cocoa powder and ground cinnamon'. And that, advertising executives everywhere will be pleased to hear, was exactly how it was.

And so to Vienna: a quick search of the sewers for a Harry Lime, borrow a white stallion from the Spanish Riding School for a tour of the city, then a spot of *sachertorte*, while Anton Karas played 'The Blue Danube' on his zither in the background.

Er, well, that was the plan, until we threw open the shutters of our hotel window and found that all the weather in the world was falling out of the sky.

With Monsieur Minne's bent and repaired forks becoming increasingly fragile, the thought of struggling into a huge city, finding somewhere to stay, then spending the day sightseeing in the pouring rain was too much for even our finely tuned sense of masochism. Instead, we climbed on the bikes and trundled all the way to Germany, thus ostracising Austria completely and leaving me with a quite unfair impression that the entire country was wet, green and lumpy, like Scotland with measles.

In the middle of the afternoon we stopped for coffee at a service station and I went off to the toilets to drain an inch of icy water out of my boots and try in vain to dry my socks by draping them one at a time over the outlet of the hot air machine. At least warm and wet is better than cold and wet, I thought, as I trudged glumly back outside, to find Patrick deep in conversation with a sociable Belgian couple returning from a tour of Eastern Europe on their Honda Gold Wing. They were model Belgians: he sported a walrus moustache and a beer gut, and she worked in a chocolate factory.

Previously I had thought the Enfield a Charles Atlas of motorcycles, but sitting beside theirs, it looked like the seven stone weakling who always gets sand kicked in his face. For the Gold Wing was not so much a motorcycle as a living room on wheels, complete with central heating, a hi-fi and a pet turtle. But our envy of it was matched by its owner's envy of our own adventure.

'Fabulous trip, you guys,' he said, in an accent somewhere between Sunset Boulevard and downtown Ghent.

We ran into them again on the outskirts of Passau, the medieval town of which Napoleon Bonaparte wrote, as he was pillaging his way through it, that it was the most beautiful in Germany. We found an inn overlooking the river, got out of our wet clothes and into a dry white wine, and went to a local bierkeller with the Gold Wing couple to consume vast quantities of pig and beer. It seemed an appropriately Belgian thing to do, in a Californian sort of way.

Now, I'm not quite sure how to put this, but I leaped out of bed next morning to be greeted by the sight of the world's largest organ.

The seventeenth-century instrument in the cathedral of Passau has an impressive 17,300 pipes and 231 registers, whatever a register is, and sits in a plumply sumptuous building above the town, which, in spite of having at various stages been destroyed by fire, high tides and Napoleon, has re-created itself as the very model of German wellbeing, whose citizens go about their business every day with a justifiably self-satisfied cheerfulness. Looking at their guileless, well-scrubbed faces in the early morning sun, it was difficult to imagine that this was a people who had ravaged Europe twice in the twentieth century. It seemed as unlikely as a sheep suddenly walking up and smacking you in the face.

Talking of which, I returned to our little inn to find Patrick, his bruises finally healed and his forks still one step ahead of the junkyard, busily engaged in the tightening of nuts, the checking of oil and the reunification of dissident parts, which are, as we all now know, part of the daily joy of owning an Enfield.

'Shall we proceed?' he said.

And so we did until early evening, when, with rain closing in, we stopped for a break at Würzburg, the town that was carpet-bombed by the Allies during the Second World War. It is the home of the Residenz, a fabulous eighteenth-century palace that just missed being flattened. On the ceiling inside is the world's largest fresco, in which, from the four continents, a panoply of overweight cherubs, Red Indians, camels, sheikhs, fops, ostriches and dervishes pay homage to the prince bishops of Würzburg, who built the palace to symbolise their wealth and status. It is, in its gargantuan and immodest way, quite sweet.

We emerged into the square to find the rain sweeping down, and Patrick turned to me.

'Listen, would you mind if we called it a day? I'm knackered wrestling with those forks. They're so shot I can't even use the front brakes.'

'Aye, no worries,' I said. 'Look, there's a little hotel on the corner.'

Inside, a very charming woman called Tina was standing behind the reception desk, looking as if she had just had a hot shower, patted herself dry with an organic free-range towel, then been lightly dusted with sunshine.

'Ah, you two are bikers,' she said brightly.

'Was it our air of rugged charm?' I said.

'Although with a hint of natural sophistication and infinite sensitivity?' added Patrick hopefully.

'No, it was more the helmets,' she laughed. 'What sort of motorcycles are you riding?'

'You've probably never heard of them,' I said. 'They're called Enfields.'

'Ah, Enfields,' she said. 'Funny, my friend Jochen Sommer is the main Enfield dealer for Germany.'

Patrick's ears pricked up. 'Bloody hell,' he said. 'Where does he live?'

'Vockenhausen, a little village on the way to Frankfurt.'

Patrick's ears pricked up as far as it is possible for ears to do, for that was on our way tomorrow. 'Can we phone him?' he said.

'Absolutely,' said Tina, dialling the number and handing Patrick the phone.

Patrick talked briefly to Jochen, his smile widening by the second.

'Incredible,' he said, as he handed the phone back to Tina. 'Incredible. He's been waiting for a delivery of forks from India for three months, and they just arrived last week.'

And so, thanks to this remarkable piece of serendipity, we found ourselves the next afternoon, soaked by yet another downpour, in the neat and clean workshop of Jochen.

All around us were Enfields – 350s, 500s and two rare 624 cc specials, a model we had never seen before. Patrick was in Enfield heaven, and it was about time, for while my machine had been humming along without a care in the world, his had had the worst of luck, what with Turkish mechanics and Bulgarian sheep. Of late he had taken to muttering about making a funeral pyre of it and buying a nice, used BMW with low mileage and one careful owner when he returned home. In fact, things had come to a bit of a head just that morning, when we left the hotel after a hearty breakfast of hand-knitted granola to find his rear tyre flat.

'Why, oh why?' he had wept into his gauntlets. 'Why does nothing ever go wrong with your bike?'

'Because it knows I can't fix it,' I suggested helpfully, as he dug into his panniers for the pump.

But now, just at this moment, watching Jochen strip down and replace his forks, Monsieur Minne was as happy as a pig in the proverbial.

'You got here just in time. These were just about to disintegrate,' said Jochen, finishing off the forks before going on to fix the puncture, replace a bent pushrod on my bike that I hadn't even known I was suffering from, and tune both our engines so that they sounded better even than when we had picked them up from Nanna.

'I can't wait to be able to brake again,' said Patrick as we rode off. 'What a luxury.'

And if you think that makes him a man who is too easily satisfied, you have obviously never ridden an Enfield.

Our Teutonically tuned motorcycles were now both humming along beautifully through the endless rain and wind. We were heading into the weekend, and what a busy little social life we had planned for ourselves: a cosy soirée in Brussels that night with two delightful girls – Pamela, who had once been a tenant in my house in Belfast, and her friend Heather; followed the next day with an evening in Kent with an ex-girlfriend of mine.

The first time I had visited Brussels, I had set aside two days for sightseeing, and finished in forty-seven minutes. Stuck for what to do, I had spent half a day searching for a pub that allegedly sold 400 types of beer, only to find when I got there that it was closed.

I'm afraid this time around things were little better. Walking through the evening streets left me with an overwhelming impression of nothing more than smug, provincial dullness. However, it did give Monsieur Minne, whose father was born in nearby Ghent, the chance to savour the experience of not being the only Minne in the telephone directory.

'Look, there are loads of us. There's even a P. Minne,' he said excitedly.

'Phone him up later and see if it's you,' I said.

'It can't be, because I'm going out tonight.'

And so we were – to eat and drink like Eurocrats in a fabulous *fin de siècle* restaurant with an air of vaguely doomed decadence about it.

After dinner, the four of us went dancing at a little salsa bar in the old quarter. We had been away so long that at first the salsa looked as impenetrable as Delhi traffic, but then Delhi traffic had looked like that at first as well, and soon I was salsaing away so convincingly that people kept coming up and asking what part of Brazil I was from, and I had to be taken away by Patrick and revived by a refreshing glass of champagne. Unfortunately, he had forgotten that Dorothy Parker's famous dictum about martinis – that one is never enough and two is always too many – also applied to bottles of champagne. As a result, we were in a particularly sorry state the next morning as we climbed on the Enfields and crawled to Ostend for the ferry to England.

Even worse, my fuel tank developed a leak halfway there.

'You can fix it with chewing gum,' I said, as Patrick looked on glumly.

'I didn't know that,' he said, surprising both of us.

'I learnt it from a Biggles book,' I said, thus making my single practical contribution to the expedition.

Half an hour later, fuel tank fixed with a wad of Wrigley's Spearmint, we arrived in Ostend and wearily got off the bikes.

'God, I am so looking forward to a huge fry and a good snooze on the boat,' I said, as a large man came over holding a small clipboard.

'Sorry, gentlemen, but when we were parking the boat last night, we bent it. You'll have to go on Calais,' he said.

'Bloody hell,' groaned Patrick, 'that's another hundred miles.'

The man looked at his watch, then at the Enfields, and grinned. 'You might just make it,' he said.

We climbed back on the bikes, and with the wind tossing us from pillar to post and the engines spluttering in protest at a diet of Belgian unleaded fuel, we did make it, but only by the skin of our carburettors.

Exhausted, hungover and relieved beyond measure, we hauled the Enfields onto their stands and pulled off our helmets.

As we sat on the saddles waiting for the queue to start

moving, a middle-aged man got out of a car several vehicles ahead and walked up to us.

'You're Geoff Hill from the *News Letter*, aren't you?' he said. 'I've been reading about you two. And is this Patrick, who killed the sheep?'

'Bloody hell,' said Patrick. 'You kill one sheep, and you never get to hear the end of it.'

We were still laughing as we rode onto the boat, polished off an onboard breakfast, which involved the premature death of several small pigs, then found a quiet corner and slept all the way to England.

For the Enfields, the leafy lanes of Kent were their spiritual home, especially with the tank full of good, old-fashioned British four-star. As for me, I wasn't quite sure where home was any more, except maybe the horizon.

'Which way is it to Yalding?' I asked a man outside a pub in Maidstone.

'Oh, that depends which direction you've come from,' he said.

'India.'

'Fair enough,' he said. 'You'll need to go through the town and look for signs to Tonbridge then,' he said.

And so, in the garden of a beautiful cottage in the little village of Yalding, we drank red wine with my old girlfriend, as above our heads a thread of jet-trail silk stitched the fabric of the stars. The next morning, Sunday church bells rang, and we had strawberries and cream for breakfast on the lawn while sunlight danced with roses and a Tiger Moth from the local flying club puttered overhead.

Then we took the long road north, and as the morning cars hissed silently past, I thought for one last time what it is that makes old motorcycles so romantic. Perhaps it is because they are so at odds with the trend in the latter half of the twentieth century towards the silent, the cool, the minimalist. Thundering mills become yuppie apartments, hushed except for the sound of gathering money. Typewriters become word processors, cine film becomes videotape, record becomes compact disc, and cars hum along so quietly that you would not even know they were running. Brocade becomes muslin, and black becomes grey becomes white. Compared to all that, the Enfield is a nasty, brutish, dirty, noisy beast. It spits in the face of post-modernism, and leaves a trail of oil all over its cool white interiors.

There. Having sorted all that out, we stopped in the Lake District at an old coaching inn whose walls were lined with blackboards advertising sumptuous fare, none of which, naturally, was available.

As I got off the bike, I noticed that the entire air filter had worked loose and was only held on by the ignition key, against which it was leaning in a devil-may-care fashion. You can take the Enfield out of India, but you can't take India out of the Enfield.

We came to Glasgow in the rain, checked into a hotel we could not afford and squelched around, leaving damp footprints on its expensive carpets and the imprint of our cold faces in its thick white towels. Then we went out drinking late into the night with women from many countries, which Patrick had impressively conjured up with a few phone calls.

At one stage I found myself sitting beside a small, dark girl who looked vaguely familiar.

'Have I ever seen you before?' I said.

'Could have,' she said. 'I'm an actress. I was the schoolgirl in *Trainspotting*.'

Now I remembered. The last time I had seen her, she was naked on top of Ewan McGregor: an image which made it so difficult to concentrate on my pint that I had to have several more.

At two in the morning Patrick went off with them all to a club, and I wandered back towards the hotel, then suddenly realised that I hadn't eaten all day. I found a café and ordered a kebab from a dark man in his thirties.

'Where are you from?' I asked him.

'I am from nowhere. I am a Kurd,' he said.

Patrick announced his arrival back in the hotel room at five in the morning with a rousing chorus of 'My Wild Irish Rose', fell into bed, then proved impossible to rouse for breakfast three hours later.

'Get up, you lazy bollocks,' I said, beating him around the head with a rolled up copy of the room-service menu. 'We've got to do a photoshoot for a Glasgow newspaper, then catch the ferry at Stranraer.'

We eventually made our way to a nearby square, had our photographs taken, and set off late for Stranraer. We stopped to refuel halfway there, and I was beginning to think we would make it after all when Patrick climbed on his Enfield and set off in completely the wrong direction.

I caught him ten minutes later, and we sped down the coast, needles of rain stabbing our faces, only to arrive at the terminal just in time to see the ferry kiss the harbour goodbye.

Wet and weary, we got off the bikes and went inside. Patrick fell asleep on a bench, and I phoned Nambarrie in Belfast to tell them the good news that we'd made it all the way from Delhi, and the bad news that we'd missed the boat.

There was nothing else for it but to wait for the next crossing, and I settled down for the afternoon with a novel I had found lying on the street in Brussels, but it was written in such a way that the words got in the way of the meaning. I left it down, looked out over the cold grey sea, and saw in the mirrors of my mind the lilac mountains of Persia shimmering in the desert sun. And then I thought of the other ribbons of water we had crossed: the Bosporus, the Danube and the English Channel. And the lands. I named them one by one: India, Pakistan, Iran, Turkey, Bulgaria, Romania, Hungary, Austria, Germany, Belgium, France, England and Scotland.

It seemed impossible that we had travelled such vast distances on the red and yellow motorcycles sitting outside, lashed with rain and looking a world more weary, worn and wise than when we had first seen them new and gleaming in the corner of Nanna's yard in Delhi. It seemed impossible that I was sitting in Stranraer, watching a television game show.

As the ferry pulled away from Stranraer, a girl aged ten or eleven, with red-gold hair and a lime pullover, stood on the jetty looking up. She gave a little wave, and I waved back, and wished her a life of adventures such as the one we had just had.

At Belfast, our friends were waiting, with gladness and champagne. We had come home at last, for there, as we rolled off the ferry, were Patrick's parents, Georges and Jeannie, and their youngest daughter Sheila. There, too, was Joris, elegant as ever and clutching in his freshly manicured hand two glasses and a bottle of vintage Bollinger.

'We'd better just have a sip of this,' I said, 'since we're expected over at Nambarrie headquarters with the tea.'

We started the Enfields and rode on in our own mini-cavalcade. Cars hooted, and drivers rolled their windows down and gave us the thumbs-up.

It was all rather splendid until we got to within spitting distance of the Nambarrie building. I was looking ahead to the small crowd of reporters and TV cameramen who had gathered outside when I suddenly became aware that it had gone strangely quiet.

'Here, is it just me, or has your engine stopped?' I said to Monsieur Minne.

Except that the world-famous Franco-Belgian motorcycle mechanic wasn't there. He was 20 yards behind, getting off his Enfield with a familiar look of exasperation on his face.

'Bollocks and buggery, but I don't believe it. We ride 7,000 miles, and it stops 200 yards from the frigging finishing line,' he said, giving the kick-start several hefty swings, which only succeeded in turning him a shade of pink that clashed rather unfortunately with the red Nambarrie T-shirt he had washed specially for the occasion.

Several minutes of fiddling having failed to produce any signs of life from the recalcitrant engine, he sighed and began to push the Enfield towards the waiting crowd. And since it would have not quite been the done thing to have roared ahead over the finishing line in a solitary blaze of glory with a cry of: 'Don't worry about Paddy. He'll be along in a minute, and anyway, I did all the hard work myself', I sighed too, switched my engine off and began to push my Enfield alongside his.

And thus it was, after seven long weeks on the road, countless missing nuts, and one dead sheep, we crossed the line together, on foot.

'Sorry we're late,' I said to Brian Davis of Nambarrie, digging the silver canister of tea out from a pannier and handing it to him.

'That's all right,' he said. 'Well worth waiting for.'

We shook hands with everyone who had turned up to wish us well and then did several interviews with the local media people.

'What was the most frightening bit?' said one particularly glamorous television presenter.

'Glasgow,' I said.

'And would you two do it again?'

'Absolutely,' I said.

'Tomorrow,' said Patrick. 'If I could get this bloody thing started, that is.'

He borrowed a mobile phone and called the AA, and we went inside, feeling simultaneously exhilarated and hollow, as I imagine celebrities do.

'Suppose we'd better make use of this,' said Brian suddenly, holding up the canister of finest Darjeeling. 'Anyone fancy a nice cup of tea?'

As the kettle in his office was coming to the boil, filmed by three television crews, the AA man arrived and set to fiddling with Patrick's electrics.

'Aha,' he said at last, holding up a piece of tinfoil. 'Look's like one of the dealer's little helpers busted a fuse and replaced it with this.'

'Bloody hell. No wonder it's been playing up,' said Patrick, as Brian emerged with a teapot.

And you know what? It tasted lovely. Although not quite as lovely as the several beers I had later that night. For after riding back to the house, which the happy tenants had covered with balloons for the occasion, we suddenly realised that in the excitement, we hadn't eaten all day.

'Don't suppose you fancy going out for an Indian, do you?' said Patrick.

'It's funny you should say that,' I said, reaching for my jacket.

We slept most of the next day, and in the evening I shook hands with Monsieur Minne and watched him ride around the corner on his yellow Enfield for the last time.

Heavens, I thought, what do I do now? And immediately went upstairs to look for an atlas.

Several glasses of wine later, I had been sitting looking at a map of the United States for half an hour when I realised that the answer was staring me in the face.

Route 66. On a Harley-Davidson.

Geoff and Harley-Davidson Road King at the start of Miller Miles,
Route 66 from Chicago to Los Angeles

Part II

Miller Miles
Route 66 on a Harley

Itchy feet

Now all I needed was a month off work, money and a Harley. And the funny thing was, that organising Route 66 proved as easy as Delhi to Belfast had been difficult.

A couple of days after our celebrated return to Belfast, I hopped on the Enfield and rode into work, where I found Geoff Martin sitting behind his desk and looking surprised to see me. Probably because when most of his staff go out on a story, they come back that afternoon, but I had been gone seven weeks.

'Sorry I'm late, boss. We got a bit held up in Quetta. And Istanbul, come to that.'

'Quite,' he said. 'Lucky for you the readers enjoyed it. Now, what can I do for you?'

'Well, I was wondering if I could take a month off to do Route 66 on a Harley.'

I left the office soon after that, since I find uncontrollable sobbing unseemly in a man, and applied myself to the task of finding my desk under almost two months' worth of unanswered letters.

The wonderful thing is, I discovered, that the longer you leave important correspondence, the less important it becomes, and I rode home that evening leaving behind several bins full of urgent requests to attend meetings, press conferences and briefings, which had come and gone, none of them any the worse for me not having been there.

Almost a month later I was at a beer promotion, when Brian Houston, the man from Miller Genuine Draft, came up to me.

'Here, you're Geoff Hill, aren't you?' he said.

'I think so, although I'll check, if it's really important to you,' I said, hoping he wasn't going to ask me to pay for all the beer I'd drunk.

'Listen, we all loved reading about the Nambarrie Run in the paper. You don't fancy doing something similar with Miller, do you?'

'What, like Route 66 on a Harley, for example?'

'It's funny you should say that. The Harley factory in Milwaukee is just across the road from the Miller brewery. And just up the road from Chicago.'

'Where Route 66 begins.'

'Absolutely.'

'Brian, let me think about this for a minute. Yes,' I said.

'Good decision. Like another beer?'

Splendid. Now all I had to do was sort out my love life. You see, shortly after the conversation with Brian, although I don't hold him personally responsible, I started going out with a girl who seemed ideal. She was a quarter Indian, a quarter sexy, a quarter voluptuous, a quarter funny and a quarter vivacious. I know that's five quarters but, as my mother always says, there are only three types of people in the world: the ones who are good at maths, and the ones who aren't.

Several months of the relationship passed, and apart from the arguments, the slammed doors and the broken glass, everything seemed perfect. Until the weekend I went away for a volleyball tournament and came back to find that she'd got religion.

Now, don't get me wrong. I've got nothing against religion. Apart from the Crusades, the Spanish Inquisition, corruption at the Vatican, child-molesting priests, sadistic Christian Brothers, proselytising missionaries, humourless fundamentalists, suicide bombers, jihads and sectarian murder, I think it's a wonderful thing.

However, I kept all these thoughts to myself. Until the morning in October she moved out. Even until the morning in November that she booked us into a one-hour Christian counselling session, then turned up fifty-five minutes late.

I sat in the office all day, glumly trying to write a humorous column and thinking that maybe life, the universe and everything was trying to tell me something about my relationships with women. Like that I should be a nun. Or gay. Maybe a gay, ascetic, hermit Buddhist eunuch nun, just to be on the safe side. Either way, I felt as if I should give up women for a while.

And then Cate walked into my life.

To be fair, I had done what all the therapists and self-counselling books recommended – you know, the ones with titles like *You can Heal Your Heart Easier than Your Liver* and *Men are from Glasgow, Women are from Planet Zog* – and given myself a reasonable amount of time between ending one relationship and even thinking about starting another. I mean, it must have been, oh, a good eight hours between when I'd split up that morning and when Cate, who had been invited to a baking party at my house by Caitriona, a mutual friend, walked through the door.

'You look a bit glum,' she said, as she handed me a bottle of wine and a big bunch of flowers.

'I split up with my girlfriend this morning,' I said glumly.

'Oh dear,' she said, squeezing my arm empathetically.

By four the following morning, everyone else at the party was drunk and having competitions to see who could bake the biggest willy. In the middle of this priapic maelstrom of flour, eggs and butter, Cate, who had turned out to be a research psychologist freshly arrived from London, was sitting talking to me about dialectical materialism. Or it might have been Cartesian dualism, logical positivism, cognitive disestablish-mentarianism or one of a hundred other things she would later prove to know inside out, upside down and back to front.

But it was not just that. It was the fact that she was not just talking to prove a point or win an argument or show how clever she was. She was just trying, elegantly and wisely and humorously, to find the truth, and it was at that moment, and for that reason, that I began to feel the first butterflies stir in my heart for her. Oh, and possibly the fact, now that I think of it, that she was tall, dark, willowy and gorgeous, with the biggest, bluest eyes and the finest bum on the planet.

Mmm. A psychologist with a gorgeous bum. It sounded like the answer to my problems, since I could solve most of them by just looking at her.

However, since she had arrived in Belfast determined to concentrate on research, and since I was equally determined not to plunge my still singed heart into the furnace of yet another affair, it was a couple of months before Cupid stepped in, in the shape of Caitriona. Fed up with us gazing meaningfully at each other and doing nothing about it, she invited us to a dinner party. With no other guests. Then left us alone in the room together.

The rest … well, the rest is hysteria.

To celebrate, I decided soon after that we would take a little holiday together, and as it was now only a matter of weeks before I left for Route 66, I thought we might ride to Ardara in Donegal on a Harley. First of all, so that I could learn to ride one, since a Harley is the size of a small house and makes an Enfield look like an anorexic Vespa. And secondly because there are more similarities between the road from Belfast to Donegal and Route 66 than you might think. Chicago and Belfast, for example, have the same number of letters. So do Ardara and Los Angeles, give or take a few. And both Route 66 and the road to Donegal are black, with white lines down the middle.

However, I had to get my hands on a Harley. I phoned Provincewide, the dealer in Ballymena, and simply asked them if they'd lend me one for the weekend. To my surprise, they said yes, so I hauled the Enfield out and prepared to set off. It had been a while since I had been out on it, and it sat there looking at me accusingly, covered in a fine miasma of dust and a delicate tracery of cobwebs until I went and got a cloth and bucket, and washed it down.

The strange thing was, though, that despite the fact I had by now ridden over 7,000 miles on the Enfield, through baking deserts, icy mountains, rain, hail and snow, even a journey of 30 miles down the road was still an adventure. You see, in a car, you just grab the keys, jump in, start up and go. But on a motorcycle, you start off by packing all your wet weather gear into the panniers, because if you do not, it will probably rain at some stage in the journey, even if there was not a cloud in the sky when you set out.

On an Enfield, you also check the oil levels and tyre pressure, spray the chain with lubricant and make sure that every nut and bolt is tight, because something will almost certainly have worked loose or fallen off since the last time you were out.

I got on my jacket, scarf, helmet, goggles and gloves and prepared for the often lengthy process of starting the bike. Much to my surprise, it coughed into life on the second kick, creating a large cloud of white smoke, which was the inevitable result of several weeks of thoughtful condensation in the petrol tank. Pushing it down the drive, like a Zeppelin pilot guiding his craft out of cumulus, I observed with interest that the exhaust was still blowing out at the manifold, made a mental note to do something about it, threw away the note, then climbed aboard and proceeded down the M2 at a gentlemanly pace with the sun shining and the birds warbling away – when will birds ever get to the point?

Because it was the first time I had been on the Enfield in several weeks, as always in such situations it was a while before I could relax and enjoy it, rather than listening with a hypersensitive ear to every hum, rattle and whirr. Suddenly, in among all the noises of an old single-cylinder British motorcycle, I noticed one I had not heard before: a deep, monotonous sound, like a man grinding a set of ill-fitting false teeth. Was I imagining it, in the manner of pilots over oceans, who become so hypersensitive to every slight change in the note of the engines that they go mad? No: first of all, I was already mad, and secondly, it was definitely there. By a process of slowing down and speeding up, then placing a gloved hand all over the bits of the bike, I finally tracked it down to the lid of the left pannier, which had been hand-built by Nanna.

Now that I had named my pain, I relaxed, made a mental note to get it seen to immediately, tore up that note and threw it away as well, and rode on, bathing in the warm sunshine and glorious scenery, and enjoying the song of the engine, the wind in my moustache and the flies in my teeth for, oh, about thirty seconds, until I noticed a distinct shimmy in the rear wheel. Was I leaking oil? No, as a glance to the rear revealed. I pulled onto the hard shoulder and got off. It was a puncture.

'I don't believe it,' I said to a small crow sitting on a fence, and phoned the AA.

Now, in the old days when you phoned the AA, you got a grizzled veteran in Belfast and said to them: 'Listen, I was heading out of Belfast on my Enfield and I've had a puncture. I'm on the M2 half a mile short of the Ballymena turnoff.' 'Righty-oh,' they would say, and send someone immediately. Now, what could be simpler than that? Nothing, unless you're an accountant. You see, the bean counters in grey suits who run too many companies these days are not interested in providing a good service for their customers. They are simply interested in making money, as a result of which they base everything in Milton Keynes, Mars or the Shetland Islands, whichever is the cheapest that month, and employ people with half an NVQ to answer the phone.

Consequently, I had the following conversation with the AA woman:

'Hello, AA Shetland Islands UK Central Headquarters, how may I help you?'

'Hello, AA. My name's Geoff Hill, and I'm a member from Belfast in Northern Ireland. I've got a motorbike with a flat tyre, although to be honest it's only flat at the bottom, so I could probably fix it myself if you send a chap with a round bottom for a motorcycle tyre. Alternatively, I could always try leaning over the front handlebars to take the weight off the back wheel and going fast enough so that the centrifugal force expands the tyre by itself. Or is it centripetal? I can never remember.'

'Where exactly are you located, Mr Hill?'

'Right beside the motorbike, thanks.'

'And where is that?'

'It's on the M2, half a mile on the Belfast side of the turnoff to Ballymena.'

'Are you on the A26?'

'No, I am not on the A26. As I said, I'm on the M2, half a mile on the Belfast side of the Ballymena turnoff.'

'I only have Junction 10 and 11 here. Are you sure you're on the M2?'

'Yes. Absolutely, totally sure.'

'Hang on, please.'

A long silence followed.

'I think I've got you now. You're between Junctions 7 and 1.'

'Splendid,' I said, wondering to myself how Junction 7 had got next to Junction 1. Maybe Junction 1 had been married to Junction 2, and they'd split up because of his habit of going into bars and asking for one for the road. Eventually his drinking had got so bad that he'd turned into a real cyclepath, so Junction 1 had moved up the road to be with Junction 7, whom she'd met at a party, made cat's eyes at and discovered a mutual liking for middle of the road music.

However, I didn't tell the woman from the AA any of this, because I didn't want her to think I was strange or anything.

It was, in the end, almost two hours before the AA man turned up at 5.30 p.m.

'Sorry about that,' he said, strapping the Enfield onto the back of his recovery van. 'They sent me to the wrong place. The funny thing is, I used to be one of the twenty-two private contractors who worked for the AA in Northern Ireland. Then the accountants decided to dump half of us to save money. Then they realised they needed us, and took us back on again.'

We arrived in Ballymena at one minute to six, and discovered that Billy at the Harley showroom had waited for us, God bless his leather trousers.

'Just leave the Enfield here and I'll fix the puncture. Your Harley's all ready to go,' he said.

I got on, started the engine and rode to Belfast, enjoying the sound of the big V-twin engine and the hefty feel of the bike, and thinking that a Harley was possibly the perfect motorcycle, except for one thing. It wasn't fitted with machine guns, in case I spotted an accountant on the way home.

Still, never mind. When Cate and I set off the next morning, we had a Harley, we had a full tank of gas, we had shades, leather jackets, faded Levis and the open road in front of us, stretching all the way over the horizon to Donegal. Well, you have to start somewhere.

Late that afternoon, frozen to our bones after the long ride from Belfast, we found ourselves in Ardara, and after asking a local man for directions and getting four different answers, we finally rode up the steep, winding lane to The Green Gate, the little guesthouse run by Frenchman Paul Chatenoud, where we were booked in for the weekend.

Which was where things started to go what I believe is referred to in the trade as pear-shaped. You see, Harley-Davidsons are built for going from New York to Los Angeles in a straight line at 55 m.p.h. They are not built for negotiating hairpin bends on steep, winding Donegal lanes at 0.5 m.p.h. Especially when the man in charge of gear selection has unaccountably picked second instead of first. That was me, and as a result of stalling the engine, I quickly found myself in the rarely used horizontal motorcycling position, while, behind me, Cate was sailing through the air with the greatest of ease to land on the part of her body normally used for attaching her to sofas.

'Oh dear,' she said. 'I don't seem to able to get up. It's either because I am paralysed, or because this lane is so steep that my head is below my feet.'

'I do apologise, dear,' I said politely, 'but even worse, there seems to be petrol leaking out of the fuel cap over the hot engine, so I may well shortly be immolated.'

She struggled to her feet and grabbed the back end of the bike, and we set to the task of hauling it upright, at which point we discovered that the problem with a motorcycle that has an engine the size of a car's is that it is a motorcycle that weighs the same as a car.

'You know,' said Cate, 'they really should build these things with sensors, so that when one starts to fall over, little stabiliser wheels pop out and stop it.'

'And a stout rope with a block and tackle, so you can haul it up steep Donegal lanes,' I said.

Eventually we got it back on its wheels, only to find that the carbs had flooded and the engine wouldn't start.

'Never mind,' said Cate, 'we can just push it to the top of the hill.'

Sadly, that proved easier said than done, and after ten minutes we had covered, oh, a good six inches.

'I think we're going to be here for the weekend, dear,' I said.

Thankfully, at this stage the engine coughed into life, and it was a weary duo who finally presented themselves at the door of The Green Gate.

We checked in, and some time later, found ourselves in the smallest of the village's thirteen pubs. Actually, when I say pub, I exaggerate. It was more of a large cupboard into which nine people, including a man from Anchorage, Alaska, had managed to squeeze. At least I think it was nine: it was hard to tell, because the smoke was so thick that you could have sliced it and sold the slices as cakes to people who were pretending to give up smoking.

The barmaid, a handsome woman in a green anorak, was wearing a flying helmet, sunglasses and an oxygen mask.

'Is it because of the smoke?' I asked an elderly man sitting in the corner, dropping cigarette ash onto a two-bar electric fire, where it flared into a brief resurrection then settled dully onto the chrome.

'No, she thinks she's Amelia Earhart,' he said.

The next day, we managed to get lost halfway up a mountain, and it was late afternoon when we finally set off for home.

We arrived just before midnight, so cold that we had lost all feeling in our hands and feet.

I phoned out for pizza, lit a fire and opened a bottle of wine, and as I touched glasses with Cate to that lovely old Turkish toast, 'Cam cam'a degil can can'a', I looked at her in the firelight.

'You know, my dear, I was just thinking. If you love me after I've flung you off the back of a motorbike then frozen you to death, you'll love me through anything.'

'Funny,' she smiled, 'I was just thinking exactly the same thing.'

Chicago

The Chicago Board of Trade, an elegant art deco skyscraper on Jackson Boulevard, is topped by a stainless steel statue of Ceres, the Roman goddess of grain. Beneath her feet is a bear pit, in which capitalism, red in tooth and claw, is unleashed every day to eat its tail.

On the trading floor, by eight in the morning, the men and women wearing child-bright jackets are already shouting and waving their arms frantically to buy and sell things that do not exist. They are trading in futures: educated guesses that the price of grain, soy beans or pork bellies will be higher on a specified future date, if they are buying, or lower, if they are selling. It is a gambling den in which 50 billion dollars are bet every day on horses not yet born. And at the end of each day of making money out of thin air, of speculation without investment, of cleverness without intelligence and knowledge without wisdom, they drive home in their limousines to their mansions by the lake, north of the city.

Economists will tell you, of course, that it is an essential system, invented to avoid the chaos of the days when farmers poured into town to sell their grain and, if they could not, simply dumped it into the river. But it is not a pretty sight, to see people devoting all their energies to creating nothing other than wealth for themselves. And the worst sort of wealth: for rather than the vast, deep riches of love and laughter, food and art, this sort is only as deep as a dollar bill.

I had flown into Chicago that afternoon, in the middle of April, checked into a hotel and wandered into the Board of Trade as I was out for a constitutional. After half an hour, I had had all the naked greed a man can take in one day, so I had a snooze back at the hotel and went out for dinner in a sports bar, an expression that might seem to you an oxymoron, like military intelligence or Scottish football.

On large televisions all around the walls, fit men dunked basketballs, rifled home pucks and slugged baseballs out of the park, watched by fat men who dunked beer, rifled home burgers and slugged their waistlines right out of their trousers. From the ceiling hung a panoply of tennis rackets, skis, tandems, baseball gloves, and ancient canoe paddles, which had almost certainly been made last month by baffled Taiwanese housewives. I ordered food that came in a thousand choices, all of them without any noticeable taste, and drank a beer that was so insubstantial that it was like liquid air with a hint of hops.

I walked back to the hotel through the velvet night, thinking, not for the first time, that America is a doomed society.

Take the catalogue of a supplier of travel goods called Magellan, which I discovered back in my room. A Magellan traveller, if the catalogue was anything to go by, was the sort of person for whom even going to the toilet is an experience so fraught with danger that it was inconceivable without antiseptic wipes, toilet-seat covers, aloe vera sprays or, may the Lord preserve us, the Uri-Mate, a sort of funnel that saves the well-padded posteriors of American women from actually having to sit on filthy foreign toilets. Heaven only knows what the kind of woman who thinks she needs a Uri-Mate would have made of some of the squat toilets Patrick and I had encountered in Pakistan. She would probably have aimed at them from across the yard, then phoned Kansas to tell the folks at home. After wiping the phone down with her handy little bottle of Virofree hospital-strength disinfectant, of course.

Magellan Woman, although she may not know it, is a soul mate of the kind of Irish traveller who brings tea bags and cornflakes when they go away, or seeks out Irish pubs, or has breakfast at that nice little place on the corner where they speak English and will do you a lovely fry, thank you very much. They are all travelling with the same fear: that the world is a big, scary, place, and that the only way to go out into it is to take home with you. Of course, the more they take home with them, the less they are actually away. And the more they are afraid of the unknown, the less they will get to know it.

A few pages further on, I found the electronic Door Stop Alarm, to stop Afghani terrorists storming your hotel room while you are in the bath, listening to the country-and-western channel on your rechargeable Shortwave Travel Radio and trimming the hairs up your nose with the ultra-compact Groom Mate. Still, even if they get past that, you'd always be able to escape from the ensuing mortar attack by simply fitting the Evac-U8 smoke hood over your freshly trimmed noggin and making a dash for freedom, using your credit-card-sized Everlasting Torch to light the way and your Walk Buddy Pedometer to work out exactly how far it is to the door.

Now, don't get me wrong. Believe it or not, I actually like most Americans. At their best, they have the eternal optimism of childhood and a wonderful belief that energy and enthusiasm can achieve almost anything. But childhood can have negative side as well, and some of them have become spoilt, cosseted, obese brats, who should be sent to the gym and made to do sit-ups until they can actually see their feet again. And then they should be given a small knapsack containing a packed lunch of peanut butter sandwiches and an apple, and sent off to explore the world like a child, and without the burden of possession, which is the antithesis of the glorious freedom that travel should be all about.

There. I felt a lot better after thinking all that. I tossed the rolled-up catalogue artfully across the room into the bin, looked at the two small bags that would keep me going for the month of the trip, and fell asleep, feeling disturbingly smug.

I woke at dawn, and went to see a woman about a motorcycle.

Anya Baboyedova was standing in the sunshine outside the lobby of my hotel. Behind her, with the door open, was a limo waiting to take me to Milwaukee, ninety miles north of Chicago. Charming and entirely Ukrainian, Anya worked for Miller, those nice people whose brewery and the Harley-Davidson factory bestride the commercial life of Milwaukee like the pillars of the temple at Rhodes. Or was that the Colossus? I can never remember.

When we arrived at Harley HQ two hours later, a row of motorcycles was sitting in the sun, and my heart started doing funny things. Yours would have too.

Inside, a tour was just starting, but for romantics like me the assembly of nuts and bolts holds little charm. Monsieur Minne would have enjoyed it, though. He would have enjoyed, too, the fact that the company now has a growing business remanufacturing parts for anyone restoring vintage Harleys. In a quiet little corner of the factory, the tedious dictums of Henry Ford have been ignored, and each of the fifteen workers can do all of the jobs.

We stepped out again into the sunshine, and found that the temperature had begun to rise. Which could mean only one thing – it was time for a beer. So we crossed the road to the brewery, which still stands on the same spot where it was founded in 1855 by a German immigrant whose name will come to me in a minute. Sprawling across 82 acres and 75 buildings, it produces 50 million bottles of beer a year. Just to put it into perspective – that's enough for 50 million people, if they drank a bottle each.

As well as making beer, Miller also sponsors the local baseball stadium, the American version of *Blind Date*, and several charities, including me. Who was, just at that moment, standing in the sun and wearing a brand new leather jacket which Miller had given me, holding a box containing a waterproof riding suit, baseball cap and knife which Harley had given me, and looking at the Road King which they had lent me to ride Route 66 for a month.

Feeling like a kid who in a spell of absentmindedness had somehow mislaid all his Christmases, then found them all at once, I threw my leg over the saddle and pressed the electric start button. Now, if you can imagine a pair of flatulent elephants making love underwater, you have some idea of the sound of a big twin-cylinder Harley-Davidson starting up. You also need psychiatric help, but we'll leave that aside just for the moment.

I adjusted the mirrors on the bike and looked up at Mike Hennick, the man from Miller. For some reason, I felt like Hardy Krüger in the scene from *The One that Got Away*. You know the one, where he tries to steal a Hurricane, only to be caught out as a fraud at the last minute. Thankfully Mike showed no sign of producing a gun and escorting me to the clink, so I kicked up the side stand and found first gear more by luck than judgement.

'Splendid,' I said. 'Now how do I get back to Chicago?'

'Well,' said Mike, 'the nicest way would be to go south on 41 then hang a right on Mitchell and stop for a frozen custard at Leon's on 27th and Oklahoma.'

I love the way Americans give directions, even though I haven't the faintest idea what they're talking about.

So I went south on 41, hung a something on somewhere, and tootled along completely happily, but completely lost. However, I find that several wrong turns often cancel each other out and become a right one, and eventually I turned a corner – sorry, hung a right – to find Leon's famous frozen custard shack straight in front of me.

Like many famous American food outlets, Leon's was actually a hole in the wall. Customers placed their orders through it, then sat in their cars and tucked in, looking like people at a drive-in movie without the movie.

I took my place in the queue and finally arrived at the window.

There was no one there, but a voice out of nowhere said: 'How may I help you, sir?'

I looked down and found that it belonged to a Chinese girl, as tiny and delicate as a sparrow.

If you've ever eaten in America, you will know that the cheaper the joint, the more complex the menu, and that the only solution is to decide what you want, order it decisively and not change your mind, no matter how many choices you are offered.

'I'll have a Special Super Sundae with pecan nut and cherry on top,' I said firmly.

'You got it. And what flavour topping?'

'Topping?' I gulped. No one had mentioned topping.

'Sure. What flavour topping?' she said, looking up at me as if I was an imbecile. Which in the circumstances wasn't far off the mark.

'Em, what toppings do you have?' I said, knowing in my heart exactly what was just about to happen.

'We got butterscotchchocolatestrawberryraspberry-maplecinnamonbutterpecanandmint.'

'Was there vanilla in there somewhere?' I squeaked optimistically.

'The custard is vanilla, sir. The flavours are not.'

Inside my head, twin searchlights of hope and despair scissored around the vast empty darkness for words describing flavours, but they were all hiding in the corners, the cowardly little buggers.

Some time passed.

'Chocolate?' I said suddenly, surprising both of us.

'Chocolate we got,' she said, tripping off across the tiled floor.

Frozen custard, you will be pleased to hear, is like very good vanilla ice cream which has just started to melt, allowing all the flavour to seep out, mostly over your shirt. And although I had ordered the smallest portion, I was quite unable to finish it, yet all around me people were waddling to their cars with tubs ranging from a pint to several gallons. I could see now what Route 66 was named after. It was the size my waistline was going to be by the time I got to Los Angeles.

I went to bed after some beers, and woke the next morning to the realisation that if I didn't start sending some stories back to the newspaper I worked for soon, pretty soon I wouldn't be working for the newspaper I worked for.

Now, as lovers of black-and-white movies on Saturday afternoons will know, in the old days journalists got their stories back to the office by picking up the phone and yelling: 'Get me Copy! I've got a story that's gonna blow this town apart!' Except in Belfast where they yell, 'Get me Copy! I've got a story that someone else has blown this town apart!'

In many newspapers they still have real human copytakers, and the advantage of dictating to one is that if you are in a lonely hotel room far from home, especially if you have talked to no one all day because you failed O-level Mandarin and the paper has unaccountably sent you to China – or Vancouver – you get the comfort of a warm, friendly voice, a bit of chat, the news from home and some feedback on whether the story you are reading down the line is likely to win the Pulitzer Prize or would be better printed out and used to prop up that wonky table in the office canteen.

In fact, the only disadvantage is the chance of getting the one copytaker – every newspaper has one – who has no sense of humour whatsoever. This results in the very dispiriting experience of delivering what you imagined to be some of the funniest lines ever written to someone whose response is at best a weary 'Yes?' and at worst a sigh and a: 'Is there much more of this?' However, the advantages far outweigh the disadvantages, which now made me wonder why, in a moment of madness, I had decided to bring a laptop and e-mail my stories back.

You see, according to the chaps in IT back home, all I needed when I got to the States was to walk into a computer shop and get an ISP. Of course, I barely know what IT stands for, unless it's I will give you a thousand complicated problems rather than one simple soluTion. But being an optimist by nature, later that morning I walked into a branch of Radio Shack to be greeted by a teenager with an air of despair about him that was troubling in one so young.

'Well, I guess all you need is a CD-Rom,' he said, hauling out my laptop. 'Ah, you don't have a drive.'

I left the shop and wandered aimlessly down the street until I found myself outside a branch of Comp USA, whose posters seemed to suggest that they could not only solve every computer problem that ever existed, but figure out who killed Kennedy as well.

'OK,' said the girl at the counter when I explained that all I wanted was to send e-mails back to the UK, 'how fast is your modem?'

'Is that the little black thing?'

'That's it.'

'It hasn't moved in two days.'

She gave me one of those looks.

'I see. What about your CD-Rom?'

'Apparently I don't have one.'

She sighed.

'Well, in that case I can only suggest an overhead underhang with a 47 Magnum and 678 gigadongles of reverse camshaft, but it'll cost you 20 dollars a month for three years,' she said.

At least, I think that's what she said. The only bits I understood were the 20 dollars and the three years.

'Can I make it 3 dollars over twenty years?' I said plaintively, thinking that at this rate I'd be dead well before then.

'Afraid not.'

I turned away clutching my tragic bundle of laptop and wires, like a space age refugee, and almost collided with the large black man behind me in the queue.

'Listen,' he said, 'just call Directory Enquiries and ask for the number for Excite. They'll talk you through changing the dialling codes on the laptop from the UK ones to local US ones, then give you a free e-mail address and Internet Service Provider.'

It was the first sense anyone had talked to me in a computer shop all day. Or possibly all my life.

I walked back to the hotel and asked the operator for the number for Excite. However, I think she misunderstood, for when I called the Excite she gave me I got a girl who had several interesting suggestions about how I could spend the evening with her, her boyfriend and a family-size tub of baby lotion.

It was very kind of her, but it was not what I was after. After several minutes of being outraged I slammed down the phone and looked in Yellow Pages instead.

Finally I tracked down a company called Earthlink, which sounded like the sort of place where nice people in check shirts all sat around a computer on a well-scrubbed wooden table and took turns answering the phone.

I called them, and for a piffling 19.99 dollars, a cheery chap called Richard set me up with an ISP account, which I could cancel at the end of the month. Then an even cheerier IT chap called Dan talked me through changing all my dialling codes.

To celebrate, I decided that evening to go for several beers at Famous Dave's BBQ and Blues on Clark Street. Outside, lightning split the sky, thunder rattled the windows and rain pummelled the streets. Inside, Rob Stone and the C Notes were pumping it up, or grooving it down, or whatever it is that blues singers do, while all around me, black couples were talking in code.

'Yo, howyadoin?'

'Doin fine. Whaddya want?'

'Whaddyagot?'

'Whaddyawant is whaddagot.'

'Mmmm, I'm gonna have me some of that.'

Whatever it meant, it meant that at some stage later they would go home and have great sex, while all the white people in the audience would go home, feed the dog, go to bed and flick through the LL Bean catalogue, trying to decide between beige and lovat in the canvas field jacket.

Not that that's what I found myself doing later, you understand. Anyway, they didn't have it in extra long.

I snuggled down on the pillow, thought about Cate for a while, then leafed idly through a copy of *Vogue*, thinking that no matter how much you are aware how Americans define themselves in terms of their possessions, whether it's clothes or cars, it's always a surprise to come face to face with newspapers and magazines containing page after page of advertisements for this shoe, or that vehicle, or the other holiday destination, tailor or health farm, many of them bearing the legend, repeated over and over again: 'You've arrived'. As if the ownership of a particular type of watch, or booking your poodle in for a colonic irrigation with the same vet who cuts the toenails of Oprah's pet chinchillas, confers a sense of destiny hitherto inexperienced outside the rigours of Zen.

Mind you, it does backfire: the previous day in a book on Route 66, I had seen exactly that declaration – 'You've arrived' – above an old advertisement for a Ford Edsel, which as you may remember was to cars what George Best was to synchronised swimming.

I slept like a log, spent the morning brushing up the leaves, and in the afternoon rode over to watch a baseball game at Wrigley Field. For Chicago sports fans, Wrigley Field is Lords, Wembley and Twickenham rolled into one, covered in ivy and plonked down carefully in the northern suburbs of the city. For them, heaven is taking the train out to the 75-year-old stadium on a Saturday afternoon, grabbing a beer and a hot dog and taking a place on the bleachers to watch the Cubs play baseball, that uniquely American sport that shares so much with English cricket: the wearing of long trousers, the act of hitting an impossibly hard ball with an even harder bat, an utterly impenetrable scoring system, and losing.

The Cubs, you see, haven't won anything important since the Second World War, and when the *Chicago Tribune* bought the ballpark from the Wrigley family of chewing-gum fame and promised to uphold all the traditions associated with the Cubs, the fans assumed that losing would be one of them. And it was. Then when the new owners finally installed floodlighting, there were howls of anguish from older fans, who felt that if God had meant men to play baseball after dark, he would have given them luminous balls.

On this particular afternoon the Cubs were playing the Florida Marlins. Outside, the owners of houses around the stadium were selling tickets to their roofs to fans who had failed to get tickets for inside, and who were standing around drinking beer, eating hot dogs and catching up with friends.

I got a ticket off a scalper and took my place on the ancient bleachers. All around me, people who had succeeded in getting tickets for inside were also drinking beer, eating hot dogs and catching up with friends, pausing only to join in the traditional seventh inning singing of 'Take Me Out to the Ballgame'.

Completely unnoticed, the Cubs actually won the game that day by four to two, although four to two what, I'm not exactly sure.

I walked outside with the crowd, started up the Harley and headed north on the highway in the late afternoon. As darkness gathered, I found myself thinking that riding a Harley into Chicago at night, with the engine burbling beneath you and that great expanse of lit skyscrapers paying homage to the Sears Tower, must be one of the great experiences of an adult life.

I went to bed early, a smile still on my face. It was my last night in the city. Tomorrow, at last, I would set out on Route 66.

Which seems a good time for a brief history of the road, so pay attention at the back there, while I try to stick to the point.

In 1926 America was booming. F. Scott Fitzgerald was still sober, and the average American was earning 1,200 dollars a year, more than most journalists today. Henry Ford's Model T had reduced the average price of a new car from a year's salary to 400 dollars, and more and more families were taking to the road and heading west for their holidays – until they got to Chicago and ran out of road. For of the 3 million miles of highway in America, only about 36,000 were suitable for cars, and all of those were in the east.

When an indefatigable Oklahoman called Cy Avery pointed this out to the government, Washington rolled up its sleeves, spat on its hands and told Avery to pick up a shovel. He was appointed head of the Associated Highways Association of America, and set to planning a new route from Chicago to Los Angeles.

By 1928, Route 66 was taking shape, but a shadow was about to be cast across the nation. The stock market crashed in 1929, and the following summer the first of several years of drought turned the Midwest into a dust bowl, sending Okies west on overladen jalopies to the promised land of California. About the only person who did well out of it was John Steinbeck, whose *Grapes of Wrath* about the exodus won the Pulitzer Prize in 1940.

Then came the war, and Route 66 became a convoy road, filled with olive green jeeps and trucks heading west on manoeuvres.

When peacetime returned, the soldiers came back, this time with their families on holiday, in third-hand Fords bought with demob pay. Bobby Troup wrote 'Get Your Kicks on Route 66', and Jack D. Rittenhouse published the first Route 66 guidebook.

In the fifties, Disneyland opened, Jack Kerouac wrote *On the Road*, and the lure of California grew even stronger. But the bright lights of Route 66 were already beginning to dim, for one of those soldiers heading west on manoeuvres had been Dwight Eisenhower, who had returned from Europe so impressed by German autobahns that in 1956 he spelt out plans for a national system of interstates that would bypass the small-town main streets, which much of Route 66 had run through, and which had earned it the sobriquet Main Street of America.

In the sixties, hippies hitched the Route and CBS ran a hugely popular series called *Route 66*, funny enough, about two adventurers who travelled its length in a red and white '57 Corvette.

But the interstates kept coming, and in 1984 the last stretch of Route 66 was bypassed near Williams, Arizona, and the last US 66 shield sign taken down from the roadside. But you know, you can't keep a good road closed, and in each of the eight states Route 66 passed through between Chicago and LA, associations dedicated to its preservation are putting up the signs again, publishing guides and selling memorabilia.

In places the old road is a dead end that runs into the weeds, but in others it is still there, ready and waiting. Not for those who believe that it is progress for you and a hard-driving friend to make the 2,448 miles from Chicago to Los Angeles in three or four days. But for the rest of us, who are in no hurry, who want to stop and smell the roses, the freshly brewed coffee or the pumpkin pie. Who feel, as the seventeenth-century Japanese poet Matsuo Basho said, that the journey itself is home.

A home where you can be handed that cup of coffee or that slice of pie from the person who brewed and baked them, or shoot the breeze with someone you have never met before and will never meet again, but with whom in that moment you feel entirely content.

Well, that's the story so far. Class is dismissed for today. Pack your bags and get an early night, for tomorrow we leave for the Main Street of America.

Illinois

The temperature outside was dithering above freezing, but in Lou Mitchell's on West Jackson Boulevard all was steamy and warm, and all the waitresses were somebody's mother. At Lou's they bring you your bacon and eggs in the skillet, then butter your home-made toast and turn the slices face to face, the way your girlfriend does when she brings you breakfast in bed. In fact, the more I thought about the temperature outside, the more the thought of forgetting about Route 66 and staying in Lou's for ever appealed to me.

'Hey, Sheri, how do you fancy adopting me?' I said to the waitress.

'I'd love to, honey, but I got three kids already,' she sighed. 'Never mind, have some more coffee instead.'

It was no use. I was just going to have to get on with it. I paid the bill and walked out into the freezing air just in time to stop a policeman giving the bike a parking ticket.

'You're packing pretty light for a month,' he said, putting his notebook away sadly after I'd fallen at his feet and begged for mercy.

And he was right. I had finally mastered the art of travelling – just bring twice the money and half the clothes you think you need. In the panniers of the Harley were nothing more than a spare T-shirt, socks, a pair of boxer shorts (the Wallace and Gromit ones) and a jar of the new combined bike and hair oil, Brylcreem GTX.

I climbed on, zipped up my leather jacket, adjusted my shades, checked that I had a full tank of gas, and rode to Grant Park on the shores of Lake Michigan, where Route 66 began in 1926. Only to discover that Chicago had made it one way. The wrong way.

As I was sitting trying to work out how much it would cost to dismantle the bike, post the pieces to LA, put it together and start from there, another policeman arrived on the scene.

'Can I help you, sir?'

'Good question. Is Route 66 one-way all the way from LA?'

'Nope. Just to the end of Jackson Boulevard.'

Very helpful chaps, American policemen, unless you're a black down-and-out vegetarian mobster.

I turned for one final look at Lake Michigan, the last expanse of water I would see until the Pacific, and then started on the long road west.

Great place, west, as is north. East may have its effete bourgeois charm, even further east its languid oriental pleasures, and south may have its sunshine and piña coladas, but west and north is where adventure lies.

Soon I was in the industrial suburbs. On the left, the huge freight trains that once hauled millions of baffled cows to their nemesis in the Chicago stockyards now seemed to be hauling nothing but Japanese cars, and on my right was row upon row of weathered clapboard houses. Outside one of them, a bright green sign hung from a lamppost; it said 'Birthplace of Ernest Hemingway, Pulitzer Prize-winning author'. (Oh, *that* Ernest Hemingway.)

I got off the bike and knocked the door. Several flakes of pale green paint detached themselves and fluttered to the porch. The door opened and an elderly woman with fluffy white hair and a bunch of dollars inexplicably clutched in her hand stood there.

'Here, it's all I got,' she said.

'No, no, I just want to know if Ernest Hemingway was born here.'

'Who?'

A younger woman came down the stairs wearing nothing but a Cubs T-shirt.

'Can I help you, honey?' she said.

'I was just wondering if Hemingway was born here.'

'Oh, him. Nah, he was born someways around here, but not in this house. We get a few people calling by, same mistake.'

'Shame. You could make some money out of that.'

'Hey, I never thought of that.'

So if you're ever passing 5414 Ogden Avenue in Chicago and you see a sign saying: 'Guided tours! See the back yard where Oh, Him shot his first rabbit! And the drinks cabinet where he stole his first whiskey!' don't believe a word of it. Even if the tour is only a dollar fifty.

I climbed back on the Harley and headed south-west, through a landscape inhabited entirely by factories, a giant plastic chicken and a truck bearing the legend 'Montana Joe's Little America Flea Circus'. It was, as you can imagine, something of a relief to arrive in Joliet, home of the forbidding prison where Elwood collected Jake in the Bluesmobile.

Sadly, I found it first time, thus depriving myself of the pleasure of riding around declaiming: 'Joliet, Joliet, wherefore art thou?'

Listen, when you're travelling alone, you get your kicks whichever way you can.

Past Joliet, you ride, literally, into America's back yard, rolling through tiny hamlets like Dwight and Odell, Cayuga and Chenoa, where you stop to let kids retrieve their ball from the middle of the road and have ludicrously polite discussions with pedestrians over who has the right of way.

'After you. Nice motorcycle.'

'No, please. Great zimmer.'

Here and there, you ride past ramshackle tourist attractions, like haunted houses or crazy golf, which some dad built in his back yard in the fifties and forgot to close. And one-man garages, with pumps outside still selling gasoline by Phillips 66, Mobiloil, Petrox, Sky Chief Supreme and Penn State: vintage toasts to America's great love affair with not only the car but the fuels that run through its veins. And at under a quid a gallon, you'd love it too.

Then, for a while, the little towns fell behind, leaving only the vast open expanses of oak-dark farmland. On the right, the interstate ran parallel to the old road – in the setting sun a glittering river of fish swimming downstream. On the left, the railroad track, that other legend of American travel, ran parallel to the old road too, flanked by a line of weathered telegraph poles. Their wires had been disconnected for decades, but they still tilted their heads this way and that, listening for news of Kennedy, Vietnam and the first man on the moon.

The moon, which rose now over the dark, flat fields, brought the rusted grain elevators back to silvery life. And then another road appeared on the right: an even earlier incarnation of Route 66, superseded and lying idle, dark weeds cracking its concrete. I slithered the Harley across the grass verge and rode the ancient road for miles in the moonlight, feeling like a ghost carrying messages that only the old telegraph poles could hear.

But then I realised that even ghosts could not have hands this cold. When I took my gloves off to inspect them, the little finger on my throttle hand had turned entirely white, and my legs were so numb that I feared if I stopped, I would simply fall over and lie there until I was run over by a truck.

I found an old motel in a town called Normal, and plunged my hands into a sinkful of hot water until I could feel them. Three words describe it. Bliss, bliss and bliss. And then I went out to see if Normal was normal.

It was, and perfectly so. It had a Normal Avenue, and a Normal Street, and when I went out for a pizza, I came back instead with 2.54 children, a Labrador and a Volvo estate.

As I leapt out of bed the next morning with gay abandon and

flung open the curtains, however, it was obvious that I had spoken too soon when I said that Normal was normal, for the weather was anything but. Lightning split the sky, thunder rattled the motel windows and commuters left the car at home and surfed to work, some of them failing to negotiate a particularly tricky whirlpool at the corner of Main and College and disappearing below the surface in a flurry of unhinged briefcases. And according to the *Pantagraph*, the local organ whose quaint name suggested a device for monitoring the rise and fall of underwear rather than a newspaper, things were going to get worse.

In short, it was not ideal motorcycling weather, but there was nothing else for it. Climbing aboard and turning down the road, I passed several frogs hitching west to dryer weather.

'Want a lift, guys?' I shouted above the rain.

'Are you kidding? We're waiting for a nice warm car,' said the smallest.

Honestly. No sense of adventure, frogs.

And after a while riding through the downpour, neither had I. Ho hum, sometimes I wish I was a normal person, happy to sit in an armchair by the fire with a copy of *Biggles Hits the Trail*. (The one with the giant Tibetan caterpillars, if you remember.) However, at this moment my thoughts were interrupted by the appearance through the mist, as if by magic, of a Harley-Davidson sign on a pole. It was the local dealer, so I stopped and squelched through the door.

'I don't suppose you have a pair of those nice leather gauntlets I saw in the Harley shop in Chicago for only 85 dollars in extra large, do you?' I said to the grizzly but sprightly chap behind the counter.

'Sure do. And we got them three bucks cheaper!' he said.

I put them on and rode west, almost falling off several times because I was admiring them so much. After half an hour the sun came out, and I stopped and put them carefully in one of the panniers, thinking with a sigh that I would probably never wear them again.

And half an hour later I was in Funks Grove, where Isaac Funk began selling the world's finest maple syrup in 1825, and where his great-grandson Steve still sells it today. On the railroad track, the noon train from St Louis to Chicago went howling by with a mournful wail, and in the silence on the other side of its departure, finches were singing in the bluebell woods. I know they were finches because of the yellowed bird identification chart in the grimy window of the Funks Grove General Store, an antique shop more antique than many of its contents, which were mostly junk deified by age.

Across the road, the equally threadbare railway depot was filled with even more junk: stuffed toys, children's dresses, old novels and a cardboard box bearing the legend 'Kohler plumbing fixture, Kohler Co, Kohler, Wisconsin'. Looks like it's about time the Monopolies Commission paid a visit to Kohler, I thought.

Half a mile up the road is the Funks Grove Cemetery, in the corner of which is a little section for the Irishmen who died during the building of the railroad out here – assorted Murphys, O'Donnells and Connors. And half a mile down the road is the famous maple syrup shop, a wooden shed whose shelves are lined with Route 66 souvenirs and jars of syrup.

'Are you Steve?' I said to the man behind the counter.

'No, I'm Steve's son. But I'm Steve too,' he said.

Fair enough. In the circumstances it seemed only reasonable to buy some syrup, or 'sirup', as they traditionally spell it in Funks Grove for reasons that would take several pages to explain.

It was delycyous, as was the bread pudding with vanilla custard in McLean, where the Dixie Truckers' Home has been making big truckers even bigger since 1928. All around me, men who spent their days wrestling eighteen-wheelers down the interstate, dressed identically in jeans or bib overalls, lumberjack shirts and baseball caps extolling the virtues of heavy machinery, disposed of herds of pigs and cows that had been variously fried and battered to death. I licked the last of the pudding off my spoon, ignored their meaty stares and made a mental note to start a Bikers Who Love Custard chapter of the Hell's Angels when I got home.

I waddled warmly to the bike, and by nightfall I was in Springfield.

Before the Simpsons came along, Springfield was best known as the home of Abraham Lincoln, and Springfield won't let you forget it. A slow walk around the town reveals the reconstructed village where he grew up, the office where he practised law, the office where he got law right and the State Capitol where he gave his 'A house divided against itself cannot stand' speech, thus establishing himself as the Senator George Mitchell of his day. Not to mention the bank where he kept his overdraft, the pew on which he placed his august bottom every Sunday, the railway depot where he left for Washington and the tomb where he was buried after his assassination at an opera in 1865, thus giving wags the chance for evermore to greet the misfortune of others with the words: 'So, apart from that, Mrs Lincoln, how did you enjoy the show?' Mrs Lincoln is in the tomb as well, along with four of their children, which must make it cosy but a bit squiffy in summer.

A quick look through Springfield's phone directory, meanwhile, reveals the Lincoln academy, chiropractic clinic, florist, golf course, soccer league, alarm company, snack supplier, taco drive-in, cab firm, lampshade shop, and tree surgeon.

But not, thankfully, the Lincoln Route 66 gas station museum, for that honour belongs to Bill Shea. I found him inside his cavern of delight in the north of the city chatting to another septuagenarian. They were sitting on the back seat of an old Chevy, but the old Chevy was no longer attached to it.

'Northern Ireland? Hell, I have a relative there – John McStay, drives a taxi in Portadown, where all the trouble is,' said Bill, springing to his feet and shaking both my hands at once.

All around him, in glass cabinets, on shelves and hanging from the ceiling, were thousands upon thousands of items of Route 66 memorabilia, from canvas water bags for crossing the Mojave Desert (Saturate before Using) to a row of petrol pumps, all intact. Somewhere in the middle was a small sign saying, 'If you write in our dust, please don't put the date.' It was like one of those theme bars you see, except it was real. And Bill doesn't serve beer.

Now seventy-eight, he had been collecting stuff from the road for fifty years and showed no sign of stopping: he'd just bought an entire 1930s gas station from up the country, which he was busy restoring in the yard. He was already halfway through, and had a sign up saying, 'Opening soon under old management'.

'Hell, I've no intention of retiring. I'll keep going until I'm ninety, then maybe work half days,' he said, in answer to the question I hadn't asked him.

The good news is that when he finally quits, the place will not quit with him: his son and grandson are already eagerly helping out.

When I finally rode off down the road an hour later, he was still waving when I got to the corner. I gave him one last wave, almost falling off in the process, and pulled in just as the rain came on at a Route 66 gas station to fill up the tank and check where I could find the Cozy Dog diner, where, as you all know, Ed Waldmire invented the eponymous hot dog on a stick in 1946.

'Sure do call by there. Ed's folks'll be glad to see you,' said the almost completely spherical gas station man.

Now, bear in mind that this was a man in the north of a city of 110,000 souls, talking about a family who lived in the south as if they lived across a village street. But then, Route 66 is not so much a road as the longest village in the world, populated both by the people who travel along it and the people who still earn their living from it, in 10,000 dime stores and nickel bars, soda fountains and pie counters, gas stations and short-order diners.

And, of course, the Cozy Dog.

Ed, in spite of being the only man in the world to look younger than his children, died in 1993, but his son Buz was behind the counter.

'You doing the whole of 66? Here, this one's on me. Besides, everyone should have their first Cozy Dog free,' he said.

In the corner by the window, a bunch of old-timers were shooting the breeze over coffee, and by the look of it, had been all year.

'Hey, young feller, come over and join us,' said the youngest, who was about seventy.

Now, anyone who calls me young feller deserves the time of day, so I went over and sat down with them and tucked into my Cozy Dog.

Bob and John and Phil and Bill and Rich were all ex-servicemen who had seen out the war in Europe. Rich had flown thirteen missions as a gunner on a Flying Fortress, the first of them only weeks after his brother died in a Superfortress over Germany.

'Do you know Raymond Baxter, the British TV commentator?' I said.

'I've heard of him. Wasn't he a Spitfire pilot?' said Bob.

'Indeed he was. He flew bomber escorts, and a few years ago he was sitting at a black-tie dinner in Berlin beside a young Michael Schumacher, who didn't know him,' I said. 'Halfway through the soup, Schumacher leaned over and said: "So, tell me, have you ever been to Germany before?" "Yes, but only in the evenings," said Baxter, in that wonderfully English voice of his.'

'I like it, I like it,' laughed Rich.

'Hey, listen,' said Bob, 'have a great trip. But just be careful around old folks like us – we're the biggest carriers of Aids in America.'

'Yeah, Band-Aids, hearing aids and walking aids,' said Rich.

I left them laughing, and headed down the road to Glenarm, for no other reason than that there's a village of the same name in Northern Ireland. And the two are almost identical, down to the dozen clapboard shacks, disused bandstand and two pick-up trucks below a large sign advertising Nickorbob's Craft Mall and the Truckers' Homestead Restaurant.

However, I was saving myself for the quaint delights of the Ariston Café. On a road famed for diners, where big truckers eat their hearts out in every sense, the Ariston, aptly named after the Greek *aristos*, or 'superior', has been an idiosyncratic legend of Route 66 since it opened in 1926. Inside, its tables were laid with sparkling linen, fresh flowers and gleaming silver, the waitresses looked as if they had just stepped elegantly from the bath – and put their clothes on, of course – and there was old dance-hall music playing on the radio.

It would have been the loveliest thing in the world to slip out of my wet clothes and into a dry martini, then decide on the trout washed down with Chablis, followed by one of the pies glistening seductively on the silver trolley in the corner. But it was impossible. There's no room for a tuxedo on a Harley; and besides, I had to meet a man called Russell Soulsby.

Over the months I had been planning this trip, he had smiled up at me every day from page 46 of *Route 66: The Mother Road* by Michael Wallis. In the photograph, Russell is standing outside the Shell station his father opened in 1926, making it the oldest on the Route, and which he and his sister still ran, keeping their accounts on the roll-top desk their father bought when he opened the business. When the interstate came along, things slowed down a little, but there was still enough work for Russell and Ola to stay open seven days a week.

'We kept steady customers. They'll stick with us always,' said Russell in Wallis's book. 'See, we try to satisfy the public. We pump the gas ourselves and clean every windshield.'

In 1970, Russell's wife died, and after a while he and Ola decided to take a rest on Sundays, if only so Russell could recover from going out dancing on Saturday nights.

'See, my father played in a string band every Saturday night, and when we were kids we always went along,' Russell told Wallis. 'He played mandolin and guitar. He was real good. Sometimes his band would play until daylight and us kids would find a place to sleep.'

Russell himself played clarinet and sax for a while, up and down Route 66 in a dance band called The Melodians. And these Saturdays, Wallis recorded, when they shut up shop for the week, Russell shaves, shines his shoes and drives down the old road to go dancing in Springfield or Sherman, Litchfield or Edwardsville.

'I don't go to the doctor or take pills. Instead, I take prize ribbons with my dancing,' was how he put it.

I liked the sound of that. And I liked the way he looked in the photograph, smiling in the sunshine outside Soulsby's Service. So that afternoon, although it was far from a sunny day, I wrapped up well and rode along in pouring rain and vicious winds. Down in the Midwest, the land is so flat that the wind gets a good run at you before it tries to kick you over. But it was a good feeling, wrapped up in scarf and goggles and helmet, leather jacket and gauntlets, wrestling with the elements on the winding road west. It felt like being a man.

In the village of Mount Olive, the freshly painted walls of Soulsby's Service gleamed through the rain from half a mile away. I pulled up outside and switched off the engine. It was strangely quiet. The door was locked, and there was a sign on the window saying that Soulsby's Service was closed. Baffled, I called at the house next door. And there they told me that Ola had died a few years ago, and Russell had joined her only last month.

You see, for every little business that somehow survived when Interstate America turned its back on Route 66, another one has died. Earlier that day, I had passed other tombstones along the way: two old Campbells trailers, with their famous galloping camel logo, rusting in a field. And a Phillips 66 gas station, its Mobil, Olympic and Imperial Ethyl pumps run dry and its Chicago Motor Club sign creaking in the wind. And then a few miles down the road, a faded wooden sign announcing 'Dining! Dancing! Cocktails!' – a ghostly holy trinity of fifties sophistication.

The day before, I had talked to Ernie Edwards, who had owned the Pig Hip diner since 1927, and he had told me that none of his ten children had been interested in taking over the business. Like Russell Soulsby's three sons, they had all moved to the city and had landed good jobs. And every Saturday, they got into their cars and drove to do their shopping in one of a thousand identical malls that have stolen the soul of the Main Street of America.

Missouri
(and a little bit of Kansas)

In November 1979, a Greyhound bus on its way from Los Angeles to New York stopped briefly in St Louis, and a young man swung down off it to stretch his legs. He had finished university in Belfast, spent the summer in California playing volleyball, and was on his way home with no money and even less of a clue as to what he was going to do when he grew up.

Inside Busch Stadium, a baseball game was in full swing as he walked around the corner to come face to face with something he had not even known existed. It was a stainless steel arch, soaring over 600 feet above the banks of the Mississippi and glowing gold in the setting sun.

'Heavens,' he said, absentmindedly taking a bite of his last peanut butter and banana sandwich. 'You never know, I might just come back here in twenty-one years, on my way down Route 66 on a Harley.'

The arch is still in St Louis, although it is not really a Route 66 landmark, having been built as late as 1965 to mark the gateway to the West, which the city had been for the early pioneers. That honour had fallen to the 66 Park-In, a drive-in cinema that I had been looking forward to going to on a motorbike, but which had been knocked down to make way for yet another shopping mall. And the Coral Court, a stunning motel built in 1941 in the rather coyly named Streamline Moderne style. Although in the years after the war the Coral Court had been booked solid for months, it sadly fell on hard times, and one of its unique features had become its downfall. For the private garages that allowed guests to enter their rooms in secrecy proved all too attractive to couples having illicit affairs, and the Coral Court became a no-tell motel and went slowly, shabbily broke.

It was bulldozed in 1993 and, much to the disappointment of locals, no trace was found of the 600,000 dollar ransom rumoured to have been stashed away in the hollow walls by resident gangster Carl Austin Hall forty years earlier. Part of it has been rebuilt in the city's transport museum, a fascinating collection which nevertheless pales into insignificance compared to what is possibly the best and certainly the maddest museum in the world, the St Louis City Museum.

Made entirely of recycled junk, the City Museum contains 4000 feet of caves, the world's largest windmill, a petrified forest, a circus, a walk-through whale, the contents of several entire buildings saved from the wrecker's ball and the world's largest men's underpants. As you wander around in the company of Jean Steck, the museum's splendidly gaga director, she is entirely likely to say at any moment something along the lines of: 'This is the room where we dyed the sheep when we had the sheep festival.'

'Have you had a Ted Drewe's frozen custard yet?' she said, as she showed me the way out past a giant silver stiletto.

'I'm just on my way there now,' I said.

Ted's frozen custard was a legend, so thick that the most popular was called a Concrete because, held upside down, it won't fall out. Since it was Good Friday, the Easter special was a Bunnycrete, made with carrot cake. It was, in fact, so thick that I was still finishing it when I arrived back at the hotel, which had, funny enough, been built on exactly the same spot where the Greyhound bus had pulled in with me on board all those years ago.

And the next morning I walked over to the arch, where I had bought a ticket to go up the inside with my last two dollars, then realised I didn't have time before the bus left for New York. Having somehow mislaid the ticket since then, I bought a new one and squeezed into the cylindrical lift with an English couple and their two children.

'Daddy, I think the rope is going to break and we're going to fall for ever and ever and ever,' said the little boy.

'Your feet are really big,' said his small sister to me.

'They have to be, or I'd fall over,' I said.

'What does that say on your T-shirt?'

'It says, "Miller Miles: Route 66 on a Harley".'

'I didn't think Route 66 existed any more,' said her father.

'It certainly does,' I said protectively, as we bumped to a stop and walked up the steps to the viewing windows.

So I finally got up the arch. And as I looked down from the top in the morning sunshine, I could almost see the ghost of a wistful young man gazing back up at me.

I took the lift down, climbed on the Harley a happy man, and rode out of town, realising almost immediately that because it was Easter Saturday, everyone in Missouri had decided to get into their cars and drive everywhere at once.

Except at Meramec Caverns, where they had decided to re-enact the crucifixion, and I will tell you about that in a minute.

But first, a little Bosnian breakfast. After all, it's not every day you see a sign at the side of an American road saying 'Bosnian Inn'.

Inside, the owner, a crumpled man in a green shirt, was cleaning up after the night before. He and his wife had arrived there four months earlier and invested their life savings in this little diner. So there was hope for Route 66 yet, even if it was only in Bosnia.

'Can I get a coffee?' I asked.

'Sure, but is only plastic coffee this morning. I haven't been out to get real stuff yet. But we have real food – no plastic, no frozen. All real.'

So I had some real *gibanica*, a cheese and egg custard, baked in filo pastry.

And now, back to the Meramec Caverns. Original owner Lester Dill, the man who also invented the bumper sticker, and painted invitations to the caves on roadside barns all the way from Chicago to LA, so that for hundreds of miles parents were tormented by plaintive back-seat cries of: 'Are we at the caves yet, Dad?'

I spotted the first one just outside St Louis, where Route 66 rolls through wooded hills past Times Beach. It was here in 1925 that the *St Louis Times* created pandemonium among its readers by auctioning off 20 x 100 feet lots for a paltry 67.50 dollars. And those were the days when 67.50 dollars really was 432 Hungarian ukeleles to the pound. Thousands applied, and the little community flourished until the seventies, when, in a spectacular piece of urban planning, the local council kept the dust down by spraying the streets with a mixture that was later found to be a highly toxic cousin of Agent Orange. The whole place was shut down and the folks moved out before they grew two heads, so that there was nothing but a whisper in the trees as I rode through. With my mouth shut.

Just south of there is Villa Ridge, where in the twenties one Spencer Groff memorably opened the world's first all-night banana stand. Tragically, all that remains of Spencer's vision today is a truck stop filled with hefty truckers, who probably wouldn't recognise a banana unless you fried it and served it with hash browns.

After Villa Ridge, the Meramec Caverns signs started again, and I had to tell myself several times to stop fidgeting or I'd go to bed without any supper. As I got closer, the signs seemed to grow larger and larger, and the delights they promised ever more impossibly exotic: cool temperatures all year round, camping, boat trips, canoes, kayaks, home-made fudge, world-famous hideout of Jesse James. The last one, however, was just a fantasy dreamed up by Lester Dill, when he found some rusty guns and an old chest in the caves in 1940.

'You wouldn't catch me getting involved in that fantasy stuff,' I said.

'Absolutely not,' said the rabbit on the back seat.

Well, I was lonely, you see, and the pet shop in St Louis was doing a special offer on rabbits. And he was the smallest one in the shop, so I felt sorry for him. Besides, he fitted nicely on the back seat. And kept my back warm.

I looked at him for a while, trying to figure out a name for him. Then it came to me: at school, whenever a teacher had asked me what something was called and I didn't know the answer, I'd always said 'Jim', to confuse them for long enough to give me time to think up the right answer.

'Hill, what's the capital of Guyana?'

'Jim, sir.'

'Did you say Jim, boy?'

'No, sir. Georgetown.'

Yes, the more I looked at him, the more of a Jim he became. Jim the Rabbit. It had a sort of ring to it, like John the Baptist, Mott the Hoople and Winnie the Pooh.

Anyway, where was I? Ah yes, pulling up at last outside Meramec Caverns, at the entrance to which the Caverns Motel nestled in a leafy glade.

A one-eyed cat was sleeping on the porch, and a two-eyed girl was standing behind the counter.

'You the travel writer who booked in?' she said.

'I hope so.'

'Travel ryder', she wrote down carefully on a piece of paper, and put it in a drawer.

'Tell me,' I said, 'just why exactly are they re-enacting the crucifixion in the caves this evening?'

'They do it every year. At Easter,' she said, taking out the piece of paper and looking at it again, then putting it away.

In the largest of the caves, which was a good five storeys high, the crucifixion was about to begin, watched by two

Stationary
Dep,t

LNER

Reminder

Kings
Cross

....

....

....

....

....

....

....

thousand evangelists, and me. It was like being in a light bulb shop when you run on gas.

Before the actual crucifixion, though, we were to have a family gospel group called The Lesters.

'And don't forget, folks,' said Lester Snr before the collection buckets were passed around halfway through, 'if you choose to contribute by cheque, your contribution is tax deductible.'

And so to the show, in which Jesus was finally crucified, although I thought some of the other actors deserved it more, and then buried in the cave while Joseph of Arimathea sang a little number entitled: 'He'll only need it for the weekend.'

Believe me when I say that I've nothing against love and faith. I just like them honest and pure and simple. I like them to be the still, small voice of the soul, not wrapped up in smarm and glitz and songs so mawkish they would make even a three-year-old throw up.

'Here,' I asked Jesus afterwards, 'do you not get fed up being crucified every year?'

'Lord, no, it's a blessing,' he said brightly, tossing back the tresses of his long auburn wig.

What a day it had been, I thought to myself, what with Bosnian breakfasts and getting to interview Jesus. I went back to the motel room quite exhausted by it all.

'Are we at the caves yet?' said Jim, as I tucked him in.

'We're going to see them in the morning,' I said, and he fell contentedly asleep.

I sat reading through some notes for a while, then realised that after all that religion, I needed a beer. So I headed down the road on the bike with early evening midges ricocheting off my teeth, looking for somewhere to dine.

After about five miles, I spotted a neon sign advertising a place called Hrunkels, or Schmurgles, or something like that. In the window, one of those notices that you make by sticking letters on a board with holes in it said: 'Saturday night fish fry – all you can eat for $4.99! Including tax!'

I got off the bike, hung my helmet on the handlebars and

went inside, where I approached a spotty teenager polishing an already sparkling counter and studiously ignoring the customers. Which was me.

'Pardon me, do you serve beer or wine here?' I said politely.

'No, this is a *normal* restaurant,' he sneered through his dental braces.

'Beer and wine is normal,' I said, refraining from strangling the snotty little git with my bare hands before I proceeded down the road to a Pizza Hut, where I was greeted, this time, by a pleasant young girl.

'Do you folks possibly serve beer or wine?' I said hopefully.

'We do have beer, sir.'

'And what type of beer do you have?'

'We do have Bud Lite.'

'That is a tautology, but I will have one nevertheless,' I said and sat down.

At the next table, a fat woman in tinted glasses was saying to another waitress: 'Honey, I need a napkin and a strawberry shake, and I need it now.'

Now, most Americans in the Midwest are entirely pleasant, but here was an exception: one of the ones who are just spoiled rotten, and as a result have forgotten the difference between needs and wants. They think that when they want something, it is a matter of life and death, which napkins and milkshakes rarely are. Even strawberry. What they actually need is to go to Ethiopia for a while. Or stay at home, wise up, lose some weight and stop thinking that every genuine emotion is a chance to write a country-and-western song about it.

There. What a cathartic thing a rant is sometimes.

I ate my pizza, had three more tautologies and rode back to the motel, completely ignoring the advice of Dean Martin, who said: 'Never drink and drive. Don't even putt.'

In the morning, before we left, Jim and I went for a wander around the rest of the caves. I thought they were splendid, and he felt entirely at home. Then, after a hearty breakfast of cold pizza, I strapped on my leathers and set out for Springfield, Missouri.

This Springfield is where Wild Bill Hickok killed Dave Tutt in the town square over a gambling debt. It is also the home of the world's first drive-through diner and the Shrine Mosque Theatre, which my guidebook described memorably as the Grand Old Opry designed by an itinerant Arab architect. It is also the queen of the Ozarks, home of good ole boys.

Good ole boys live at home and love their mom. They salute the flag, stand for the anthem, drive pick-up trucks and consider ZZ Top a bit too avant-garde for their liking. They have dinner at lunch time, and supper at dinner time. They wear big boots, baseball caps on backwards and camouflage suits, except in bed, when they wear camouflage pyjamas. For no matter how much good ole boys love sitting at home eating biscuits and gravy made by their mom, there is something they love more, and that is going out into the woods and swamps of the Ozarks, finding small furry creatures, and killing them. And when they go out to shop, they shop in Pro Bass in Springfield, probably the biggest huntin', shootin' and fishin' shop in America, and therefore the world.

I rode up to it that afternoon and, after carefully hiding Jim in the saddlebag with a couple of back issues of *Lettuce Weekly*, I strode inside trying to look as if I wanted to kill something too. The front ends of assorted deer, bears and one petulant turkey looked down glassily from the walls on everything from a 99 cent coffee-mug warmer to a 32,000 dollar speedboat, which wouldn't keep your coffee warm at all. For 25 dollars you could buy a fish that would flap and belt out a rousing version of 'Take Me to the River', and for about the same a hunting video-game for rainy days. I had a go, and scored two trees and a barn door. They were asking for it, believe me.

There were videos on advanced strategies for stalking dominant whitetail bucks, and if you found those gave you a headache, there were pillows in the shape of fish to rest on. There were baseball caps saying 'If It Flies It Dies', which will be disturbing news for airlines everywhere. In one corner I thought I heard a flock of kamikaze ducks, but it was just a bunch of good ole boys trying out duck calls near a pond, in which several nervous trout were swimming around trying their hardest to look like good ole fish.

There was even a section for good ole girls, which was doing a special offer on White Lilac Silky Body Spray. Well, even a good ole boy's gotta leave his mom sometime.

There were, in short, enough guns to supply an army, enough boots to march them, enough duck feather and down to keep all the Eskimos in Christendom warm, and enough Gore-Tex to keep even Tyrone dry.

I returned to the bike and opened the saddlebag.

'About time,' said Jim. 'It's so cold I was beginning to think this place would be the death of me.'

'You never spoke a truer word,' I said, starting the engine and heading for the centre of Springfield.

Now, let me explain something before I go any further. The American street system is the simplest in the world. Generally speaking, everything runs either east to west or north to south. At each junction, a number tells you how far you are in any given direction. Only an idiot could get lost.

So why was it that every way I went, I was getting further away from the centre of Springfield?

On second thoughts, don't answer that.

Finally, I stopped to ask a passer-by, a black teenager who was bouncing along the pavement as if someone had stolen his basketball and hadn't told him.

'Pardon me, but is this the way to downtown?' I asked.

'No,' he said, concisely, if not entirely helpfully, and bounced on.

I gave up. Turning my back on the delights of the Wild Bill Hickok shootout, the Shrine Mosque and the world's first drive-through diner, I turned west. Only to be joined overhead by a large black cloud, which immediately began sharing its burden of torrential rain with me.

After ten minutes, I realised that I was not being paranoid and that it actually was following me. It was, honestly. I stopped, got off the bike, and put on my waterproofs. But by that time I was already completely soaking, so that as the wet clothes inside warmed up to slightly above freezing, my goggles steamed up. And if things weren't bad enough, my rugged outdoor shoes had started letting in water. I couldn't believe it. I must have paid a good 17 dollars for those shoes in Philadelphia, and that was only two years ago.

As darkness fell, by which time I had trundled about 240 miles through the rain, I found a warm bed for the night at the rather splendid Grand Avenue Inn in Carthage, a Victorian town of leafy boulevards, and woke to a bright, cold morning, and the sound of the courthouse clock striking thirteen. It did that once in a while, but nobody bothered too much about it, just as nobody bothered too much when some joker slipped turnip seed into the mix for the town lawn.

Inside the Main Street Mercantile General Store, Harold and Gene were as close to the stove as it was possible to get without bursting into flames, and Harold's dog Julie wasn't far behind. A coffee pot was sitting on the stove, and their draughts board was four square on top of an old barrel. Behind the counter, Shea was topping up the candy jars, and around her the shelves were groaning with everything from flower seeds to the dulcimers she takes down every Friday night to play at the bring-your-own-food party.

'Here, young feller, pull up a seat and grab yourself a cup of coffee,' said Harold, looking up from the draughts game.

A crop-spraying pilot for many years, he had been left with a permanent limp after a crash and was now well into retirement after several spells in hospital.

'Spent all the money I saved on doctors. Your move, Gene,' he said, as the bell above the door chimed and the postman walked in.

'Hell, Bryce,' said Gene, ignoring Harold, 'you're running late this morning.'

'Yeah, hour and a half,' said Bryce. 'Still, I'm so late there's no point in hurrying.'

He sat down and grabbed himself a cup of coffee.

Then the candy-jar man came in, and Julie wandered over in the hope of a treat.

The candy man sat down too, and an hour later Bryce had gone, but I was still there. We had been through the price of gas, the great dynamite factory explosion, which blew half the town apart, the Civil War, the troubles in Ireland, and the reason why you can't get a decent head in a wet beer glass.

From time to time Harold would toss a quarter to the corner of the store, and Julie would raise herself with a weary sigh and retrieve it, returning with a look that said humans were easily pleased.

By the time I left, they had moved on to the Cuban problem in Miami. By nightfall they would have solved that too. And the next morning they would wake up having forgotten everything, and start all over again.

As I rode down Main Street, Bryce gave me a cheery wave. He was standing chatting to a farmer, having got about 100 yards in an hour. On the way out of town, the old 66 Drive-In was alive and well and showing *My Dog Skip*.

Through woods and dappled horse meadows, I came at last to Kansas. In Riverton, the sign outside the Eisler Brothers General Store said 'Welcome Route 66 Cruisers', so what could I do but stop and go in?

Behind the counter, where they had been serving customers since 1925, manager Scott Nelson fixed me one of his special baked ham and Swiss toasted sandwiches.

'Lucky you didn't come through here yesterday. Tornado north of here wiped out six houses,' he said.

I ate the sandwich with a Dr Pepper on the sunny porch. On the radio, Dolly Parton had been ditched again. That girl, will she never learn that men are only after two things?

As I left Kansas, the birds were singing in the trees, the clouds were piled high in a blue sky and spring was just around every corner. I could see why Dorothy had wanted so much to come home.

By mid-afternoon it was time for a coffee and a slice of pie. In the little diner I stopped at, the special that night was fried chicken, coleslaw, mashed potatoes and beans (no substitutes). Across the road, the Green Acres motel was not flourishing. The only car parked outside had cellophane for half its windows. Thankfully, I was staying somewhere else: at the Claremore Motor Inn down the road, where according to my guidebook, the man behind the desk was a former highway patrolman with many tales of the old road.

However, when I got there, the receptionist was a 36-year-old from Bombay.

'You'll not be the former highway patrolman, then,' I said.

'No sir, he retired.'

Still, since the cowboys had had it all their own way around here for so long, it was about time the Indians made a comeback.

Oklahoma

The Oklahoma School of Poodle Grooming in Tulsa was closed. And I had been looking forward not only to seeing how to groom a poodle – well, you never know when it might come in handy – but giving Jim a good tidy up after long days on the pillion. Heartbroken, I rode on, passing several times the corpses of armadillos by the roadside.

You may wonder what armadillos were doing in Oklahoma. Well, after years of persecution by the Aztecs, they flew north on improvised hang gliders, and because of the prevailing winds were never able to return.

'You're losing it,' said Jim from the back seat.

'Hey, what do you know? You're only a rabbit,' I said.

Anyway, if he thought I was going loopy, on the right of the road was a bright blue whale sitting in a lake – an aquatic amusement park, which had for years been a welcome sight for travellers on hot summer days.

In Stroud, the Rock Café had been another must stop for Route 66 riders since it opened in 1939, well before the Hard version. As I stepped inside, fans stirred the languid air, and on the unvarnished wooden walls were original advertisements for the 1954 Buick Roadmaster, Frank Sinatra's latest album, and Shirley Temple's Christmas single. At the corner table, a couple were celebrating their 42nd wedding anniversary with a helping of the daily special, a chicken dish called Zuri

Gshnatzel. And while I'm normally quite happy to eat things I can't pronounce, I was on a mission for Bikers Who Love Custard, and there was a very nice Peach Cobbler with ice cream on the dessert menu. In fact, it was the only thing on the dessert menu. It was, I am pleased to report, the best so far.

In Chandler I found the grave of Bill Tilghman, a frontier lawman who in 1924 died in the last gun battle of the old West near here, and on the outskirts of town one of the last, genuine, hand-cranked, steam-powered gas stations still working on the old road. I filled up and rode on through the rolling plains, on a section of Route 66 that was built, as the guidebook aptly put it, by men who drove rather than men who budgeted. And they made a fine job of it, for there can be few finer sounds in the world than a Harley snoring through one of their banked curves at 55 m.p.h.

Alongside it ran an older stretch of the road, with a sign saying: 'Historical Attraction: part of the original 1926 stretch of Route 66. Private land: trespassers will be prosecuted'. Honestly, that's like someone saying: 'Hi, I'm a gorgeous nymphomaniac. Now take your hand off my leg.'

I rode along part of it anyway, just as a protest, and came to Arcadia, which in spite of its thirties ambience was obviously a progressive town, if the 'Clint Loves Angie and Tiger' graffito on the outskirts was anything to go by.

However, it was not Clint's open-mindedness that Arcadia was famous for, but the Round Barn. Built in 1898, in a shape that would withstand tornadoes, it was used for hay and cattle until someone realised that its roundness created acoustics so good that when you heard a pin drop, it meant someone had dropped a pin. After a complete renovation by enthusiastic pensioners, the old barn was once again the Friday night venue for old-timers to dance the night away, while fiddle players serenaded the harvest moon. But not square dances, naturally, I thought, as I rode into the suburbs of Oklahoma, the city that went up in a day, and almost came down in one.

On a bright spring morning in April 1889, a single gunshot

signalled the opening of the land to white settlement, and what was empty prairie at dawn was by nightfall a city of 10,000. Then, on another bright spring morning in April 1995, a single explosion at the Federal Building killed 168 and almost brought the city to its knees.

But through all of the years of boom and bust, oil and dust, discovery and despair, there is one word that has summed up Oklahoma since the day and hour it was born. Cattle. For to the stockyards in the south of the city, cowboys have driven 100 million of the critters a year for as long as anyone alive can remember.

It's strange, I thought, as I motored down there, how herding cows caught the popular imagination, and other animals didn't. I imagine it's because all men want to be heroes, and John Wayne herding a flock of truculent sheep across the Rio Grande doesn't quite cut it in the heroic league.

Down by the stockyards, it was a quiet afternoon, and men poured straight from the Wayne mould were buying their saddles from the National Saddlery, tucking into their former charges at the Cattlemen's Steakhouse, getting their hair cut at the Cattlemen's Barber Shop, treating themselves to a new stetson or pair of boots at the Cattlemen's Western Wear Store or booking into the Cattlemen's Hotel then heading over to the Cattlemen's Club for a cold one.

Hell, when you know what you want, you don't need no fancy names for places. Which is why the National Cowboy Hall of Fame in the north of the city is called just that. There you will find every cowboy in the world except the last plumber you hired.

There was, in truth, little that was heroic to being a cowboy: just long, dusty days spent in the country they called the High, Wide and Lonely, living on beans, tobacco and cheap coffee on a dollar a day, and then being fleeced in some end-of-trail town by broads and barmen.

But for Hollywood, a myth is as good as a mile, and standing in the entrance hall surrounded by old posters of John Wayne,

Tom Mix, Roy Rogers, Gene Autry and Will Rogers, it was difficult not to come over all wistful for my lost childhood, as if I was back on Thursday nights watching on an old black-and-white television the double bill of *Shenandoah* and *The Rifleman*, with Chuck Connors cocking his Winchester at the start. There was a photograph of the Virginian, and Doug McClure as Trampas. And Ben, Adam and Hoss from *Bonanza*. Even the news, not that John Wayne was really Marion Morrison, which I knew already, but that Robert Taylor was originally Spangler Arlington Burgh failed to cheer me up.

And it was about to get even more wistful, with a quote from Will Rogers: 'I only have two things that I will always die very proud of. One was that I used to teach Chet Byers tricks with a rope, and the other is that I waved at the train Queen Marie was on, and I will always believe she saw me.'

Oh, what a pure and simple life, when rope tricks and an imagined wave from Queen Marie of Romania was enough to make a man happy!

I wandered in a melancholy daze through rooms of saddles and hats, boots and spurs, chaps and lariats, Colt revolvers and Winchester repeating rifles, until I found a television showing an old John Wayne movie. But it was too late. The sun was sinking low, and I had to be hitting the trail.

'OK, let's mosey on out, rabbit,' I said as I popped Jim on the pillion and turned gloomily west.

But it was all right in the end. The sparkling waters of Lake Overholser, graced by two daft-looking ducks and a somnolent fisherman in a dinghy, spirited away my nostalgia for my lost boyhood.

In 1941, Pan American's graceful Clipper flying boats would have risen from these waters, filled with passengers convinced that transcontinental seaplane travel would be the next big thing. However, by the end of the war the world was covered in long concrete runways, and Lake Overholser was left to the ducks.

Just down the road in El Reno, the huge building on the right was all that was left of the Oklahoma exhibit at the St Louis World Fair of 1904, the event that introduced hot dogs to the world. Not only that, but El Reno itself is the town where they invented the onion-fried burger, and where every May they cook the world's biggest – a 650-pounder. Not including the bun, of course.

You see, American history is so new that everyone can remember when things were invented, and all along Route 66 you see signs like, 'Ed's diner: inventor of the Cozy Dog'. I mean, in Ireland you never see signs saying: 'Bridget Murphy's: World-Famous Home of the Soda Farl'. (Now, how would yez like yer eggs – fried or boiled?)

After the overnight rain, the endless acres of spring wheat all around me as I rode along were a shimmering, iridescent green in the sun, and it was hard to believe that this was the area drought and wind had turned into the vast dust bowl of the thirties. The dust had covered everything. The sky turned black for days on end. Schools closed, transport stopped, cattle died of thirst, flocks of geese blinded by the grit crashed to the ground, and people died of dust pneumonia. And a third of a million Oklahomans strapped all they could onto third-hand jalopies and headed west for California or bust.

Behind them they left the Indians, from whom they had taken the land in the first place, and whose legacy now ranged from a very fine cultural centre to cheap tobacco shops and bingo halls. In the Cherokee Trading Post, I'm afraid all you could buy was tacky and mawkish junk. Some very expensive tacky and mawkish junk, but junk all the same. Personally, I found it all a bit sad.

And so back to the road. Over the years Route 66 was straightened and resurfaced several times, but here it had the original slabs of pinkish concrete with the little curved kerbs that were supposed to help drainage, but which actually turned hollows into large sheets of icy water. The reason I know is because I soaked my bum going through one. I was alone on the old road, apart from the occasional farmer, who used the same greeting as their Ulster equivalent: an index finger raised from the steering wheel.

At the diner in Weatherford, where I stopped for coffee and pie, the waitress was called Kim.

'You a travel writer? Cool. What's your favourite country?'

'Japan, I think.'

'Naw, I wouldn't like to go there. They eat dogs and kids. Y'all have a nice day, now.'

Americans. They're so friendly, but some of them don't get out much. I mean, everyone knows you can't pick up a dog with chopsticks.

In the middle of the afternoon I pulled up outside the Route 66 Museum in Clinton, and switched off the engine, feeling strangely as if I'd arrived home. And indeed, the ladies inside were as sweet as several mothers rolled into one.

For someone who had been on the old road for miles, it was a very peculiar experience finding a whole building dedicated to it and realising that you hadn't imagined it after all. The tour of a chronological history of the road was narrated by author Michael Wallis, in a voice as dark as tar and as sore as all hell about the way in which America had almost allowed its Main Street to die.

'The road brings us back to a time when the country was not littered with cookie-cutter housing developments, franchise eateries and shopping malls selling lookalike merchandise to people who have lost their own identity,' he said. 'This highway of phantoms and dreams is the romance of travelling the open road, the free road. Whenever we think of Route 66, we think of the road to adventure.'

And so long as someone hums 'Get Your Kicks' or reads *The Grapes of Wrath*, the road still lives. Or even better, climbs on a Harley and rides off into the sunset.

Which is exactly what I did, although to be honest, I only got as far as across the road to the Tradewinds Hotel, where I was due to have dinner with the Doc. Or, to give him his full title, Dr Walter S. Mason Jnr, the entirely charming former vet who now owns the hotel, which, it just so happens, was a favourite stopover of Elvis's on his way between Memphis and Vegas or Hollywood.

Since the King didn't like flying, he and his entourage would travel in three black limousines, arriving outside the Tradewinds at dead of night, and Elvis would sneak into Suite 215, which had been booked weeks earlier under a false name. They would sleep most of the next day, ordering from room service, then leave as secretly as they came. Until one morning in 1964, when the housekeeper found out who the secret guest was and told a friend, making her swear not to utter a word. The friend did the same to another friend, and by noon the whole town was gathered outside.

Elvis came out, played ball with the local kids, got into his limo and was driven away. He never came back.

'Would you like to see his room?' said the Doc. 'We've kept it pretty much the same.'

'Absolutely.'

But the ghost of Elvis had locked the door. The key failed to work, and the next one too.

When we finally got in, all was black leather and satin, just the way Elvis liked it. I sat on both the chairs, just to say my bum and Elvis's had something in common. Before he put on the weight, of course.

'C'mon and I'll take you for a drive around the town,' said the Doc.

We climbed into his car, an ancient brown Lincoln with 140,000 miles on the clock, and went weaving by the old Hawkes Hotel and the place where Pop Hicks's diner burnt down, going the wrong way down a one-way street and missing death oh, maybe, half a dozen times. It was tremendous fun, and since everyone in town knows to watch out for the Doc, I was still alive when I woke up the next morning.

Unlike Elvis.

And what a fine feeling it was to finish a breakfast of

buttermilk pancakes and ham that would keep a grizzly full for a week, climb on the Harley and hit out west again.

There is something very special about travelling by motorcycle, and especially on that fresh spring morning, for since Oklahoma is a helmet-free zone, I had stashed mine and was enjoying the wind in my hair. I know, very irresponsible. If I had died, I'd never have forgiven myself. And Cate would have killed me. It is the simplest and most carefree of lives, I thought, as I rode along unburdened by the adult cares of mortgages, of rising damp and the falling pound. A life in which the only decisions are whether to choose the almond cake with lemon curd or the French Silk chocolate pie at the Country Dove in Elk City.

Mmm. Tough choice. I went for the chocolate, and it was the best so far. I know I always say that, but it's always true. Unlike, for example, the great Indian uprising down the road in Sayre, where in 1959 a bunch of high school kids barricaded the road and told motorists that Indians had burnt the bridge and were on the warpath. For most of that day, the state highway patrol had their hands full with speeding motorists fleeing for the Texas border.

Those drivers were just lucky they weren't around two decades earlier, when an over-zealous patrolman named Officer Elmer made nearby Erick the worst speed trap in the nation. Using a black 1938 Ford with Oklahoma overdrive, Officer Elmer could catch anyone, and did. He even booked Bob Hope, and the comedian joked on a subsequent radio show that the next time he went through Erick, it would be on a donkey. On dark nights, travellers on this old road say that a black Ford V-8 still appears sometimes in your rear-view mirror, but I cruised through the sleepy little town untroubled by the ghost of Officer Elmer, and pulled up at a motel.

Inside, a man called Harley was standing behind the desk.

'Anywhere good to eat in this town, Harley?' I asked him as I checked in.

'No,' he grinned. 'This here's a little ole redneck town, so they've no need for good food.' He handed me a plank, on which had been roughly written the words 'MOTER CYCLE'. 'Here, Geoffrey, you park your stand on this, so it don't dent the asphalt.'

I parked my moter cycle on the plank, and went out looking for some bad food and a beer.

Erick, as I soon discovered, is so small that the 'Welcome to Erick' and the 'Thank You for Visiting Erick' notices are on the front and back of the same sign. It is, in truth, too small to be a hamlet, but it is where Roger Miller, the songwriter who penned 'Little Green Apples', was raised. Now, if you've always thought that his lyrics are slightly loopy, you are not alone. For everyone at his school thought Roger was loopy too. Except for Mrs Bessy Kelly, his teacher, who encouraged him to write poetry, until he was expelled for messing about once too often.

I bought a burger and a beer in the local store and returned to the motel. To while away a couple of hours, I watched television but found that the choice seemed to be between a plumply unctuous evangelist in a bright blue suit holding sway over an audience of people who were urgently in need of a good psychiatrist, chat shows in which the hosts were more interested in themselves than their interviewees, and laxative advertisements.

Finally I found *The Thirty Nine Steps*, and fell gratefully asleep to it.

At four in the morning I was awakened by a huge storm, which tumbled the power lines and sent the wind howling and screaming around the darkened motel like a banshee.

Then a sound. There was someone else in the room!

I fumbled for the light switch, and saw on the floor the pages of the book I had been reading earlier that evening flicking idly to and fro in the draught from the door – *Haunted Highway: The Spirits of Route 66*.

I laughed and shivered at the same time, and went back to sleep.

Texas and New Mexico

Half an hour after breakfast, I was in Texas. Not the one you and I are familiar with in the UK – the DIY store where they have every widget in the world except the one you want – but the real one, where it is illegal to carry a cigarette in a public park, but not a handgun. And where they are so polite that, by law, criminals must give their intended victims twenty-four hours' notice, either orally or in writing, and explain the nature of the crime to be committed.

Indeed, it was not long after I crossed the state border before I discovered my first crime. Someone had stolen all the trees, hills and fields. Immediately I had the feeling I had left behind the cluttered east and was facing something raw and primeval. A land in which there was only the sky and the horizon, on which I could already see Shamrock, the first town in the Lone Star State.

Named in 1893 by George Nickel, a homesick Irish immigrant, Shamrock had not forgotten the old sod, and I don't mean George. Every St Patrick's Day, thousands of Texans flood to the town to drink green beer, salute Miss Shamrock and Miss Irish Rose and attend a traditional Irish rodeo. Riding into town, I was confronted with a sign for the Blarney Inn, with a splendid-looking leprechaun announcing 'A Wee Bit of Ireland here in Shamrock'. Disappointingly, the U-Drop Inn across the road, the finest piece of art deco architecture on all of Route 66, was closed for renovations. In fact, everywhere in Shamrock seemed to be closed, except for a friendly little eatery run by folks called McDonald. Even though I assume they are Scottish, when they heard I was Irish, it was as if I had announced I was the love child of Dolly Parton and the Pope. Nice little place, and they did a very nice burger called, quaintly, a Big Mac. I think they'll go far.

Unlike Alfred Rowe, the English rancher who founded McLean further down the road. In 1912 Rowe left behind the thriving little town to revisit England and never returned, having booked his passage back on a brand-new unsinkable ship called *Titanic*. Since then, only three things have happened in McLean. The first was that Route 66 came. The second was that it went, leaving behind a town in which the paint is fading in the sun and the tumbleweeds gather around the doorway of the Avalon Theatre, below posters for films whose stars have also seen their glory days. And the third thing about McLean is that the old Sears bra factory at the edge of town became the world's only barbed-wire museum. A thorn in a D-cup, you might say, if you were inclined towards dreadful puns. Thankfully, I'm not.

Well, I don't know how much you know about barbed wire, or bob wah, as they call it down here, but after half an hour in there I certainly knew my Brinkerhoff from my Kittelson and my Nadelhoffer from my Edenborn. My favourite was definitely the Brinkerhoff: stylishly simple yet effective, if you know what I mean.

I had obviously been out in the sun too long and needed a beer. But unhappily McLean has never had a saloon. The Lord was speaking to me, and he was pointing the way to Amarillo.

I climbed on the Harley and rode west, singing Johnny Cash so badly that you should consider yourself lucky you weren't there. I launched into the second verse as I passed the sign announcing the city limits of Amarillo, which was named after the Spanish for 'yellow'. Some say it was because the early settlers got a job lot of yellow paint and painted all the houses with it; some say it was after the yellow soil; and some more romantic souls say it was for the little yellow flowers that wave in the prairie breeze when spring comes to Texas.

Whatever the case may be, it is a place where you are likely to be felled by a plummeting chicken. For down on 6th Street, in days not too long gone, the local grocer took to promoting his daily specials by the innovative marketing strategy of tossing live chickens from the roof. So what? you may say: chickens can fly. Except when they've had their wings clipped, of course.

As you can imagine, I drove down 6th Street with my helmet on, but there was no sign of a flying chicken by the time I got to safety at the Natatorium, a wonderfully strange building, described memorably by Tom Snyder in his *Route 66: Traveller's Guide and Roadside Companion* as being 'like an architectural Appaloosa horse with a Moorish-Camelot front joined to a steamship posterior'. Well, Tom may have been on drugs, but he wasn't wrong.

The Nat once boasted Amarillo's only indoor swimming pool, now turned into a dance hall and one of the string of antique shops that ends further down 6th Street at Harvey's.

I could tell I was going to like Harvey's from the sign: 'Collectibles and Weird Stuff'. Inside, just behind the dummy wearing a fur coat and gas mask, Harvey and his assistant Harold were surrounded by everything from an individual egg-weighing machine through jukeboxes to a complete Russian horse-drawn troika.

'Harvey, I'd buy the lot, except I can't fit it on the bike,' I said.

'Don't worry, we'll ship.'

'How much do you want for this little King of Hearts key ring? I think my girlfriend would like it.'

'In that case you can have it for nothing. Tell her it's a present from Amarillo.'

Although Amarillo deserves to be famous for Harvey, it is for something even more generous: for several miles back down the highway, signs offer free steak at the Inn of the Big Texan. There are only two catches. One is that it's 72 ounces. The other is that you have to eat it an hour. Plus a baked potato, shrimp cocktail, salad and a roll. With butter. Surprisingly, several have done it, including a kindly 63-year-old grandmother, a baseball player who did it in 11 minutes, a 385-pound wrestler named Klondike Bill, who ate two, an 11-year-old boy whose parents watched in disbelief, a man who ate it raw, and a local chap who has done it 21 times.

'Anyone tried it recently?' I asked the girl as I checked in next door at the Big Texan Motel.

'An Australian guy tried it yesterday. He barfed everywhere,' she said sweetly, handing me the key to a room on the second floor.

'Is it true it's still illegal here to shoot buffalo from the second floor of a hotel or break wind in an elevator?' I said.

'It's OK,' she said, 'we don't have buffalo or an elevator.'

I walked across to the inn and wandered into the dining room filled with resolve. Until Daryl the waiter brought out a raw steak on a tray, with the trimmings squeezed around the edges. It looked like a meat doormat without the Welcome sign.

'Daryl, I have a problem. My mother always told me to finish what was on my plate, but she didn't mean me to explode in the process. And I don't like the look of that shrimp cocktail.'

'Don't worry, I'm not too fussy on shrimp cocktail myself,' said Daryl, as he took away the doormat and put it back in the fridge. 'So where ya headed tomorrow?' he said when he came back.

'I'm going down to Palo Duro Canyon. I hear it's where Texans go when they've forgotten what vertical means. It's north of here, isn't it?'

'South, actually.'

'Well, I was close.'

'Here, let me help.' He tore a piece of paper off his pad and drew an arrow and a capital N on it. 'There, that's north. Take that with you wherever you go,' he said, then drew me a map of how to get to the canyon.

I thanked him, ate a 7 ounce steak, tried to imagine eating nine more, and failed. Still, never mind, they might have a restaurant in Los Angeles offering the Californian equivalent: Drink Three Glasses of Wine – and Get Them Free!

Afterwards, I visited the adjacent gift shop to see if they had any 'I Wimped Out on the 72 oz Steak' T-shirts.

'Well hello, Mr Route 66,' said the girl behind the counter when she noticed the logo on my jacket. She turned out to be Becky and the head of the Texas Route 66 Association. 'So, how far you headin' tomorrow?'

'Tucumcari, I guess.'

'You stayin' at the Blue Swallow?'

'I plan to.'

'Let me call ahead and book for you. Might be getting a little busy at this time of year.'

And she did. I went to bed, feeling as if everyone in Amarillo was looking after me.

Just outside the city the next morning, I found ten Cadillacs buried nose down in the desert.

Not a lot of people know this, but they are all that is left of the first American space programme in the fifties. President Eisenhower, a notorious tightwad, was reluctant to spend huge amounts of money on real rockets, and reckoned that since America was the finest country in the world and Cadillacs were the finest cars in America, they would do nicely if the windows were wound up tightly. Amarillo, sitting on the world's largest helium deposits, was chosen as the launch site. On 21 May 1956, the Cadillacs were filled with helium to make them lighter, powered up by ethyl nitrate and lined up on the launch pads.

'Ready for take off!' said the drivernauts in very squeaky voices, and the ten went powering into the clear blue sky, only to plunge into the earth in a neat line two miles outside the city.

Fortunately, every single one of the drivernauts was unhurt: after hurtling through the windscreens, they floated around for most of the afternoon until rescued by the Amarillo Butterfly Collectors' Club.

'Is that true?' said Jim from the pillion.

'No, but it's a good story.'

The truth, if you want to be pedantic about it, is that the Cadillac Ranch was the 1974 brainchild of Stanley Marsh III, for whom the Cadillac represented the American dream in all its aspects of aspiration, fantasy and excess. Marsh, a helium billionaire, rancher and art collector, lived with his wife Wendy in the ranch house named Toad Hall. As well as llamas, peacocks and tattooed dogs, he kept a pig called Minnesota Fats as a drinking companion until Fats died after eating too many chocolate Easter eggs. Marsh had him stuffed with beans and hung from the office ceiling.

'On second thoughts, maybe your story isn't so weird,' said Jim.

'Are you cold back there?' I said.

'Freezing.'

I wasn't surprised. They say that the only thing between Texas and the North Pole is a barbed-wire fence, and most of the time it's fallen down. Although it was May Day, the wind would not only have cut corn, but frozen it for Christmas, as it swept across what is in many ways like a vast sea of grass in which those of us who travelled across it became sailors of the land, whose heart lifted at the distant sight of a spire, a tower, or a café neon sign: anything, in fact, that marked a shelter from the biting wind.

Inside the Adrian Café, in the town of the same name, the coffee was hot and the waitress was as sweet as the pecan pie. In the cold outdoors was a sign marking the halfway point of Route 66. I sat there drinking coffee with my feet on the way to Chicago and my head on the way to LA, and when I could feel my fingers again, I went outside and was just about to take a photograph of the Harley in front of the sign when a passing

Romanian truck driver offered to do it instead.

'I won my green card in a lottery, and now I am saving to bring my family out. How is your motorcycle proceeding?' he said.

'*Moturul are aprindere regulate* (the engine is firing well),' I said.

'You speak Romanian?' he said, his face stunned with happiness.

'No, it's the only sentence I know.'

I shook his hand and rode on, hardly believing my luck that at last I had been able to use the only sentence I knew in Romanian.

By now, I was on the final few miles of Route 66 in the state. Down the road in Glenrio, the 'Last Motel in Texas' sign, which on the other side reads 'First Motel in Texas', had gone the way of all neon, and the wind sang and whispered in the empty rooms, gently mocking the hopes and dreams of yet another town that had been ignored by the interstate. Only a mile away, through the broken windows, cars and trucks hurried endlessly down it. What were they seeking? Not the lost heart of America, for it was here, in these empty rooms, their doors forever ajar and their bathroom sinks forever dusty, and in the one-man garage down the tumbleweed street, the tools still hanging on its walls and outside, on the forecourt, the rusting hulks of old Pontiacs and Chevrolets, which will now never be ready on Thursday. These are as much a statement of a lost America as Stanley Marsh has made down the road, and in their way they have cost much more than a million Cadillacs.

Down the long main street of Tucumcari, New Mexico, the motel signs beckoned me in the dusk, some of them no more than ghosts: Pony Soldier, Palomino, Lasso, Apache, and Cactus. But of them all, a neon blue swallow called the most.

The Blue Swallow, you see, is the sweetest little motel in the world. For years it was run by Lillian Redman, and her black cat Smoky. Lillian had come out west in her father's covered wagon in 1915, and when she died a few years back, it was bought by Norwegian and Brazilian husband and wife Dale and Hilda Bakke, who fixed the neon swallow out the front, freshly painted the dusty pink walls, laid new gravel in the courtyard, and greased the sliding doors of the little garages beside each room, where I parked the Harley beside an open window with a geranium on the sill. And even better, above the fireplace in the office hangs a little ceramic blue swallow owned by Hilda's grandmother long before Hilda had even heard of this place.

'I do love serendipity,' I said to Jim, who was busy doing cartwheels on the bed.

Suddenly, the little white telephone on the bedside table rang. Good grief, I thought, who could it be? The editor, looking for tomorrow's copy? The bank manager, demanding that I return home, deal with my overdraft and get a proper job immediately? My mother, checking that I had clean underwear?

'Pinch punch, first of the month, and no return. Hello, my love,' said a familiar voice.

God, I'd forgotten how sexy she sounded.

'Hello, my darling. What a lovely surprise.'

'I just called to hear your voice. And to wish you long-distance hugs.'

'Right back at you, hon. Although I'm afraid I've a confession to make. I've been a bit unfaithful to you.'

'How can you be a bit unfaithful, dear?'

'Well, I've been sleeping with a rabbit for the past few weeks. If it's any consolation, he's imaginary. I just made him up because I was feeling lonely without you.'

'You're very sweet, dear. What's he called?'

'Jim, of course.'

'Of course. Do say hello to him for me.'

I hung up the phone just as Jim, miscalculating a backward somersault, landed on my lap.

'What's imaginary?' he said, looking up at me.

'It's like real, only better,' I said.

In the morning sun I filled up the tank at a nearby gas station before setting out on the long ride to Santa Fe.

'How much did you put in there?' said the owner when I went in to pay.

'Good question. I think it was two fifty.'

He whipped a pair of binoculars from under the counter and zeroed in on the pump. 'Two fifty it is.'

Twenty miles out of town I stopped for breakfast at a diner in the middle of exactly nowhere.

Which was, funny enough, just where a wonderfully strange US Navy officer and explorer called Lieutenant Edward Fitzgerald Beale found himself, in 1858, on a plain even the Indians avoided because there were so few watering holes. As he was surveying the desert one day for the government, Lieutenant Beale came up with the bright idea of using camels for carrying mail and supplies across it, and when he got back east, he put the idea to Jefferson Davis, the Secretary of War.

'Good thinking, young Beale,' said Davis, and seventy camels were immediately imported from Egypt and Arabia, along with their alcoholic drivers.

'I look forward to the day when every mail route across the continent will be conducted with this economical and noble brute,' said Beale. About the camels, not the drivers.

Sadly, when the Civil War erupted, the camels were honourably discharged and either sold to circuses or mining companies or turned loose to look after themselves without even a credit card.

I finished my eggs, bacon and coffee and walked outside to find a big black Harley and a purple customised Yamaha and their owners admiring the fact that I hadn't cleaned my own bike in several days.

'Howdy. Where ya headin'?'

'Santa Fe by nightfall. What about you?'

'Well, we been down from Wyoming three days. First night we slept on a picnic table, second night in a fleapit motel and third night at his old folks' place. Tonight we aim to be in Kansas.'

Kansas! It had taken me a week to get here from there. I was obviously not sleeping on enough picnic tables, I thought, as they climbed on and roared off with a wave.

There is a tremendous camaraderie among bikers. You see one coming the other way, and as you close you see that he too is suited up in helmet and goggles, jacket and gauntlets, and his bike is loaded up for travelling far, and as you pass both of you hold your left hand out in the traditional greeting. There is a very distinct hierarchy about this greeting. If the other rider is on a sports bike, he may not even wave, and may just dip his head in salute. If he is on a cruiser, but it is not a Harley, he will raise his hand aloft as he sails past. And if he is riding a Harley and meets another Harley rider, the two of them will simply hold out their left hand, palm down, to each other.

There is something knightly about it, in the same way that there is something knightly in the very act of climbing on a motorcycle and riding off on what is the modern equivalent of the horse. Although don't tell a horse that. There is even something knightly in the clothes that riders wear: the armoured suit and boots, the gauntlets, the helmet with its hinged visor.

If you are a cynic, of course, you may think that this is nonsense, and it is all just boys dressing up and playing with toys, but you'd better not say that or you are very liable to get covered in custard by a boyish but enraged biker.

Talking of custard, it was nearly time for my daily research into the best pie on Route 66.

Outside Santa Rosa, a sign said, 'Cline's Corner: New Chef. Good Food', which didn't say much for the old one. But I was holding out for the Club Café, where since 1935 Ron Chavez has staged a one-man war against the fast-food joints, which he blames for what he calls the blanding of American cuisine. 'They've ruined food. It comes out of machines and is made of plastic and has chemicals in it,' Ron says in Wallis's book on

Route 66. But when I got there, I found Ron was no more, and the Club Café was a car park.

Still, I found another diner nearby, but as I drove away after a large helping of chocolate pie, I couldn't help but think that they should have a sign up saying, 'Serving the Worst Pie on Route 66 since 1956! Made from Plastic and Chemicals!'

Ron, you were right, wherever you are.

However, at this stage my thoughts on pie were distracted when I was passed by a house. Mind you, it was on a trailer, which is what Americans do when they flit, rather than bother putting everything in boxes and trying to get Granny off the sofa, but it was obvious that, as the Wyoming boys would have said, I was taking it too slow.

The road ahead was straight and true, and I wound the speedometer up ... 80 ... 90 ... 100, until I was climbing through the snow-capped mountains and out onto the high chaparral. In front of me, huge storms brewed and boiled, pouring their contents onto the dry earth. I danced between them like a pilot flirting with the clouds, and came by evening time to Santa Fe, whose dappled sidewalks are no longer stomped by priests and cowboys, but by the art lovers and adobe aficionados that have made it the chicest town west of the Pecos.

I rode into town, checked into the El Rey Motel, and discovered that the price of being in the chicest town west of the Pecos is that motel rooms cost three times as much. And then discovered that at 7,000 feet things like breathing, staying upright and staying awake become strangely difficult. I dumped all my stuff on the bed, then promptly fell asleep beside it, and woke just in time to go to dinner at a nearby Mexican restaurant.

There, Eddie, the security guard, came over as I was parking the Harley, and we got to talking about bikes. A former motorcycle cop, he spent ten minutes regaling me with merry tales of riding through alleyways at 65 m.p.h., falling off, broken hips, banjaxed knees and twisted spines.

'Eddie, remind me never to go riding with you,' I said, and I walked into the restaurant, ordered a glass of wine and immediately felt completely paralytic.

So paralytic, in fact, that when I looked in my notebook during the main course, I discovered I had written down the following conversation:

Me: Don Hernandez, I have fallen irretrievably, irrevocably, irrecoverably and irremediably, to misquote John Donne, in love with your daughter Maria, and wish for nothing more than to marry her and start a Chihuahua ranch. May I, in all humility, ask for your gracious permission?

Don Hernandez: My great friend, it would give me more pleasure than anything I can imagine in the entire world, except perhaps that night with Consuela in –

Maria: Papa!

Don Hernandez: But my dear friend, your eyes fill with tears, and on such a happy occasion.

Me: I'm sorry. I always get weepy when confronted with empathy.

Maria: My darling, I think that being confronted with empathy may well be an oxymoron.

Me: How right you are, my little chilli pepper.

(Dim lights, cue Rodrigo's Concierto de Aranjuez in C Minor, and exit me, Maria and Don Hernandez left, followed by Jim the rabbit, in tears and sombreros.)

As you can see, it was probably wise for me to leave the restaurant at this point.

In the car park, I met Eddie.

'Sir, how ya doin'? Good meal?'

'Absolutely, although I feel even stranger than usual.'

'Aw, that's just the altitude,' he said with a grin.

I can't clearly recall getting back to the motel, but I must have made it, because I woke up the next morning after a troubled night's sleep, during which I had a recurring dream that I was just about to resit my A-levels and had somehow forgotten to do any revision.

I had breakfast and then headed out to explore Santa Fe. And what a strange old town it is.

Set on a high plateau at the foot of the stunning Sangre de Cristo Mountains, it was founded by Spanish missionaries in 1609 as their northern colonial capital, a full ten years before the Pilgrims set foot on Plymouth Rock. Later it became the end of the Sante Fe cattle trail from Kansas, almost 900 miles north-east. And today, with its adobe and baroque architecture not only perfected but re-created in everything from high-rise parking lots to petrol stations, it is the art capital of the west, living on a reputation firmly established by the patronage of D.H. Lawrence, Ansel Adams, and Georgia O'Keeffe, whose overtly erotic paintings of flowers pre-empted Robert Mapplethorpe by half a century.

Wandering around the old town, you will find many classic Mercedes convertibles, a lot of sensitive artistic types who look as if they would faint if you walked up behind them and said 'The Simpsons!' loudly, and 250 art galleries selling O'Keeffe paintings, Adams photographs, Lawrence quotations, and sculptures which run the gamut from utterly exquisite to 'Pardon me, miss, but do you mind if I throw up in your shop?'

In short, Santa Fe looks like Mexico would if it got an arts council grant.

I looked in all the museum shops, which is the cheater's way of seeing museums, since the shops have all the best stuff anyway, and hit out of town for the Santo Domingo Indian Trading Post, where, according to my guidebook, owner Fred Thompson had not only hosted President Kennedy and *Life* magazine, but sold everything from Dr McLean's Volcanic Liniment to the old Frazer sedan that had been sitting out the front for thirty years waiting for a buyer.

But the sedan, the trading post and Fred had all gone. Another Route 66 landmark had bitten the dust. In fact, the old road itself had bitten the dust around here, buried under the interstate for the next ten miles until I could get off the rat race and back once more to a world of back yards, native pueblos, school playgrounds and barking dogs.

I stopped once to check the map and an old man came over. 'Are you all right, señor? Would you like a cool glass of water?' he said.

Down the road, a mechanic was tinkering with a 1954 Mercedes sportster in a garage forecourt, behind him a graveyard of Detroit's finest: hugely finned and chromed Cadillacs and Imperials from the fifties, abandoned and baking in the sun, but looking as if a quart of oil and a turn of the key would bring them thundering into life again.

Yesterday I had been frozen in the mountains, and today it was 33 degrees in the shade. Except there was no shade. Huge black ants ran over my shoes as I walked back to the bike.

An hour later I was rolling through the outskirts of Albuquerque, and not liking what I saw. The whole city seemed to consist of pawn shops and loan sharks. I pulled over and stopped a youngish couple who were walking by. They were both blond, and she was wearing a badge saying 'The Leather Love Line'.

'Pardon me, but am I headed the right way for Central Avenue? I'm looking for an old Route 66 motel called El Vado,' I said, pushing up my goggles.

'Absolutely. Just take a right four blocks down,' she said, handing me a business card, across the top of which was written 'Dominant-Submissive Love, Fetishes, TV, Unique Erotica'.

'Tell me, are you into S and M?' she added sweetly.

'No, M and S,' I replied, 'although recently their socks have been a bit dull.'

I spent the night in the adobe El Vado Motel, the window open to let in the cool night air, and woke to find a small green lizard sitting on the bedside table looking at me with one eye, while admiring with the other a particularly fetching O'Keeffe print on the wall.

At the 66 Diner, where I had breakfast, the waitresses wore white socks and bee-bop skirts, the milk shakes were the best in town and Elvis was on the jukebox. I had me a meat-loaf sandwich and a vanilla malt, and headed west down Central Avenue, wobbling pleasantly because of the breakfast and steaming gently because I had washed my jeans the night before and they hadn't quite dried.

Central Avenue is where Route 66 ran through the city, and the old places are still there: the rococo KiMo Theatre, the art deco El Rey Cinema, and the El Vado Motel, where I had stayed.

I crossed the Rio Grande and climbed Nine Mile Hill to where, once upon a time, a stuffed polar bear was kept in a glass case at the old Rio Puerco Trading Post. The bear disappeared one night, and as I rode past, the trading post had disappeared too, leaving only a white wall bearing a sweating skull and the grim warning: '700 miles desert'. Beyond, the road disappeared into a bleached wilderness of sand and cottonwood scrub.

After half an hour, with no sign of life whatsoever, I began to think how frightening it would be to be stuck out here with a dead engine and a dwindling water supply, a hundred miles from the nearest milk shake. There were few signs marking Route 66 and no way of knowing I was on the road, apart from the old maps and guidebooks I had brought with me, and those almost constant companions of the old road, the railroad track and the telegraph poles. Few people care about Route 66 in this desert, simply because there are few people here, and they are too busy scratching a living from the arid land.

And in the strangest of ways, a few miles on, in the middle of nowhere, I passed a roadside stall selling martial arts supplies, whose sign – 'Give Your Kicks on Route 66' – won the wittiest of the day award, along with the one outside the Internet Café in Albuquerque saying 'Get Your Clicks on Route 66'. Mind you, selling black belts in the desert is only one of the many signs of the gadabout optimism that America was built on, and within the next 50 miles I had passed the Bluewater Motel, sadly derelict, and a sign on an even more derelict trading post saying: 'Welcome to Paradise Acres: lots for sale from $100 up'.

At Cubero there was only the long closed Villa de Cubero Café, a trading post and a handful of houses, yet it was here that Ernest Hemingway came to write much of *The Old Man and the Sea*. Standing here on the scorching sand, it was hard to comprehend such splendid perversity, and yet he must have known it was only out here in the desert he could summon up the feat of imagination that would produce such an extraordinary book about the nature of the sea.

In the trading post, a local man was buying two dozen cans of beer for lunch, and there was no sign that Hemingway had ever been there. Back east, there would have been books, videos, T-shirts and an interpretative centre run by a spindly yet lucid spinster. But then, as Georgia O'Keeffe once said, it is not what is written or said about you that matters, but what you have done with where you have been.

In the lilac dusk I came at last to Gallup, through a landscape that has been the setting for films from *Redskin* in 1929 to the *Superman* series. And when Tracy and Hepburn, Bogart, Hayworth and Peck were here, they stayed at the El Rancho, where a thirsty Errol Flynn once rode his horse into the bar.

Each room is named after the stars who stayed there, and I was in the Marx Brothers Room. There were forty-seven of us, including me, Jim, Groucho, Harpo, Chico and Zeppo, four chambermaids, three Russian aviators looking for their beards, two waiters, a sommelier and a polar bear.

Arizona

Arizona is Zane Grey country. Those of you of a certain age will have forgotten his romantic Western novels, in which the hero always triumphs and rides off through the purple sage into a crimson sunset with his tough but tender sweetheart.

Well, my tough but tender sweetheart was at home, which left me with Jim. As we walked and hopped towards the bike this morning to leave New Mexico for Arizona, I realised we were in for another blazing day, and nipped into the Wal-Mart next door to buy him a pair of cheap sunglasses.

'Kewl,' he said. 'When am I getting my Biker Bunnies leather jacket?'

'You can borrow mine,' I said, for it was getting so hot that day by day I was discarding more and more clothing, and would soon have to form a breakaway Hell's Angels chapter called Nude Bikers Who Love Custard.

We climbed aboard, donned our shades, and soon were at the Arizona State border. A fort marks the site where the old *F-Troop* TV series was filmed. If it looked familiar to me, it was because I had been here before – my Greyhound bus to New York had stopped there for half an hour in 1979.

And what do you know, there was one sitting at the same

spot with New York printed on the front.

'Can I get on to see if it makes me younger?' I said to the driver.

'Hasn't worked for me,' he said, pulling out to join the interstate east.

I turned the other way down the old road, across a landscape devoid of features, or hope for anyone stranded in it. And as the landscape changed, the language changed too: out here, a travel centre is not somewhere at which you plan to travel, but somewhere you do exactly the opposite, stopping to fill up with essentials such as burgers, milk shakes, fuel and rubber tomahawks. And signs for camping do not mean a damp farmer's field in which two of you can bed down in a pair of sleeping bags in a cramped tent, but a miniature metropolis to which you can hook up your recreational vehicle, the American term for a house on wheels, which usually comes with the family car towed behind. As soon as they can invent a machine that projects passing scenic landscapes onto the outside of the living-room window, so that Americans can just sit and eat burgers without going anywhere, I imagine they will do that instead.

In Holbrook I booked into a teepee at the Wigwam Motel, a famous old Route 66 stop.

Taking off my jeans to go to bed, I felt something in the back pocket. It was the business card of Nancy, the S and M woman from whom I'd asked directions in Albuquerque. Out of curiosity I plugged the laptop into the phone socket and dialled up the website. It seemed to consist entirely of scantily clad ladies, who for 119 dollars an hour would be nasty to you over the phone.

'A hundred and nineteen dollars!' said Jim. 'I'll do it for twenty and an iceberg lettuce.'

'No way. Have you seen the price of lettuce these days?' I said, switching off the laptop.

'Five dollah, five dollah, love you long time,' said Jim, skipping coyly around the teepee.

'You know, Rabbit,' I said, 'I worry about you sometimes. What would your parents say?'

'As if I even knew who they are. You know what rabbits are like.'

Finally he fell asleep, wearing his new sunglasses because he liked them so much. And as I nodded off myself, it came to me why I had been in such a grumpy mood all day. I had been deprived of my coffee and pie stop, for they don't do pie in Arizona. Still, at least now I knew what Lieutenant Beale meant when he said, 'Arizona is altogether valueless. After entering it, there is nothing to do but leave.'

'Any idea where I can get dessert in this town?' I said to Diane, the owner of the Jack Rabbit Trading Post in Winslow the next day. 'I'm suffering badly from pie deprivation syndrome.'

'Afraid not,' she said. 'Arizona isn't big on pie.'

In fact, things had got so bad that morning that I'd called in to the Twin Arrows Trading Post purely because they had a sign outside saying, 'Today's Special: Braised Rattlesnake Hips', thinking that might take my mind off the longing for pie. Only to find that the rattlesnake hips were just a joke and they didn't serve pie either.

'Hey,' Diane said, interrupting my reverie, 'you planning to go to the fun run in Seligman tonight?'

'Well, I won't be in Seligman for a couple of days yet. What's the fun run?'

'Loads of vintage cars from all over the States. Tonight they'll have a big street party. You gotta be there, believe me.'

I wandered thoughtfully down the street, wondering if pie would be on a street party menu, past the site of the Wigwam Saloon, where one of Winslow's most bizarre murders had started in 1905.

Two young cowboys, John Shaw and Bill Smith, had just wandered in and put their money on the bar for a drink when they spotted 600 shiny silver dollars on a dice table run by Frank Ketchum. Pulling their guns, the improvisational bandits crammed the lot into their pockets and hats, made for their horses and lit out of town.

But the sheriff and his deputies weren't far behind, and when the posse cornered the duo in Diablo Canyon, the ensuing gunfight left Smith wounded and Shaw dead. They buried him there and returned to Winslow, where that night a bunch of drunken cowboys suddenly remembered that Shaw had paid for a drink and not drunk it.

'That fella has a drink comin' to him and he should get what he paid for!' shouted one, grabbing a bottle of liquor and leading the rest out of the bar.

When they got to the canyon, they dug up Shaw and poured his last drink between his lifeless lips. One of them took a photograph, and it hung for years in the saloon.

'Come on, Rabbit,' I said, 'we're burning daylight.'

On the road out of town, virtually all the old Route 66 motels were closed and tumbled down, and those that remained were reduced to advertising the fact that they were quiet. That they were. Out here you could hear a pin drop, and you'd never find it again. Past Joseph, the old route itself petered into dirt track and dead end, and I was forced to join the interstate.

By late afternoon we had crossed the baking desert and were climbing into the piney sweetness of the San Francisco Mountains, between little farmhouses flanked by daisy meadows. After days of sand and burning sun, it felt like paradise on earth.

In Flagstaff, I sat in a café and pondered my options over a coffee. Seligman was another 75 miles west on Route 66, and I hadn't planned to be there for a day or two. Mind you, the fun run sounded like a grand idea, and down the interstate I could make the distance in about an hour. Then I could find somewhere to stay nearby, backtrack to Flagstaff, and start again.

There was only one way to decide. Democracy.

'Hey Rabbit, you fancy a party?'

'Let's go,' said Jim, slipping on his shades.

We'd covered half the distance when he tapped me on the hip.

'Pardon me, but do you realise you're singing "Take it Easy" over and over again?'

I hadn't, funny enough. I stopped, just to keep him happy, and half an hour later we were in Seligman.

America's long love affair with the automobile has produced some beautiful children, and it seemed as I rode into town that most of them were lined up on either side of Main Street. There were Corvettes, Mustangs and AC Cobras. There were little deuce coupes and big limos, hot rods and street racers, convertibles and sedans, and not one, but two, half-size Chevys, lovingly hand-built by a man from Los Angeles. Where else?

It was the Beach Boys and *Wacky Races* rolled into one and stretched over a mile of Main Street, complete with music and dancing, burgers and beer and a constant parade of cruising cars. There were engines that purred past like fireside tabbies, and engines that roared like distinctly annoyed lions. And there were engines that bore mute witness to the fact that their owners were boring farts who polished their cars, chromed their engines down to the last nut, bolt and washer, then took them everywhere on a trailer so they could win the *concours* award. God forbid they should actually get behind the wheel and enjoy driving them.

Sadly, I couldn't stay and party, since I had to find somewhere to stay for the night. So after winning the Dustiest Harley section, I picked up a burger and some beers and raced back down Main Street towards Flagstaff, trying to find a motel for the night before the beef got cold and the beer got warm. I felt like one of Zane Grey's heros, riding through the purple sage into a crimson sunset with my tough yet tender rabbit by my side.

Yes, quite.

However, because so many people had poured into Seligman for the fun run, the only motel I could find with a vacancy was a dismal affair about 35 miles away, in a dusty hamlet so small it didn't have a name. I parked the Harley outside the room and sat on the bed, munching cold burger and guzzling warm beer and flicking through the increasingly dire television channels until, finally, on the History Channel, I found something interesting: a documentary on the twentieth-century in America. Not even the ads every ten minutes for athlete's foot and haemorrhoid creams spoiled it. Or the fact that to describe the motel room I was staying in as a fleapit would have insulted any self-respecting family of Mr Flea, Mrs Flea and all the little Fleas. But if I thought I had problems, the room next door was occupied by a Mexican couple and their four children who looked as if they had been living there for months.

'Rabbit, dear, pass me over a beer, if you please,' I said, getting up off the bed and settling down on an armchair, which immediately collapsed.

'Thanks, I'll have one myself,' he said, hunting around in the bag for the Swiss army knife.

I later changed my mind about the History Channel, after a programme called Lost and Found, which had unearthed the first microwave, Hitler's limousine, Gandhi's bloodstained dhoti and Haydn's skull, which had been lost for years, but presumably found after a game of Haydn seek.

Anyway, it was time to go to bed, for tomorrow I had a little adventure planned for rabbit and myself.

I woke him at eight.

'Why are we getting up when it's still dark?' he said.

'It's still dark because you've got your sunglasses on, and we're getting up early because we're going to see the Grand Canyon,' I said.

How sweet it was to ride through the high country in the cool of a summer morning, with the song of the wind in the sky above, the song of a big V-twin below, and me in the middle, with a smile on my face. Especially since it's not every day you see the Grand Canyon for the first time.

Even the bare statistics of it are beyond imagination. The sluggish Colorado River began to form the canyon around 12 million years ago, and it began to take its current shape around 2-3 million years ago. Today, it is still deepening, at the rate of an inch every 500 years. It is between 4 and 18 miles wide, and over a mile deep. At the bottom lives a tribe of Havasupai natives, whose predecessors have been there for 2,000 years, and who are the only people in America who still have their mail delivered by mule.

The first Europeans to discover the canyon were Spanish colonists in 1540, but thinking it impenetrable, they failed to explore it, and it was not until 1869 that the indefatigable Major John Wesley Powell led a completely lunatic expedition in three boats down the river.

The rapids were so fierce that Powell lost one boat and several men, and close to the end, three of the party announced that they could take no more and would find their way out of the canyon on foot. They were never seen again, and after one more rapid, Powell and the survivors emerged safely into calmer water.

The only way to comprehend such a landscape at first glance is from the air, so half an hour later I was strapping myself into the seat of a De Havilland at Grand Canyon airfield.

'Can I fly it?' said Jim, struggling to get the seat belt around himself.

'No, you need very expensive sunglasses to fly aeroplanes,' I said.

No matter how much you have seen or heard of the Grand Canyon, the first sight of it is astonishing. It is quite impossible to bring enough superlatives with you to describe it, and the authorities should really leave large boxes of assorted Goshes, Wows, Good Heavenses and I Says at the park entrance, which you can then leave back for future visitors.

Even at 2,000 feet above the rim, or almost 7,000 feet above the river at the bottom, its curves and whorls, crenellations and layers, fill your vision to the horizon. It is a kingdom of its own, formed by an ancient alliance between river and rock, its codes incomprehensible to us.

When we returned to earth, I rode to the rim and sat there as the sun went down, at first in glories of gold and then shadows of lilac, until in all the blackness only the silver of the river was left under a crescent moon.

What a grand day, I thought, as we rode home, in spite of the fact that I had dropped my dictaphone into the toilet at the airfield. However, after a spell under the hand dryer, it had begun working again, which was almost as astonishing as the Grand Canyon.

'What a day, Jim,' I called back over the roar of the wind.

But he was asleep, and had been for some time.

The next morning I found myself in Flagstaff, a town which could have been the movie capital of the world. For on a stormy spring morning, just before the First World War, a talented and ambitious young man was steaming west on the Atchison, Topeka and Santa Fe railroad. In his bag on the rack above was the screenplay for *The Squaw Man*, the world's first full-length feature film, and in his mind's eye he could see exactly where it was going to be made, for he was fed up trying to re-create the Wild West in a gloomy studio in Long Island. No, this one was going to be made with real cowboys and real Indians, under a real Western sky. And he had read enough Zane Grey novels to know that Flagstaff was the perfect location for his epic.

But when the train arrived there, it was snowing. And not just snowing: great, mushy flakes were piling on the mounds of slush already lying on the platform. For young Cecil B. De Mille, one look was enough. He stayed in his carriage all the way to an obscure suburb of Los Angeles called Hollywood, and the rest ... well, you know the rest.

Today, Flagstaff is one of the pearls on the necklace of the old road, draped over the peaks and canyons of the San Francisco Mountains of western Arizona. Some of them are still shining brightly, some have lost their lustre, and some have dropped off the string entirely. A busy college town, Flagstaff thrives as a gateway to the Grand Canyon and on its connections with Route 66.

So too does Williams down the road, whose main street, called Bill Williams Avenue, is lined with Route 66 diners, souvenir shops and icons, like the Sultana Cinema, the first in the state to show talkies in 1927. Now, it is rather wonderfully shared by a bar and the First Assembly of God religious group. In the nearby Pine Country Restaurant, where I stopped for a coffee this morning, a Japanese couple were having a late breakfast and two mustangers were having an early lunch. Across the road in Pancho McGillicuddy's Irish-Mexican cantina, the only two customers were slumped over the table, either with a hangover or severe ethnic confusion.

Back in October 1984, this street was an emotional scene when Williams became the last town on Route 66 to be bypassed by the interstate. In tears, Bobby Troup sang 'Get your kicks' to huge crowds lined along it. Named after a Baptist circuit rider who was ambushed and killed by Indians in 1849, the town passed into folklore in 1954 when a group of local citizens got together to form the Bill Williams Mountain Men, dedicated to perpetuating the 'lore, memory and romance of the mountain men of old'. Once a year these otherwise sane businessmen grow beards, dress up in buckskins and ride on horseback to Phoenix, 150 miles to the south.

Honestly, how silly, grown men acting like that, I thought, putting on my leather jacket and getting on the bike to ride 130 miles to the west.

As I rode along, I thought what a beautiful thing it was that the line on an old map can become the concrete blurred beneath your feet, and the ink smudges beside it, cottonwood bushes dancing in the wind. Which, actually, had grown so strong through the morning that by lunch time I was riding along at 45 degrees, and had got so used to it that when I got off the bike in Seligman, I walked at the same angle into the barber shop.

'Why are you walking like that?' said Angel Delgadillo.

'It's the wind,' I said, and promptly fell over.

Seligman is the start of the longest single remaining stretch of Route 66 in existence – 156 miles – and Angel won't let you forget it. For although he's seventy-three, he's not only the town barber, but head of the state Route 66 association. He was born in Seligman, and his father was the town barber before him. During the Depression, things were so bad that the house was boarded up and the family's Model T loaded up to head out west. Then his brother Juan came home with some money from playing music, and they stayed to sing a hymn to the old road.

'People are getting excited about Route 66 these days. Even a lot of young folks, whose parents or maybe grandparents drove down it, want to come back and see for themselves. It was nearly dead, but people wouldn't let it die, and it's alive again,' said Angel.

Juan, who's even older, runs the Snow Cap Restaurant next door, where an old pick-up outside had been turned into an impromptu flower basket, and there were two signs in the window. One said: 'Today's Specials: Hamburgers without Ham, Cheeseburgers with Cheese, Dead Chicken', and the other, 'Slightly Used Napkins and Straws For Sale'.

Down the road I rejoined those faithful old companions, the telegraph poles and the railroad tracks, on which this morning a freight train was hauling wood. Like all American freight trains, its front end had arrived in Kingman before the back end left Santa Fe.

By now the wind had become stronger still and I was being attacked by kamikaze hordes of tumbleweed, leaving thorns embedded in my ankles and once, memorably, in my forehead. It was time to take a break, and according to the guidebook, at the Frontier Café in Truxton the coffee was good, the food was some of the best on the Route and the stories were on the house.

Pie! They might have pie, I suddenly thought.

I got off the bike, strode inside optimistically, and took a seat. The walls were lined with photographs of award-winning sheep and cows, and a solitary sign saying: 'Old-Fashioned Service for a New Millennium'. There were no customers, and two waitresses. The youngest was about eighty, and the older one had a zimmer frame. They ignored me for several minutes, perhaps because they had not realised I was there.

I coughed loudly, and the younger one looked up with a start, then hobbled over.

'Hello, young man. What would you like?' she quavered.

'Do you have any pie, at all?'

'What was that?'

'I SAID, DO YOU HAVE ANY PIE?'

'Pie? Oh yes, we have apple and peach.'

'AND WHICH IS YOUR FAVOURITE?'

'Oh, neither.'

I had the peach, which tasted of apple anyway.

Halfway through it, the phone rang. The older waitress showed no sign of having heard it, so the younger waitress picked it up, and had the following conversation: 'Frontier Café. Oh, it's you. No, you can't. Goodbye.'

'WHO WAS THAT?' said the older waitress.

'It was her.'

'WHAT DID SHE WANT?'

'She wanted everything, as usual.'

'DON'T GIVE HER NUTHIN'. SHE'S ALREADY GOT ALL YOUR FURNITURE.'

In the toilets, a rusty machine contained condoms which in shape and texture resembled the minarets of the Blue Mosque in Istanbul. 'She'll love you for using it!' said the legend below the coin slot.

As I drove away, I looked back to see the younger waitress pulling down the blinds and turning the sign in the door to Closed.

As Arizona creeps ever closer to California, the old road swoops and dips between peaks and plains, as if reluctant to enter the last few days of its journey. This is the Wild West of childhood memory, and behind every rock in every dusty gulch hides a desperado or an Apache, eager to see you to a sticky end. I stopped at Bert's Store, a canyon shack whose advertising slogan was 'Country Dancing and Cold Beer', and bought Jim a cap gun so he could ride stagecoach, just in case.

Above, the sky was wild and free. Squadrons of cumulus marched north in formation, unmoved by the transparent temptations of dancing horsetails. Tumbleweed cartwheeled across the road, and on the plain below, a tornado twisted and turned.

In Hackberry, John and Kerry Pritchard had turned the general store into a living shrine to Route 66, down to John's 1957 Corvette parked in front of the vintage petrol pumps outside.

Just when you think you've bought all the Route 66 souvenirs there are, you find another one, I thought, as I wandered outside holding several postcards and stickers and a bottle of cold soda made from cactus juice.

Three bikers and their girlfriends were sitting in the comfortable wooden chairs on the porch.

'Pull up a chair,' said the oldest guy, 'and tell us where you're headed.'

The sun was well down over the canyon rim before I left, and it was dark as I descended the 20-mile straight into the twinkling lights of Kingman, feeling more like I was landing a plane than riding a motorcycle.

In Kingman, as a result of my dedication to staying only in authentic Route 66 motels, I ended up in an establishment which made the one a couple of nights ago seem like a shrine to hedonism. Both motels were recommended in Jack D. Rittenhouse's 1946 guide to Route 66, and I really must dig him up and have a word with him. Only the lack of a good lawyer prevents me from naming the one in Kingman, but suffice it to say that the curtains were held up with sticky tape and the television was lovingly inscribed with the names of several previous occupants. When I turned on the shower, a screeching and howling like several cats being slaughtered by a posse of flatulent banshees was followed by spurts of water at random temperatures ranging from freezing to boiling. A statistician would probably tell you that meant the average temperature was entirely acceptable, which just goes to show how much they know.

To make up for it, I took myself out for a steak dinner, then went to bed and dreamt of large, fluffy towels, remote control television, room service and king-size beds.

After a fleabitten night, I spurned the shower next morning and went for a swim in the motel pool, emerging covered in a thin film of oil and with such an impressive collection of dead insects in my hair that I had to have a shower after all.

Trying to decide whether I was scalded or frozen, I walked up the road to Mr D'z Diner, where my grumbling to myself was interrupted by a remarkable sight. For lo and behold, if it wasn't an Enfield motorcycle and sidecar, sitting in the car park.

It was piloted and co-piloted by Dave and Chris Williams, who had been given it by one of the growing number of Enfield dealers across the States to publicise a Route 66 website, which the Williamses were currently researching.

'Amazing. I rode one of these from India to Belfast a year ago,' I said.

'Did every bit of yours fall off too?' said Dave.

'Absolutely.'

Still, it made me feel quite wistful for the days of the Nambarrie Run, spent happily braving Indian fleapits, Pakistani roads, Iranian truck drivers and Bulgarian sheep with Monsieur Minne. I really must get him off on an another adventure, I thought, as I motored along the old road, which climbed through desert scrub into the mountains, turning this way and that, as if uncertain which was the best way up.

Back in the old days, when most cars didn't have enough power to make it to the top in first gear, the locals had no doubt about which was the best way up – backwards. In those days, as your radiator boiled and your fan belt frayed, you were likely to be overtaken by a gold miner going up in reverse at full speed, steering by rear-view mirror, and with a cigarette in a hand dangling out the window.

Over 36 million dollars worth of gold was taken out of these mountains in the nineteenth century, and the mines were still worked until 1943. Then, when Route 66 bypassed this section and even that source of income dried up, stops like Goldroad and Oatman became ghost towns overnight. The folks in Goldroad had a pretty nifty solution, though: they burnt the whole town to the ground to save on taxes, and today there are only a few adobe walls and stone foundations left.

Just over the summit, Oatman was pretty quiet, too – apart from the souvenir shops every three yards and coachloads of tourists buying carrots to feed the burros, which are the descendants of those released into the wild by the miners before they left, and which wander around so amiably I suspected they were really student volunteers in donkey suits.

Halfway down the only street is the Oatman Hotel, where on the night of 19 March 1939, much to the surprise of the girl behind the counter, Clark Gable and Carole Lombard walked in and asked for a room. The two had met in 1936, but she thought him stuffy and he found her rude and boisterous. Then, at a white-tie society ball that year, they finally got talking. That night, she had two white doves slipped into his room while he slept, and they were married on 19 March three years later, in the Methodist church in Kingman. Heading back to California after the service, they had only made it up the mountain road as far as Oatman by nightfall, and walked into the hotel.

They never came back to this little town, of course: she was killed in a plane crash only three years later, and he died of a heart attack in 1960. But Room 15 is exactly as they left it, with a sweet little white iron bed, a small dressing table and a gramophone. And in its bright and airy optimism, the ghostly but almost tangible memory of the first morning they woke as man and wife.

I closed the door, tiptoed down the stairs, and rode out of town.

And if I'd thought the road up the mountain to Oatman was bad, it was a pussycat compared to the road down the other side – down and round and down again, past giddy precipices and inches away from impossible drops. The thought of getting down it as an Okie in the thirties in an old jalopy overloaded with one wife, two chickens, three mattresses, six kids and all the family belongings was enough to make me want to take to an armchair and never leave home again. It was so bad, in fact, that I was actually relieved to get down into the baking desert on the other side, the sweat drying on my forehead as I tootled along, glad to be alive, between palm and tamarisk trees waving in the hot breeze.

And then, a smack of blue in the golden sand: it was the Colorado River, opening into a lake. I could understand now why the Joad family in *The Grapes of Wrath* had got down off that mountain, stopped their car and just walked out into the shallows. And that's exactly what I did.

Suddenly I spotted a snorkel unzipping the water towards me, and a familiar figure emerged dripping from the water, wearing a diving mask and flippers.

'Rabbit, what on earth are you doing?' I said.

'The name's Rabbit. James Rabbit,' he said, in a remarkably good Sean Connery accent. For a rabbit, I mean.

At Needles I stopped and filled up with fuel.

'Where's good to stay in town?' I said to the gas station owner as I handed over 5 dollars.

'Nowhere,' he said, which spoke much for his candour, if little for his chances of employment with the Needles Tourist Board. 'Why don't you head 20 miles north to Laughlin? You'll pick up a great room there for around 25 bucks.'

I was halfway down the road before I realised I had forgotten to ask him why the citizens of Laughlin were so generous with their hotel rooms.

The answer, of course, is that they can afford to be: Laughlin is across the state border in Nevada, the gambling capital of the world. And although Laughlin is a sleepy little retirement town, whose streets are filled with the tinkle of colliding zimmer frames, on its outskirts lie miles of enormous casino hotels in every architectural style you can imagine, and a few you wouldn't want to.

I stayed in a hotel called the Colorado Belle, the shape of a huge riverboat that sails forever through the desert. I was in room 51014, which gives you some idea of the scale of the place. The room itself was the size of a planet and cost me the princely sum of 24 dollars, and the T-bone steak and beer I had for dinner were 8 dollars, all thanks to the subsidy of the suckers who night and day line the rows of slot machines, blackjack tables and poker schools, hoping against hope that this quarter or this next turn of the card will be the one that will make them rich and unhappy rather than poor and unhappy.

California

California! The promised land, where the air smelt of orange blossom and you could almost hear the crash of the surf on Pacific beaches.

Like the pioneers and the Dust Bowl families, since I left Chicago and struck out west, I had been whipped by wind and soaked by rain, baked by desert days and frozen by mountain nights. I had climbed the dreadful road to Oatman, then descended the even more dreadful road down, and faced the California state border guards, who in the past had prowled the lines of jalopies waiting to get in, turning away anyone with plants or animals or a hint of disease that might bring pestilence to their golden land. In their hearts they saw a future in which ragamuffin children in straw hats and overalls would throng the volleyball courts of Redondo Beach, trying to sell flea-ridden chickens to beautiful people whose most difficult decision every day was between latte and mocha.

And like the pioneers and the Joads, I had bathed in gratitude in the waters of the Colorado, and been glad that the worst was over.

And then, I looked west and realised that the worst was yet to come.

The Mojave Desert.

Many before me had looked out at the bright and cruel sands and, beyond that, a jagged range of mountains a thousand feet higher than the ones they had just crossed. And beyond that, a range higher still, carrying the snows of winter even though it was already above 40 degrees where they stood. All had trembled. Some had left their prairie schooners or steaming jalopies sitting there and just walked out into the burning sands, never to be seen again.

I thought about it for a while, and decided to have breakfast.

And, since this was California, I had wheat and milk and honey, raisins and freshly squeezed orange juice, wholemeal toast and marmalade. Goodbye to grits and hashbrowns. Goodbye to fried eggs and Polish sausages and pastrami and salami and all those other amis. Goodbye to fat people feeding quarters into slot machines, and farmers who had never seen the ocean.

California! I could almost smell the salt sea breeze from here. I would become a surf bum, my skin so dark and my hair so blond that I would often be mistaken for an infra-red photograph. I would play volleyball on the beach and be wooed by a former beauty queen with a bottom like two oiled ball bearings, only to have to tell her that I had a tough but tender sweetheart at home and a rabbit to look after.

'Come on, Rabbit, surf's up,' I said, striding to the Harley and riding west, where in the crucible of the desert my bright new future would be forged.

And my suntan, come to that.

Half an hour into the burning sands of the Mojave, the old road has been battered and worn by the many weary wheels that have passed along it. Out here, you are on your own and every change in engine noise becomes a breakdown, every twitch in the suspension a wheel just about to come off.

I was glad after an hour in the relentless sun to see Goff's General Store, a favourite stop for old Route 66 travellers because it was exactly halfway between nowhere and nowhere else. Inside, Bob, the owner, was serving breakfast to Tom from the Fisheries Conservancy Board, although you wouldn't think at first glance that there would be a lot of fish to conserve out here.

We talked about old motorcycles for a while, and I finished my coffee.

In the toilet, a sign on the wall said: 'Notice: If you cannot reach the Urinal, use the Crapper.'

'What's the temperature looking like today?' I asked Tom as I walked out the door.

'Looking like 103 in the shade. If you can find any,' he laughed.

This is where over half a century ago General George S. Patton brought two million men to train for the North Africa campaign, knowing that after the Mojave, Rommel's Panzer Corps would be a relief. Patton could have brought twice as many, and still lost them in this vast inferno. I was doing 60, 70 then 80 m.p.h. and barely seeming to move through it.

At last I climbed into the mountains, only to be confronted on the other side with more desert.

I had forgotten completely the colour green and the concepts of cool and wet by the time I reached Amboy, which is the nowhere that Goff's was halfway to. 'Population 20', said the sign, as I pulled up outside Roy's Motel Café, which had been serving Route 66 customers since 1933. Today, the only ones were me and, proof that I was not mad after all, a whip-thin Dutchman called Maarten from Arnhem, who was cycling from San Francisco to Albuquerque.

'Then I go home. I have been travelling for a year, and it is enough,' he said.

He filled up his water bottles, climbed on his bike and pedalled east.

'Damn punks,' said the owner, who was neither the original Roy nor his son-in-law Buster, 'they live on welfare and go travelling for months. Me, I can't even get ten days off.'

I drained my coffee and continued west, returning the population again to twenty.

Outside the town limits, the land turned dark and frightening, and south of the road rose the black and menacing plug of the Amboy volcano. But like the owner of Roy's, although it looked angry, it had been dormant for years.

Halfway from Amboy to Siberia lie the dusty remains of Bagdad, and in the middle of them the Bagdad Café, inspiration for the eponymous film. Inside, the waitress was a striking redhead called Monique.

'*Bonjour, Monsieur. Qu'est-ce que vous désirez?*' she said, handing me a menu.

'*Ah, vous êtes française,*' I said.

'No, I'm just practising.'

'Ah. You wouldn't happen to have pie, by any chance? I haven't had a decent pie since Oklahoma.'

'Sure. We got chocolate, cherry, vanilla, strawberry and coconut.'

I felt like a satyr who had wandered into a brothel.

As I was tucking into the chocolate – and delicious it was, too, especially with ice cream – the man at the next table said, 'Nice motorcycle you got there.'

Middle-aged and moustachioed, his black T-shirt declared: 'I Can't Believe I Once Thought Forty Was Old'.

'Thangsh,' I said, my mouth full of pie.

'You own it?'

'I wish I did, but I have to hand the keys back to Harley in a few days when I finish Route 66.'

'Hell, I been travelling that old road for years.'

'Really? What's your favourite part of it?'

'Right here. No parties, no bullshit, no nothing. Just peace and quiet.'

'How long have you lived here?' I said, torn between continuing with the conversation and continuing with the pie.

'Three weeks. Pulled in right outside on a 1200 Sportster to let her cool down and the engine blew up on me. Got a job on an ostrich farm near here, so I can save up to get her fixed.'

'Hell, that's funny,' said the man at the table behind. 'Me and Alice here were riding an FLH 1500 just west of Gallup when the engine blew on us. Got a lift here with some Navajos.'

'Yeah,' said Alice, 'we was trying to outrun a dust devil. Doin' ninety and that critter was still sittin' on our shoulder.'

It could only be a matter of time before the man behind Alice turned around and said: 'Hey, it's funny you should say that, but ...'

I got up and paid the bill.

'*Merci beaucoup, monsieur. Vous êtes très gentil,*' said Monique.

'*Et vous, Monique.*'

I rode carefully down the road, listening to the engine, but all was well, and by nightfall I was in Barstow checking in at the El Rancho Motel, which was made entirely of railway sleepers and had a sign outside pointing out helpfully that it was almost exactly halfway between London and Tokyo.

'Boy, am I glad to get out of that desert,' I said to the man behind the desk. 'What's on the other side of Barstow?'

'More,' he said.

'Anywhere good to eat around here?'

'Yeah, there's a really good doughnut place at the next stoplight,' he said.

'Does it serve beer?'

'Nope. If you want a beer, go round the back of the doughnut place. There's a vacant lot, and at the back of that there's a place called Hooz in One.'

I walked out, leaning against a hot desert wind, and found the place, which was a sports bar filled with all the local girls having their weekly night out at the pool table.

'I'm not a local girl,' I said to the barmaid, a large blonde with a small nose. 'Can I have a beer anyway?'

'Hell, sure. Though if you're looking for food, all we got left is steak and mushroom sandwich. Where you come from today?'

'Came down from Laughlin by way of Needles and across the desert.'

'Well, you come a ways today,' she said, handing me the coldest, wettest beer I had ever tasted.

It was the first time anyone in America had ever told me I'd come a ways today. And in America, that meant something.

On the next bar stool, a man called John in a Lakers baseball cap was bemoaning his luck to a man called, apparently, Dork.

'Whaddya mean, ya can't drive?' said Dork.

'Listen, Dork, I mean I can't drive. I had one pitcher of beer and the cops busted me on the way home. So I can't drive. One lousy pitcher.'

I sipped my beer and waited for the steak and mushroom sandwich to arrive. On the big screen, the basketball game between the Lakers and the Jazz was interrupted by a sports newsflash: Pitcher arrested for domestic violence.

That lousy pitcher. First he gets John busted, then he beats up his wife.

I checked out next morning, and at the last stoplight west of Barstow, I met a cyclist coming the other way with a mesh shopping bag over his head.

'Bugs,' he said, before I had a chance to ask him.

The freedom of the open road does weird things to people. But then, this was California, where it is illegal to set a mousetrap without a hunting licence, or ride a bicycle in a swimming pool.

I rode on, over the high desert plain, occasionally passing signs saying, 'Don't Litter Your Desert', although they could just as well have said, 'Don't Desert Your Litter'.

It was beautiful in the early morning: a place of lilac grey shadows and multicoloured birdsong. And although it was desert, it was a doddle compared to the previous day in the heart of the Mojave. Even better, soon it became mountain roads, which were made for motorcycling, swooping and banking their way up and then down to Victorville for a breakfast of pancakes and honey, after which I was completely stuffed.

And so, funny enough, was Trigger.

For in the nearby Roy Rogers-Dale Evans Museum, the cowboy couple not only sent the famous horse off to the taxidermist, but also Trigger Jnr, Bullet the dog, Dale's horse

Buttermilk, and several animals shot by Roy on safari.

What a strange man, I thought, as I wandered through the magnificently hagiographic exhibits, while the sound of 'Happy Trails' wafted overhead. He was one of the all-time American heroes, yet belonged to Egyptian, Arabic and Scottish chapters of the Masons. Who regularly told people to support their country, yet rode a Honda. Who reminded me on television every Saturday morning to be kind to animals, yet went around Africa shooting them. Not to mention stuffing Trigger because he loved him too much to bury him.

I walked around half expecting at any minute to bump into Dale and the rest of the Rogers family stuffed as well, but instead emerged into the sunlight to find two baffled pensioners wondering if they could afford the entrance fee to the museum.

'I wouldn't go in there, if I were you. They stuff horses,' I said, getting on the bike and riding through the last mountains of Route 66 into icy mist. It was bloody freezing, and I had to stop and get out fleeces and scarves and gloves I had thought long defunct.

Down the mountain in San Bernadino, the old California Theatre had been restored almost as well as Trigger. In the thirties, all the sneak previews of Hollywood movies were shown here, and the Santa Fe railroad out from Los Angeles became a commuter line for stars trekking out in furs and jewels to find out whether their latest effort was a skyrocket or a squib. Like every other restored theatre in the world, it was currently showing *Joseph and His Amazing Technicolor Dreamcoat*.

San Bernadino was also where that nice McDonald family whose little diner I spotted in Shamrock, Texas, were born. I told you they would do well, and isn't it funny how so many Scots succeed in the food business? Like Duncan Donuts, for example.

I was wondering why none of them had turned their hands to solving the great Arizona pie crisis as I rode into Chino. This, since you ask, is not the place where chinos were invented, since Americans call them khakis, a term invented by the British, who now call them chinos. There, that's that explained. It is, however, the place were thousands of Allies and Axis aircraft were flown after the war to be broken up and melted down for scrap, a sight which so appalled nineteen-year-old Ed Maloney that he started dragging assorted Mustangs, Messerschmitts and Mitsubishis home. Finally, when the field at the back of his parents' house was full, he realised he'd better open a museum, and since 1957 the Planes of Fame Museum has been one of the delightfully hokey attractions that children plague their parents to pull off the old road for. Me, I took little persuasion, and spent a couple of hours happily poking about in a state of vicarious Bigglesworthiness.

West of Chino was once the land of orange blossoms and fruit picking, where the Dust Bowl families found their first steady employment since leaving Oklahoma. But now the only signs of that aromatic heritage are in the names of the avenues: Orange and Cherry, Mango and Mulberry. Or the occasional field of strawberries, a man at the edge of the road selling them fresh. And here and there, faded signs from the glory days of American travel in the fifties and little motels, the doors of their rooms draped with orange blossom and bougainvillaea.

But even though you are still 60 miles from Los Angeles, you can already see the smog, sense the urban sprawl gather around you, and feel threatened by the armed guards at the gates of exclusive housing estates, the same way you feel guilty walking through customs even when you're not smuggling anything.

But then you see a little thirties filling station on a corner in the leafy suburb of Monrovia, and realise that the old road is still alive. It was just playing with you, that's all. After all, it was born in 1926, has been through several near-death experiences, and deserves a bit of fun with the people who still love it. And through all those years, it has earned all the names it was given – the Mother Road, the Freedom Road, the Main

Street of America.

By contrast, the Los Angeles freeway, which buried it almost within sight of the ocean, must be the most inappropriately named road in the world. Los Angeles means 'the angels', and it is obvious what freeway means, yet this is a road on which cars become trapped and the people inside them become devils, cutting in and refusing to give way, taking advantage of any sign of good nature, cursing at everyone else on the road and shouting into their mobile phones. This is a road that has forgotten what being a road means.

At Sunset Boulevard, the old road emerged again, and my heart sank at the mish-mash of tacky shops on either side, then lifted at the first glimpse of the famous Hollywood sign up on the hill as I rode onto Santa Monica Boulevard, the final stretch of Route 66, which leads down to the ocean. It was being dug up, and looked more or less like the main road into Lahore, although I could tell I was getting close to Beverly Hills when I saw the first pet spa and psychic counsellor, inside which countless Fifis were having colonic irrigation and aura analysis.

Then Beverly Hills itself, an oasis of lilac Rolls-Royces, freshly watered lawns, mansions snoozing smugly in the shade of jacaranda trees, and what must be the most sparsely attended church in the world, the Beverly Hills Presbyterian.

I had gone 20 miles, and it had taken me almost four hours. I needed a break, and I knew just the place: Harry's Bar and American Grill, just across the road from the Century Plaza, where they have a competition every year to see which of the customers can write most like Hemingway.

I walked through the doors. It was dark after the heat. There were some men, and we ate the high soluble fibre, low-fat, low-sodium bread of that country. It was good. We drank the rough Chablis spritzer which men drink. It was good. Then they left. They had to go to the mountains to see a man about real estate, and I had to go west with a rabbit who had never seen the ocean.

Back on the bike, almost immediately I caught the first sea breeze, and with it that unique smell of California, which I remembered from when I lived here all those years before, and which occasionally came to me in dreams: a combination of citrus, cocoa butter, fresh sweat, hot sand and salt sea air.

And then, at last, the sudden blue smack of the ocean!

I drove along the coast until I came to Redondo Beach, where I had played volleyball. Arby's was gone, and the Red Onion, where the waitress had told me in all seriousness that she was Irish and her family name was Kowalski. She was, I imagine, one of the Strabane Kowalskis.

I rode up Pacific Coast Highway, and there, on the corner of Ward Street, was the house where my coach, Jim Joy, had lived. I had called his old number a week ago and had got no reply, and now, when I knocked on the door where we would leave for matches every Saturday morning, there was still no reply, and the neighbours told me that although he still lived there, he was away on holiday. It seemed that not only the icons of Route 66 were vanishing, but also the icons of my own personal road.

As the sun sank over the ocean, I rode back to Santa Monica Boulevard, where Route 66 ended the journey it had begun 2,448 miles ago in Chicago, and where I would now end it too.

I sat on the grass under the waving palms and thought how trips like this can change a man. For one thing, it would take a while to get used to waking up every morning and realising that you don't have to ride a motorcycle for hundreds of miles through icy rain, savage wind or baking heat. But it was more than that. Journeys like this awaken the restlessness which is in all of us.

I looked down the coast at where I had lived for a summer when I was a young man, and then out at the ocean as it finally accepted the dying sun, and realised that my life would never be quite the same again. But then I realised that it had never been quite the same before.

I walked across the road, found a bar and a greengrocer's,

and came back with two martinis and an iceberg lettuce.

'Well, Rabbit,' I said, 'it's the end of the road. Any plans?'

'I thought of going back to St Louis, now that I've finally seen the ocean,' said Jim, sipping his martini. 'But I've decided to stay here and become a movie star.'

'Oh, really? Who are you going to base yourself on?'

'Warren Beatty, of course.'